THE REAL COST OF CAPITAL

FT Prentice Hall
FINANCIAL TIMES

In an increasingly competitive world, we believe it's quality of thinking that will give you the edge – an idea that opens new doors, a technique that solves a problem, or an insight that simply makes sense of it all. The more you know, the smarter and faster you can go.

That's why we work with the best minds in business and finance to bring cutting-edge thinking and best learning practice to a global market.

Under a range of leading imprints, including *Financial Times Prentice Hall*, we create world-class print publications and electronic products bringing our readers knowledge, skills and understanding, which can be applied whether studying or at work.

To find out more about our business publications, or tell us about the books you'd like to find, you can visit us at
www.pearsoned.co.uk

PEARSON
Education

OCLC Record

THE REAL COST OF CAPITAL

A business field guide to better financial decisions

Tim Ogier, John Rugman and Lucinda Spicer

FT Prentice Hall

FINANCIAL TIMES

An imprint of Pearson Education

London • New York • Toronto • Sydney • Tokyo • Singapore
Hong Kong • Cape Town • New Delhi • Madrid • Paris • Amsterdam • Munich • Milan

PEARSON EDUCATION LIMITED

Edinburgh Gate
Harlow CM20 2JE
Tel: +44 (0)1279 623623
Fax: +44 (0)1279 431059

Website: www.pearsoned.co.uk

_____

First published in Great Britain in 2004

ISBN 0 273 68874 X

British Library Cataloguing in Publication Data
A catalogue record for this book is available from the British Library

Library of Congress Cataloging-in-Publication Data
Ogier, Tim
    The real cost of capital : a business field guide to better financial decisions / Tim Ogier,
    John Rugman, and Lucinda Spicer.
        p. cm. — (Financial Times series)
    Includes index.
        ISBN 0–273–68874–X (alk. paper)
        1. Corporations—Finance. 2. Business enterprises—Finance. I. Rugman, John.
    II. Spicer, Lucinda. III. Title. IV. Series.

    HG4026.O337 2004
    658.15'2—dc22

                                        2004043637

10 9 8 7 6 5 4 3 2 1
08 07 06 05 04

This publication is designed to provide accurate and authoritative information in regard to the subject matter
covered. It is sold with the understanding that neither the authors nor the publisher is engaged in rendering legal,
investing, or any other professional service. If legal advice or other expert assistance is required, the service of a
competent professional person should be sought.
    The publisher and contributors make no representation, express or implied, with regard to the accuracy of the
information contained in this book and cannot accept any responsibility or liability for any errors or omissions that
it may contain.

Index by Indexing Specialists (UK) Ltd
Typeset by 70
Printed and bound in Great Britain by Bell and Bain Ltd, Glasgow

The Publishers' policy is to use paper manufactured from sustainable forests.

In memory of Jim Dezart,
a valued colleague

CONTENTS

AUTHORS' ACKNOWLEDGEMENTS

Where to start? From concept to completion this book has taken five years, and along the way we received much assistance and encouragement (and some abuse) from a large number of people.

The idea of writing a book on the cost of capital stemmed from a global cost of capital initiative in which the authors were heavily involved at PricewaterhouseCoopers (or rather Price Waterhouse as it then was). This initiative was all about approaching cost of capital estimation in practical commercial situations, and a number of papers were produced from the findings. Some of these papers inspired the material covered in this book.

Our work benefited from the enthusiasm of a large group of PwC people from across the world – the sun truly never sets on the PwC cost of capital empire! We have drawn heavily on their ideas and insights and were driven in our mission by their intelligent and practical contributions to the debate. Particular thanks must go to Franchee Harmon who joined the authors on the steering group for the initiative, and Anthony Maybury-Lewis who helped us manage the process of academic review of the findings. The PwC team that participated in the initiative stretched from Jim Dezart in Los Angeles to Steve Smith in Auckland, taking in core technical contributions from Roger Grabowski and Dave King in Chicago; most of the words were, however, spoken and written in London.

Thanks also go to the financial economists from around the academic world who kindly agreed to review the fruits of the initiative's labor and helped us in our workshops – to Geart Bekaert, Ian Cooper, Campbell Harvey, Steve Kaplan, Robert Korajczyk, Bertil Naslund, Ajay Patel and James Petersen. They, of course, bear no responsibility for any errors or omissions in our work, and do not necessarily endorse any of the views expressed in this book, but we benefited enormously from their advice.

Then came the book. As the manuscript gradually took shape we were grateful for the input of many colleagues. Our thanks go to Amit Aggarwal, Levent Aydinoglu, Chris Chua, Kelly Devine, Ben Dubow, Khalid Hayat, Julian

Herbert, Naz Naini, Andrew Porter and David Smith for guiding our thinking, helping with data, or commenting on drafts. We owe a particular debt of gratitude to Nick Forrest and John Raven who contributed significantly to Chapters 5 and 8 respectively.

As it neared completion we were grateful to those colleagues who reviewed the manuscript – to Peter Clokey and Charles Sword, and to members of Wim Holterman's PwC Global Competency Centre team, notably Pieter van Oijen, John Redmayne and Christian Wulff.

Secretarial support was crucial in helping us to juggle authorly duties with the demands of our clients, and to interpret our jottings and mumblings into usable text. Able assistance was provided by Sarah Clarke, Marcia Ledger and Karen Miller.

Last but not least, our thanks go to those who played important, albeit less direct roles, in the book's completion. To Philip Wright and our publisher, Richard Stagg, who believed in us through the five years; to our clients, who often distracted us from the task of writing, but on whose real-life situations the book draws heavily; and to our spouses, Debbie, Jo and Ernest, for putting up with us during the protracted gestation period.

PUBLISHER'S ACKNOWLEDGEMENTS

We are grateful to the following for permission to reproduce copyright material:

Figure 2.1, Tables 2.4 and 7.13 from *www.thomson.com*, Thomson DataStream; Figures 2.3, 2.4, 2.5, 2.6, 2.7, 7.1 and Tables 6.2 and 6.3 from *www.Bloomberg.com*, © 2004 Bloomberg L.P.; Figure 3.1 from *Triumph of the Optimists: 101 Years of Global Investment Returns*, Princeton University Press, (Dimson, E., Marsh, P., and Staunton, M., 2002); Table 3.1 from *The Equity Risk Premium: Another Look at History*, The Utilities Journal, Oxera, (Jenkinson, T.J., April 14-16 1998) and *The BZW Equity Gilt Study*, (now Barclays Capital) (1997); Tables 3.3 and 3.4 from *Stocks, Bonds, Bills and Inflation® Yearbook* ©2004 Ibbotson Associates, Inc. All rights reserved. Used with permission; Example 5.2 from *National Grid Annual Report 1999–2000*, National Grid Transco plc.; Tables 5.2 and 5.6 from Standard & Poor's; Tables 5.4 and 5.5 from *www.bondsonline.com*, Bondsonline Group, Inc.; Figure 6.3 from *Mobius on Emerging Markets, 2nd edition*, FT Prentice Hall, (Mobius M. 1996), ©International Finance Corporation (1996). Reprinted with permission; Figure 6.4 from *Country risk and global equity selection*, Journal of Portfolio Management, Institutional Investor, (Erb C., Harvey R.C., and Viskanta T., Winter 1995).

In some instances we have been unable to trace the owners of copyright material, and we would appreciate any information that would enable us to do so.

The cost of capital world is a real world

Imagine you are standing at the edge of a river. You can see stepping stones ahead of you – but only some of these are safe. Your lunch is on the other side of the river and you are hungry. You turn to your traveling companion for advice on how to work out which stepping stones are safe and which ones are not and he begins to tell you about velocity, turning moments, viscosity of water, and the probability of loose stones on the stream bed.

After some minutes of this, you stop listening to him, shut your eyes and jump.

There is a parallel between this situation and the world of international investment today. Investors want to make informed decisions – but most of the brilliant thinking brought to the problem of finance and investment returns is inaccessible and tucked away in the small print of academic textbooks, learned papers, and in footnotes to the products of providers of data on the financial markets. The textbooks have gaps, particularly in the area of practical application of international principles, and in the area of actually doing the calculations and making the decisions. Nowhere is this more apparent than in the area of cost of capital and it seems that to survive, you have to spend a lifetime immersed in the subject.

In addition to investors, quoted companies are also held ransom to the cost of capital. Corporate boards want to understand their relationship with the capital markets – but the tools they can use are earnings/dividend/cash forecasts and results, which investors translate into a share price using a cost of capital which the board seemingly cannot control. Some of us are too old, too tired, or too busy to go back to school and learn all this stuff. Our book is here to help.

Our mission is to use our experience to help the business world to use the cost of capital for real.

What should you expect from this book?

The cost of capital is the fundamental financial tool for decision making. It drives measures of value creation and destruction; it forms the basis of decision making using cash flow and other frameworks. This book describes the key issues in understanding and using the cost of capital today, taking principles from the world of managerial finance and putting them into the context of major investment decisions which is where much of the difficulty lies.

There is an additional theme in this book, which is that of valuation. It is impossible to give real insight into how people use the cost of capital without looking at how it is combined with cash flows.

We (the authors) spend much of our lives piloting traveling companions across this great river of business life. We have seen many scramble back onto the bank, paralyzed by the analytical nature of the environment in which they are trying to navigate. We think you need a goal to keep you on course, hanging in there to the other side. So here are seven areas you might consider in the world of international investment, risk and return, and valuation with supporting questions:

1. Should a company use its own cost of capital to appraise new investments and acquisitions? For example, what cost of capital should a US regulated utility use when considering an acquisition in the construction or transport sectors? What if it can fund this acquisition by borrowing at a cheap rate?

2. What cost of capital should a US company use when appraising an investment in, say, the Philippines? What kind of risks should you be reflecting in the discount rate in international valuation and which are in cash flows – which emerging markets deserve a higher discount rate and why?

3. For a typical investment, which type of risk is more important – specific risk or systematic risk? How should these risks be reflected in, say, a venture capital situation?

4. Debt is cheaper than equity – so why don't companies raise more debt than they do? Why isn't the world full of companies financed using high gearing levels, or is there an optimal capital structure that can be achieved?

5. Most practitioners use the weighted average cost of capital ('WACC') in valuation and appraisal – but do they understand when it should not be the preferred approach and how to use other approaches?

6. Risk can be reflected in valuation through the use of real option modeling – how does this so-called innovative thinking sit with a net present value approach and discount rates?

7. Are global capital markets integrated? Does the equity market risk premium differ across markets and how should it be calculated?

We chose these because if you can answer them, it shows that you have already mastered some of the key financial navigation tools. In that case, our book may give you cause for debate and reflection. On the other hand, if you can't answer them fully now, at the end of the book you should be able to – and you'll have worked out the answers for yourself.

The agenda for this navigation lesson is divided into three main areas. These are covered in ten chapters:

Concepts

■ Risk and return revisited.

Field guide to the cost of capital

■ CAPM @ work.

■ The great EMRP debate.

■ CAPM is dead: long live CAPM.

■ The cost of debt and optimal capital structure.

■ International WACC and country risk.

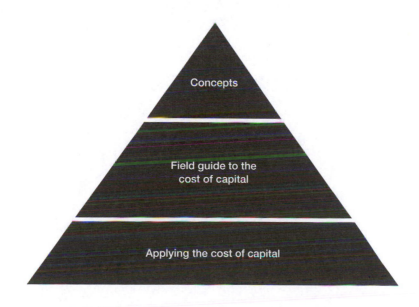

Applying the cost of capital

- Cash flows, the dot.com bubble, and all that.
- Using the cost of capital in business valuations.
- International valuation and appraisal.
- Premia and discounts.

We have gone into some theory as well as giving a real user's perspective on the issues and explain the strengths and weaknesses of some approaches. However, recapping on theory is an exciting diversion, because it gives us the power to set cost of capital theory up against the demands of practical decisions taken in today's world.

Deliberately, academic references have been avoided where possible; to reflect the environment of the business world, references to websites have been considered. We have created a website, *www.costofcapital.net*, which contains some current links. The site also carries financial games, and gives access to tax rate information and financial data relevant to using cost of capital around the world. Our objective is to make sure that the corporate planner, student, advisor, or decision maker, when he or she is on the road, can simply open the book or dial in and take advantage of a wealth of decision-making support, without the pain of extended academic study.

Examples in the book are drawn from real situations, simplified and disguised as necessary. No particular theory is espoused or recommended – where theory breaks down and where textbooks fall short, suggestions are made that meet the test of accepted principles.

But is this relevant to me?

If you are a person who makes, or even hopes one day to be in a position to make, financial decisions, then it is certainly relevant. If you manage a private company – then you need to understand the framework you can use to make better financial and investment decisions. If you own shares in a listed company – then you need to understand how to judge whether your investment is performing well or badly and some of the bases for shareholder-value measures. If you are studying financial matters, you could probably use a few war stories about what valuation practitioners struggle with in accomplishing their daily duties. And if you are a valuation practitioner or an economist – welcome home!

1

RISK AND RETURN REVISITED

This chapter deals with the concepts that underpin the application of cost of capital.

Companies obtain capital from both shareholders (equity) and lenders (debt). Both types of capital come at a cost. This is because investors require a return to reflect the opportunity cost associated with committing their money over a period of time. For debt this cost is the rate of interest that the lender charges – this varies with the amount of risk to which the lender is exposed.

In the case of equity, things are more complicated. Companies do not have a contractual obligation to reward shareholders at a specified rate. Indeed, shareholders can receive negative returns if stock prices fall and dividends are not paid. The cost of equity is the return on investment that shareholders expect to receive. While this is not guaranteed, firms that do not meet these required returns will find it difficult to attract equity capital, with a damaging impact on their businesses and the valuation of those businesses.

The cost of capital increases with risk. The riskier an investment, the higher the reward needed to attract investors. The only risks for which investors require a return are systematic risks correlated with the market as a whole. Risks specific to the investment do not affect the cost of capital as they can be eliminated by holding a well-diversified portfolio of different investments. Specific risks are nonetheless highly important as they affect expected cash flows and hence value and returns.

Introduction

The primary focus of this book is a practical, not theoretical one. It attempts to set out as clearly and nontechnically as possible what practitioners need to know about the cost of capital based on a knowledge of cutting edge academic, corporate, and advisory practice.

This is as it should be. The understanding of the cost of capital is of fundamental importance in taking key business decisions. To aid real-life decision taking it is necessary to have a practical approach to the area, not an academic or textbook one.

Against this objective for the book as a whole, this chapter rather bucks the trend. It is concerned with the theoretical underpinnings of the analysis of cost of capital. It considers the fundamental factors which determine the level of the cost of capital – the rate of time preference, the opportunity cost of investment, the relationship between risk and return, and the importance of the concepts of arbitrage and rationality to the theory. In order to comment on these fundamental relationships it necessarily contains material from the area of financial economics which is theoretical rather than practical or empirical in nature.

For this reason, if you are a reader who is looking purely for practical guidance on cost of capital issues, you may be tempted to move straight on to subsequent chapters. While this is possible (the material in later chapters is directly aimed at you, and does not presume a thorough acquaintance with the contents of this chapter) it would be a shame. A 'soup to nuts' understanding of the conceptual basis for cost of capital theory is an important part of the practitioner's armory. It rewards study, because in the real world situations continually arise which require adaptation of standard textbook analysis. The practitioner who understands from first principles why the accepted approach to cost of capital is the way it is will be able to adapt the theory with confidence to new situations as they arise.

Furthermore, some of the implications of the theory are not intuitive, and others are downright counter-intuitive (see Example 1.1). An understanding of the theory can help the practitioner to become more comfortable with such apparently counter-intuitive findings, and explain them more confidently to others who may be skeptical of the implications of the insights of cost of capital theory.

Example 1.1 Counter-intuitive findings

Among the nonintuitive results of financial theory, the most common ones which cost of capital practitioners are called upon to explain are:

- The finding of portfolio theory that investors do not require any reward for accepting risks which are specific to the company or project in hand (despite the fact that these are generally the most significant risks associated with any investment).
- That even if a company is able to fund an investment by borrowing money at a cheap interest rate, this does not mean it should appraise that project using the same low discount rate.
- Because individual investors are able to diversify their investments more easily than firms, diversification of business activities within a firm does not inherently add value to a company.

In order to make this chapter as practical and readable as possible, the theory is explained in a simple way, leaving out some of the complexity. It is structured as follows:

- It begins by defining the cost of capital – what is 'capital,' and in what way does it have a 'cost'?

- Next, it explains why individuals require a positive rate of return on investments, even when they are risk-free.

- It then introduces the concept of risk, explaining why individuals require high returns on risky projects.

- The discussion of risk and returns is then widened to explain theories of portfolio diversification of risk for investors, and the implications these have for the treatment of systematic and specific risks.

- Finally, we end with a discussion of the concepts of rationality and arbitrage which underpin the theory of the cost of capital.

Towards a definition of the cost of capital

Why the cost of capital matters

There can be little doubt that the cost of capital is an extremely important business and financial tool. It is used in corporate business models to help determine company valuation and shape corporate strategy. Governments use estimates of the cost of capital to regulate prices charged by some industries. Most importantly, the cost of capital is used by companies, individuals, and governments to help them take decisions regarding investment. In this sense, the cost of capital shapes the world we live in, by determining the balance between investment, consumption, and economic growth at the macroeconomic level, and how many factories, hospitals, and roads are constructed at the microeconomic level.

Given the role it performs in corporate and economic life, therefore, it is important to define clearly what is meant by the cost of capital. A useful starting point is to consider what is meant by the term 'capital' in this context.

What is capital?

Normally when economists refer to 'capital' they are referring to real, physical assets – buildings, plant, machinery, raw materials, semi-finished products, etc. 'Capital' in this sense is one of the two *factors of production* (the other being labor), which are combined by firms to produce output.

This is not the definition of 'capital' applied by financial economists and other practitioners when they refer to the 'cost of capital.' In this context, 'capital' refers to the financial resources or funds that businesses, individuals, or governments need in order to pursue a business enterprise or implement an investment project. It is essentially a monetary rather than a physical concept. Indeed, the trading markets in which companies and governments sell financial assets (or securities) in order to obtain their finance are referred to as *capital* markets.

> 'Capital' refers to the financial resources or funds that businesses, individuals, or governments need in order to pursue a business enterprise or implement an investment project.

The two apparently differing uses of the word 'capital' by economists can be reconciled. In the simple microeconomic approach to the firm, with only two factors of production (capital and labor), only capital requires the commitment by the firm of resources in one period in order to allow the firm to produce output in a subsequent period. Labor is purchased on an 'as needed' basis. In this simplified world, therefore, the only need the firm has for capital (in the financial sense) is to fund capital (in the sense of 'real' physical assets).

The essential definition of capital in the context of this book is one of timing – a company, individual, or government needs funds (capital) where resources are committed and/or paid for in advance of the business, enterprise, or project to which they are being committed delivering a payback.

While this concept is most readily understood in relation to 'real' capital assets (e.g. a machine with a productive life of 10 years purchased in year 1 will continue to generate cash until year 11), there are also real-life situations where financial capital is applied in the purchase of labor (e.g. a major infrastructure project involves a lengthy initial construction period before operation; during this period expenditure will be incurred on labor).

What is the cost of capital?

Having concluded that the appropriate definition of capital in the context of this book is a monetary one, meaning financial resources which must be committed to an enterprise or project with a delayed payback, it is now appropriate to consider what is meant by the 'cost' of this capital. Ignoring for the time being some of the more complex ways in which companies raise finance, there are essentially two forms of capital:

- *Debt.* Companies may draw down bank loans or issue bonds. In either case, the firm must promise to make payments over the period that the loan is outstanding (interest payments in the case of a bank loan, and coupon payments in the case of bonds) until the debt matures, at which point the original sum borrowed will need to be repaid.

■ *Equity*. Firms issue shares, representing a claim on the value of the firm after debt has been repaid. Shareholders receive dividend payments from the firm and can also benefit from any increase in the value of shares.

The cost of debt

If all capital were raised in the form of debt the cost of capital would be relatively clear and unambiguous (and this book could be significantly shorter!). It could be simply proxied by the rate of interest paid[1] by a company, individual, or government on its overdraft, bank loans, or bonds. There would still be a need to understand why this rate of interest varied between different organizations and for borrowings over different periods of time, but it would be clear to everyone that there is a cost of raising capital, and that this must be met in the form of payments of real money.

Why is there a cost of equity?

The remuneration of equity, however, introduces far more complexity. Companies do not commit themselves to paying a certain level of dividends. Share prices can fall as well as go up. There is therefore no clearly defined contractual cost of raising capital through issuing equity, the most common source of capital for companies.

But while the payments that companies must make to shareholders are not contractually defined, that does not mean that equity finance is free. Indeed, because the payments that equity investors receive are not determined on a contractual basis, and because equity investors receive payments only after debt payments have been made, equity finance is more expensive than debt finance – companies need to reward equity investors for bearing a higher level of risk than debt investors.

How is the cost of equity determined?

But if there is no contractual arrangement between a company and its equity investors regarding the level at which the firm remunerates the providers of equity capital, how is the cost of this type of capital determined? It seems at first glance odd even to refer to this as a 'cost' when it is clear that there are real world examples where companies, far from paying equity investors for the use of their capital, have actually given them negative returns.[2]

The opportunity cost of equity investment

There are two elements to the explanation of this apparent mystery. The first element concerns the economic concept of 'opportunity cost.' Individuals can choose among a range of opportunities when deciding whether to invest their money as equity in a business. For example, they could make equity investments in other businesses; they could lend it to a bank, company, or individual; they could invest it in an enterprise themselves; or, indeed, they could decide to increase their level of personal consumption.

> In order to attract equity capital from an individual a firm must convince the individual that the return on such an equity investment will be at least as great as the return on the best alternative opportunity foregone.

An individual behaving rationally will therefore choose to invest in the equity of a company only if he or she believes that this is the best option given the other opportunities available. In order to attract equity capital from an individual, therefore, a firm must convince the individual that the return on such an equity investment will be at least as great as the return on the best alternative opportunity foregone. This latter concept is the equity investor's 'opportunity cost of capital' – it is this return which provides a floor on the expected return which the equity investment must yield.

Expected versus actual returns

This brings us on to the second element in deriving the cost of equity – it is defined in terms of 'expected' or 'required' returns on investment, not actual or achieved returns. When individuals make decisions regarding equity investments there are no guarantees regarding the returns they will actually receive. Based on information available on a company and its prospects they will have views on the likely level of returns which will be achieved, but there is no guarantee that these expectations will be fulfilled. The actual outcome ('ex-post' in the jargon) could be either higher or lower than that which was expected ('ex-ante').

To attract equity investment, therefore, a company must convince investors that if they invest in the company the likely returns they will receive are at least as high as those for the next best alternative opportunity. Ex-post, actual returns could be higher or lower than ex-ante expected returns. However, any company which habitually delivered lower returns than alternative investments would quickly find it difficult to attract equity investment (because potential investors would reduce their ex-ante expectation of returns and reject such an investment in favor of alternatives).

The effect on the company would be devastating. It would be unable to attract new equity capital (e.g. through rights issues) or indeed debt finance (because its share price would fall, thus affecting its credit rating). It would have difficulty in financing its operations, its share price would fall further and it would become prone to takeover or in the most extreme case, failure.

The weighted average cost of capital

There is thus a cost to a business in obtaining capital. For debt, this cost is defined in terms of payments the company must honor contractually. For equity, the business must offer the expectation that the returns on its equity will be as good as those available from other opportunities – and over time it must achieve these returns.

The overall cost of capital of a business is simply the weighted average of the cost of debt and the cost of equity, where the two costs are weighted by the relative proportions of the business which are financed by debt and equity. This forms the basis for the formula for the weighted average cost of capital (or WACC):

$$\text{WACC} = K_e * \frac{E}{V} + K_d * (1 - T) * \frac{D}{V}$$

where

K_e	=	Cost of equity
K_d	=	Cost of debt
E	=	Market value of equity
D	=	Market value of debt
T	=	Corporate tax rate
V	=	Market value of equity plus market value of debt

This WACC formula is extremely important. We will return to it, and the calculation of its components (the cost of debt, the cost of equity, and the relative shares of each in the capital structure) regularly throughout this book.

Understanding the principles that determine the cost of capital

The previous sections of this chapter have explained that a fundamental defining characteristic of capital for the purposes of this book is one of timing – there is a delay between the commitment of financial resources and the receipt of returns. They have also shown how the returns investors require for providing capital are set with regard to the opportunity cost of that capital – the higher the returns investors could achieve through other uses of the money, the higher the returns they will demand for providing capital.

Consider a risk-free investment (we will turn to exactly what we mean by 'risk' in a moment). Because interest rates on risk-free investments are positive (for example, the average yield on 10-year US government securities, which can be regarded as risk-free, was 4.25% at the end of 2003) it is obvious that no one would invest capital in any other risk-free investment that was not expected to give a return at least equal to this rate of interest.

It is clearly reasonable that the interest rate on a risk-free investment should compensate investors for expected inflation. But an important question is why risk-free interest rates should be positive in real terms. This is not a subject generally considered by financial textbooks. They usually simply note that there are opportunities to invest risk-free at positive real interest rates, and therefore it would be illogical for individuals to make investments which did not at least match these available returns.

Why is the real risk-free rate of interest positive?

To understand why the real return on a risk-free investment should be positive requires an understanding of a branch of economics that has developed largely separately from that which considers the cost of capital.

There is a positive rate of interest for a risk-free investment because, empirically, individuals have an innate tendency to attach a higher value to money in the present than in the future. In the jargon, economists refer to an individual's 'rate of time preference,' the rate at which he or she is willing to substitute consumption in one period for consumption in the next (i.e. the additional consumption he or she will require in a subsequent period to compensate him or her for investing – and hence foregoing consumption – in an earlier period).

Interested readers may wish to visit our website at *www.costofcapital.net* for a formal economic exposition of this.

Why should individuals in general attach greater importance to consumption today than consumption tomorrow, in the absence of risk? The standard approach suggests three possible explanations:

- *An inherent or 'pure' rate of time preference*. This suggests that individuals attach less value to future utility arising from future consumption and income relative to that in the present, simply by virtue of it arising at a later date. It is not clear why this should be the case. Indeed, concepts of 'saving the best until last' and 'getting it over with' would suggest the opposite. Nevertheless, some empirical studies of savings behavior suggest a small positive interest rate value for this effect.

■ *Changing life chances*. If people believe that the risks of death increase over time then this would explain why less weight is attached to future consumption and income ('you can't take it with you'). This operates at a number of levels. Clearly for an individual the risk of death does increase with age. Some commentators have also suggested that perceptions of the risk of the total destruction of society will influence the rate of time preference.

■ *Expected income in future years*. It is plausible to assume that the extent to which individuals will be prepared to substitute consumption in one period for another will be related to their consumption in each period. As in general it is anticipated that economies will grow over time, and hence the average individual will be better off in future years than now, this is a reason why individuals may apply a positive time preference rate to future income and consumption compared to that in the present.

While it is difficult to obtain reliable empirical estimates for these factors, and hence the range of possible values for the rate of time preference is relatively wide, the best estimates suggest figures which are broadly in line with historically observed values for the risk-free rate of interest.

Introducing risk

The preceding discussion set out the reasons why the equilibrium return on a risk-free investment is likely to be positive in real terms. It is now time to discuss what we mean by 'risk' and consider how risk affects the cost of capital.

Most people would agree that, in general, individuals wish to avoid risk (they are 'risk averse'). Offered a choice between a particular level of income with certainty, or the same expected level of income but with a degree of uncertainty (the actual outcome could be higher or lower), most individuals would prefer the certain option.

Once again, interested readers can visit our website at *www.costofcapital.net* to read a formal economic treatment of this.

The implications of risk aversion for the cost of capital are clear. Capital is committed in one period in the expectation of returns in a subsequent period or periods. The investment is made with certainty – the resources are committed. In most cases, however, the expected future rewards are uncertain. A risk averse individual will therefore require higher expected returns in the future to compensate him or her for accepting this risk.

All risks are not equal

That investors require higher returns for investing in more risky projects is hardly an earth-shattering finding and is one with which we suspect most readers will be completely comfortable. However, now comes the conceptually difficult bit – not all risks are equal. If an investor holds a diversified portfolio of equity investments then he or she will require a return to compensate only for those risks which contribute to the risk associated with the portfolio as a whole.[3] Risks which are unique or specific to a particular equity investment are 'diversified away' by holding the portfolio, and the investor will therefore not require any additional return as a reward for bearing such risks.

This is an extremely important result in financial economics, but unfortunately it is also one that is highly counter-intuitive and is often misunderstood in business life.

Take the example of an oil company considering an investment in drilling a new oil well. Overwhelmingly the preoccupation of the company in contemplating what is likely to be a large up-front investment will be the prospects that the well will turn out to produce large quantities of oil at a reasonable cost per barrel. If the well is dry the investment will prove fruitless. If it turns out to be a gusher, it is likely to make a very high return. The company will therefore put a lot of effort into geological surveys to give itself the best chance that it drills in the right place to find the oil. If you were to ask the project manager about the risks involved in the investment, he or she would talk mainly about the very real danger that oil would not be found in sufficient quantities to make the well commercially viable.

Diversifiable good, undiversifiable bad

However, the risks associated with finding oil are *specific* to this investment. They therefore do not affect the expected returns that an investor with a well-diversified portfolio of equity investments requires in order to compensate him or her for the risks to which he or she is exposed by such an investment. This is because, on average, those investments in an equity portfolio which perform poorly due to specific factors will be balanced by ones which perform above expectations. In terms of the oil well example, for every dry well another may turn out to be a gusher. Or, indeed, poor returns on an investment in an oil exploration company might be offset by high returns on a completely unrelated investment in a different sector.

As long as an investor has a well-diversified equity portfolio, therefore, these specific risks are eliminated. The only risks to which an investor with an equity portfolio remains exposed are systematic risks which affect all investments and therefore cannot be 'diversified away.' Investments in most shares would perform badly if, for example, the rate of economic growth were to slow (since that would reduce demand for most products).

How portfolio diversification reduces risk

The implications of portfolio diversification for risk and return were first explored by Harry Markowitz in an article written in 1952. He pointed out that individuals can reduce the variability of the returns on the investments they make (i.e. reduce the risk) simply by investing in a number of different companies or investments.

> Markowitz pointed out that individuals can reduce the variability of the returns on the investments they make simply by investing in a number of different companies or investments.

The practical implications of diversification are most easily illustrated with a simple example. Figure 1.1 shows the monthly returns for the two year period from July 2000 to June 2002 for two companies picked at random from the Standard & Poor's 500: El Paso and Fox Entertainment Group.

Figure 1.1 shows that the returns on an investment in El Paso over this period varied from −36% in one month to +18% in another. A good measure of the volatility of returns (and hence risk) is the standard deviation of returns.[4] For El Paso in this period the standard deviation was 47%. Returns on Fox in this period were similarly variable, ranging from −25% to +20%, with a standard deviation of about 50%. These standard deviations measure the total variability in returns for each of the two companies, whether caused by company specific or systematic risk factors.

Now consider Figure 1.2. It shows the returns on a portfolio consisting of equal amounts of money invested in El Paso and Fox. One might expect that such a portfolio would have a standard deviation of around 48.5%, halfway between those of El Paso and Fox. In fact, the standard deviation on this portfolio is only 38%. Some risk has effectively 'disappeared' because in some periods poor performance on El Paso stock is offset by good performance on Fox (and vice versa).

FIGURE 1.1

Volatility of returns on two randomly chosen stocks

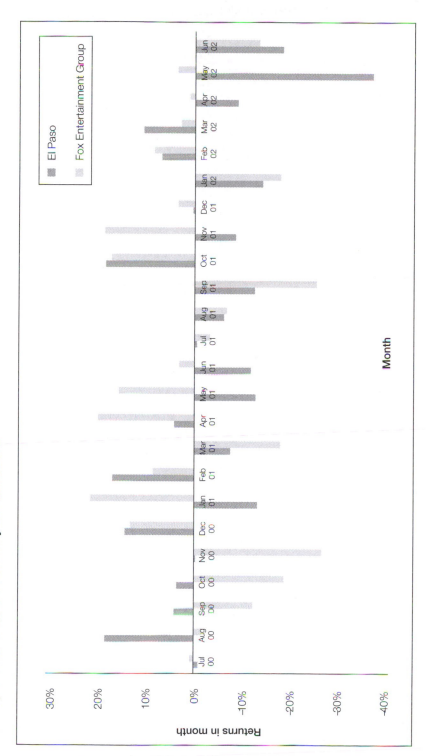

FIGURE 1.2
Volatility of returns of the two-stock portfolio

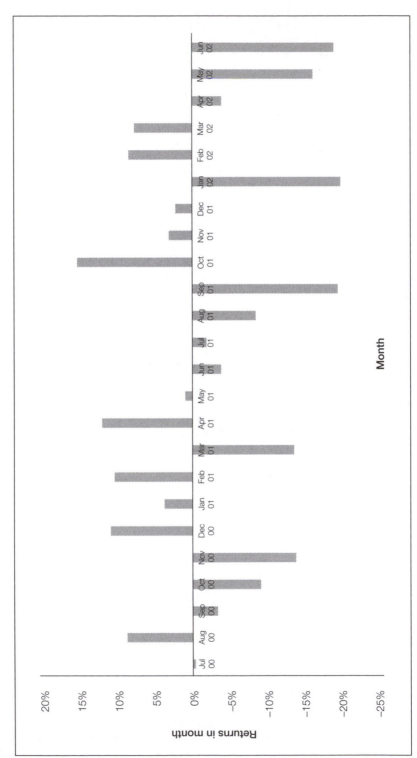

When considering investments in only two stocks, as in Figures 1.1 and 1.2, it is possible to put bounds on the extent to which risk is reduced. If the returns on El Paso and Fox were perfectly correlated (i.e. if they always moved in step with one another) then the standard deviation of a 50%–50% portfolio of the two stocks would simply be the average of the individual deviations (i.e. 48.5%). If, on the other hand, the two stocks were perfectly negatively correlated (i.e. when the returns on El Paso go up the returns on Fox go down by the same amount, and vice versa) then the standard deviation of the 50%–50% portfolio would be 0. In such circumstances, an investment in El Paso would effectively provide insurance against an investment in Fox, giving the investor absolute certainty of returns.

> In a well-diversified portfolio the risks to which the investor remains exposed are purely those associated with the market as a whole; risks specific to a particular stock or investment are not relevant.

In real life the returns on most companies are positively correlated but not perfectly correlated. In other words, the returns on investments and companies vary because of a range of uncertain factors, some of which are specific to the particular company or investment, and some of which (most notably changes in the economic environment) affect all companies together.

As more and more investments are added to a portfolio, the contribution to variability of returns of the factors which affect only an individual company or investment declines, and the importance of the correlation between variations in returns begins to dominate. Essentially this happens because, if a portfolio contains a sufficient number of diverse stocks, then on average in any period the lower returns on investments which perform adversely due to specific factors will be offset by higher returns on those which perform well due to favorable specific factors. At the limit, once a sufficient number of stocks has been added to a portfolio, all the variability in returns is associated with those factors which influence all of the stocks systematically – the factors which cause returns on individual stocks to be correlated. Hence, in a well-diversified portfolio the risks to which the investor remains exposed are purely those associated with the market as a whole; risks specific to a particular stock or investment are not relevant. To illustrate how this happens, Figure 1.3 shows how the standard deviation of returns changes as more stocks are added to a portfolio.

In Figure 1.3 we illustrate the effects of increasing the number of stocks in a portfolio using monthly data for July 2000–June 2002.

The standard deviation associated with investment in a portfolio of two stocks is that for a portfolio invested in El Paso and Fox Entertainment Group (as in Figure 1.2). Figure 1.3 then shows the influence on the standard deviation of adding more and more companies selected at random from the Standard & Poor's 500 to the portfolio.

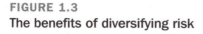

FIGURE 1.3
The benefits of diversifying risk

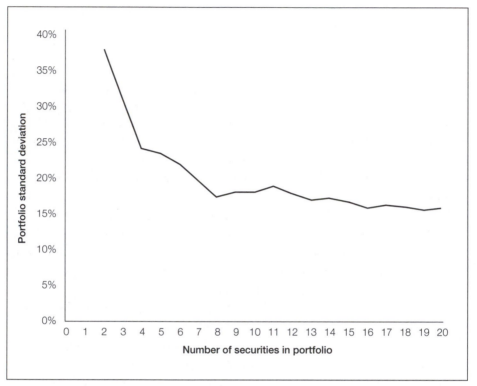

It can be seen that the overall variability of returns falls rapidly as stocks are added, before leveling out. Generally, there is little reduction in risk through adding more stocks beyond 20 to 30. At this point, the only risk associated with a portfolio is that for the market as a whole.

Systematic and specific risks

Thus, it is clear from this analysis that, by investing in a portfolio of stocks, an individual can diversify away the specific risks associated with an individual stock. If equity investors with well-diversified portfolios contemplate investing in additional stocks then the only risk to which they are exposing themselves is that which contributes to the overall riskiness of the portfolio. This comprises that part of the variability in the new stock which is correlated with the variability of the overall portfolio (systematic risk) and not risk uniquely associated with the stock itself (specific risk).

Table 1.1 gives examples of systematic and specific risks.

TABLE 1.1
Systematic and specific risk

Examples of systematic risk	Examples of specific risk
Growth in gross domestic product (GDP) is faster than expected	Construction of a new plant is cheaper than expected
Interest rates rise	There is a labor force strike in the factory
The local currency appreciates	Products need to be withdrawn due to a safety scare
The rate of inflation falls	A rival company goes out of business
There is an increase in the world price of oil	An oil well turns out to be dry

It should be noted that some of these examples would have a favorable impact on returns. As we shall see later, this is important. When the theory refers to risk it means *variability* about an average. It does not refer simply to the possibility of downside movements. This is why in Figures 1.1 to 1.3 we measured risk in terms of the standard deviation of portfolio returns, a measure of variability around the mean.

The relationship between risk and return

Portfolio models of the cost of equity

As we shall see in Chapter 4, most models of the cost of equity are based on the assumption that equity investors hold well-diversified portfolios. These models therefore assume that the cost of equity for any investment will increase only with the extent of systematic risk to which the investment exposes the equity investor.

This is true of the most commonly used model for calculating the cost of equity, the Capital Asset Pricing Model (CAPM). This model gives the formula for the cost of equity as:

$$K_e = R_f + \beta_e * EMRP$$

where K_e = Cost of equity

R_f = Risk-free rate

β_e = Equity beta of investment

EMRP = Equity market risk premium

The CAPM derives the cost of equity by adding to the risk-free rate (of interest) a premium for risk. This risk premium is itself a product of the equity market risk premium (a measure of the reward required by investors for investing in an equity of average risk) and the investment's beta (a measure of the relative systematic risk of the particular equity investment being considered). So the CAPM suggests that the cost of equity will vary between different investments only to the extent that investments exhibit differing degrees of systematic risk.

We will return to the CAPM in much more detail in later chapters.

Do specific risks matter?

Calculating the return an investor will require to compensate for the risk in investing in a stock, therefore, involves identifying those risks which are correlated with the portfolio or market as a whole. Hence, models such as the CAPM are concerned with measuring the degree of correlation between movements in an individual company's or stock's return, and the returns on the market as a whole. They do not concern themselves with the total variability of returns of an individual company or stock, as much of this variability is specific to the company or stock, and is therefore irrelevant in terms of the contribution to the riskiness of the portfolio as a whole.

While the logic is compelling, and the arithmetic in Figure 1.3 cannot be disputed, practical business people often have difficulty with the implications. In part, these difficulties are caused by the lack of a practical explanation of the theory as it impacts on businesses.

A big hole in the way the theory is normally explained is its lack of clarification of the importance of project or company specific risks. The financial theory textbooks tend to dismiss these risks as unimportant because they can be diversified away. However, as the oil well example above indicates, much of business life is concerned with these risks. Does this mean that companies are misguided in how they direct their resources? Or does it imply that the theory is too academic and out of touch with the realities of corporate life?

As we shall see the answer is that company-specific risks are incredibly important, and investors should be extremely concerned about them. They should look for companies which have decision makers with the expertise to manage their impact. Implicit in the portfolio analysis are the assumptions that:

■ Project or firm-specific risks are symmetrical. In other words, these factors could equally well result in higher returns as in lower ones. Readers need to be absolutely clear that in the context of cost of capital analysis 'risk' normally means 'variability,' i.e. the possibility of fluctuations in returns, whether below *or above* the expected or required level.

■ By investing in a portfolio of shares, the investor can be confident that for every share which suffers a slump in returns due to unfavorable company specific circumstances, there will be another which enjoys higher returns for specific reasons.

The importance of specific risks to investors

These points have two extremely important ramifications for the attention which investors and managers should pay to company specific risks.

First, for it to be reasonable to regard specific risks as being symmetrical, it is vital that managers and investors always look at true expected cash flows associated with any business or project. Implicit in the theory of a portfolio approach to the cost of capital is an assumption that the cost of capital is being applied to a probability-weighted assessment of cash flows, so that variations about the cash flows can be properly regarded as symmetrical.

> It is vital that managers and investors always look at true expected cash flows associated with any business or project.

Generally business people do not regard the possibility of above-expected returns as a 'risk,' but cost of capital theory does. The whole theory is based on the assumption that investors calculate the expected returns from an investment. The estimate of expected returns should take into account all the possible outcomes, weighting each by the probability of it being the actual outcome. Having performed such a calculation, by definition the amounts by which the cash flows for an investment might fall below their expected value are exactly matched by the upside risks. There is thus no innate risk to the investor that the investment will return below expected returns. Rather, the investor is exposed to the volatility of returns around this true, probability-weighted value.

This calculation takes into account all the risks that can affect the returns on an investment, both specific and systematic. So specific risks do matter to equity investors, as they affect expected cash flows and hence expected returns and value.

Second, all investors, however well-diversified, should be aware of the specific risks associated with companies and projects, and should invest in businesses which have decision makers who are highly capable in managing these risks. This is because the theory that such risks are diversified away is based on an assumption that for every stock which performs badly on the basis of specific risks, there is another which performs well, providing insurance and stability. Achieving successful outcomes and avoiding unsuccessful outcomes is down to good management of the project or company specific risks.

Specific risks and the cost of debt

Debt finance provides a further reason why specific risks do matter. Debt providers have no upside on the promised yield on their investment. In the event that the company or project is successful the investment is simply remunerated at the appropriate rate: the principal is repaid, together with the promised contractual interest payments. In the event that the company or project is unsuccessful (whether due to systematic or specific factors) there is a possibility that the returns on debt will be less than promised.

Thus, for a debt provider, diversification provides no protection against downside risks associated with specific factors.[5] If one investment fails to pay adequate returns due to specific factors there are no offsetting higher returns from other investments – those which are successful will simply reward debt at the contractually required rate.

This asymmetrical risk profile means that debt providers do require a higher promised return on their investment to reflect company or project specific risks.

Diversification by companies

As diversification reduces risk, does this mean that it is sensible for a firm to diversify itself?

An implication of the analysis is that, if it is assumed that investors have already diversified their investment portfolios through their choice of investments in the capital markets, then there is no additional cost of capital benefit to them of a firm diversifying itself. Furthermore, it is cheaper for shareholders to diversify risk than companies – it is a purely financial transaction for shareholders. As a consequence, investing in a new business area is a decision which should be taken on its own merits. Firms should not reduce the cost of capital used to appraise investments simply because those investments diversify the firm's business interests.

This is often a difficult result to explain to managers who assume that there are benefits in spreading company risks across a wider range of activities. Indeed, for the managers, who are generally not diversified in their choice of career and job, the attractions of such a policy appear obvious. This is not to say that diversification at the company level cannot enhance shareholder value. It may well do so, but the source of such additional value must be through improved expected cash flows, not a lower cost of capital.

There are several ways in which a move into a new business area could increase the value of a business. A new venture might simply generate value in its own right, which might be boosted by any synergies with the existing business. Or there may indeed be cash flow benefits of diversification per se, irrespective of inherent value and synergies. For example, diversification into a different business area may reduce the risk that a temporary downturn in the core business would result in the company going into financial distress, creating costs which investors would need to bear (such costs of financial distress are discussed in Chapter 5). The expected value of these avoided costs might help justify the policy of diversification. Similarly, it may be difficult to attract the right calibre of managers, or encourage them to take appropriate business risks in the shareholders' interests, if they are concerned that their jobs are not secure in an undiversified business.

Diversification at the corporate level might therefore yield benefits if it improved the management of the core business. The key point here is that any such benefits impact on shareholder value through improvements in expected cash flows, not a reduction in the cost of capital. Diversification at the corporate level cannot be assumed to reduce the cost of capital.

Arbitrage and rationality

The preceding sections have established that there is an opportunity cost of capital because investors who commit money over a period of time expect to earn a return on this investment, both because there is a general tendency to attach more value to consumption today than consumption tomorrow, and because making such investments exposes them to risk. Because most risk can be diversified away by investing in a portfolio, the only risks for which investors need to be compensated are systematic risks which affect the whole portfolio.

Returns on nondiversified investments

This assumes that individuals will take advantage of the benefits of diversification. It is plausible to make this assumption because most investors have access to pension and mutual funds in which they can invest relatively small sums of money across a very wide range of stocks. Because they have access to such funds, and it is rational for the investor to pursue a policy of diversification, companies should assume that their investors are diversified.

However, in real-life situations it is common to observe individuals who do not hold a diversified portfolio. For example, an entrepreneur may invest all of his or her money in a single business venture of doubtful reliability, effectively betting that the venture will be successful and will achieve much higher returns than would be available on a portfolio of stocks.

Furthermore, it is clear that the highest returns accrue to those who do not diversify. By definition, the returns on a diversified portfolio are likely to be close to the average returns on stocks in the market as a whole – strong performing stocks are balanced by those which perform less well. An undiversified investment strategy, by contrast, can pay off spectacularly well (see Example 1.2).

Example 1.2 A successful undiversified investment strategy

In July 1999 *The* (London) *Times* newspaper reported the case of a man in West Yorkshire, England, who had inherited a £6.3 million fortune from his parents. This was accumulated as a result of a decision around 50 years earlier to invest about £1,500 in Glaxo, a pharmaceutical company. By 1999 Glaxo Wellcome was one of the top three pharmaceutical manufacturers in the world. Had the money been invested in a diversified portfolio of UK stocks, *The Times* estimated that it would have risen in value to less than £500,000.

Why an undiversified investment strategy is foolish

This in no way invalidates the analysis. Ex-ante an undiversified investment strategy represents a poor risk–reward tradeoff. Consider the example of an investor considering investing in the shares of a completely new venture, anticipating that in the event it was successful the share price would rocket. Suppose that this investor took the view that, because he or she was less risk averse than other people, he or she would be prepared to put all his or her funds into this single share and would reason that there should be a reward for the extra firm-specific risk to which this exposed him or her.

The problem for our risk-taking investor is that other investors who behaved rationally would be considering whether to invest in the same share on the basis that this would form just one investment in a diversified portfolio of investments. This would drive the expected returns available on the share ex-ante down to those required to compensate for systematic risks only – if the share price were low enough to offer an expected return in excess of this, more investors would choose to invest in the area, increasing the share price and thus driving down anticipated returns for everyone who invested.

While our risk-taking entrepreneur might not view the investment as being associated with a portfolio, because other individuals behaved rationally and did invest in a portfolio, the expected return associated **An undiversified investment strategy represents a poor risk-reward trade off.** with the share would be driven down to the levels of return required by such individuals. The entrepreneur's investment would therefore look extremely unattractive – ex-ante, the expectation would be for low returns, but he would be exposed to the entire risk (both specific and systematic) associated with the share.

Of course, as noted above, ex-post returns *could* turn out to be extremely high. The investment might do spectacularly well. Our entrepreneur would then appear to have followed a sensible investment strategy by putting all his or her eggs in one basket, while those cautious souls with diversified portfolios would in all likelihood find their high returns in this venture offset by losses or low returns in other areas.

Newspapers are full of stories about nondiversified investments which pay off spectacularly. One example was given in Example 1.2. But for every such success story, there is another where the investment backfires equally spectacularly (see Example 1.3).

Example 1.3 An unsuccessful undiversified investment strategy

In October 2001 British newspapers reported the case of a prominent former UK amateur sportsman who invested his life's savings of £70,000 in shares in a single company, Railtrack, the company which operated the railway infrastructure in Great Britain. Unfortunately for him he made this investment only hours before the UK government withdrew its financial ▶

support and put the company into administration. The man, who runs a financial training company, was quoted as saying 'I'm an opportunistic spiv and I like a punt' and 'Even though I'm a fellow of the Institute of Chartered Accountants, I am obviously pretty dumb.'

Because in a competitive market the expected returns available when money is invested will reflect only the risks to which a diversified investor is exposed, overall a policy of nondiversified investment will not adequately reward the undiversified investor for risk – it is a bad bet.

The importance of arbitrage for expected returns

The process by which expected returns are brought in line is called 'arbitrage.' If there is an opportunity available for investors to make excess returns they will take advantage of this, and in efficient markets where capital is able to flow freely to take advantage of the best available opportunities, any anomalies will be closed as soon as they open. There will thus be a 'going rate' for the returns available and required for investments with a given risk profile, and all investments will need to be in line with this. Any investment which paid a low return relevant to its risk would be starved of funds.

Behaviorial aspects of the cost of capital

In much of the preceding discussion we have implicitly or explicitly relied on investors behaving rationally and markets being competitive. This provides the basis for assertions regarding portfolio diversification and arbitrage.

Such assumptions are conventional in economic analysis, because by and large they hold true for the majority of people. It seems reasonable to conclude that investors will want to maximize their wealth and minimize their risk, and will act accordingly. It is also difficult to make predictions about the nature of markets where such basic patterns of behavior are not assumed.

Nevertheless, the cold logic of rationality is demonstrably at odds with some patterns of behavior readily observable in society, and it is worth considering some of these briefly before taking our theory out into the real world.

Irrationality and risk assessment

The analysis above relied on investors being able to assess risk effectively. Evidence suggests that when it comes to matters of probability and risk this may be a dangerous assumption.

Consider this well-known puzzle. You are offered a choice of three boxes. In one of them is $1,000, but the other two are empty. After you have chosen, one of the other two boxes is opened to reveal that it is empty, and you are given the choice of either staying with your original selection or changing to the other unopened box. Does it make any difference whether you change your mind or not?

Intuitively most people do not think that it makes any difference, and some are suspicious that the offer to change is some sort of trick on the part of the organizer of the puzzle. But in fact, if you change your choice you actually *double* your chances of winning the $1,000. This is demonstrated in Figure 1.4.

FIGURE 1.4
Double or twist?

Assume $1,000 in Box A

Strategy 1 – Don't switch	Initial choice	Box opened	Final choice	Result	
	A	B or C	A	$1,000	1/3
	B	C	B	$0	} 2/3
	C	B	C	$0	

Strategy 2 – Switch	Initial choice	Box opened	Final choice	Result	
	A	B or C	C or B	$0	1/3
	B	C	A	$1,000	} 2/3
	C	B	A	$1,000	

Essentially what happens is that there is a 2/3 chance that the $1,000 is in one of the two boxes *not* selected. Because the organizer does not choose at random which of these two boxes to open (he or she chooses to open an empty box) effectively the 2/3 probability that the money is in one of these boxes is concentrated in the remaining unopened box. By staying with the original choice your probability of success remains at 1/3, the probability at the start of the process. By reacting to the new information (the opened box) a rational person can double his or her chances of success.

The fact that most people get this puzzle wrong emphasizes how difficult it is for people to react rationally and relate to matters of risk and probability.

Following different agendas

We have generally assumed above that people will be motivated to increase their wealth and reduce risk. In fact, they may be motivated by other concerns, including altruism or megalomania.

This is particularly true in the case of managers. Sometimes the interests of managers and shareholders are not aligned. We saw earlier how diversification at the level of the firm does not reduce the cost of capital (assuming that investors are already well-diversified), but that managers may see a benefit in such diversification because of the risk to their own job prospects of working for a firm exposed to the specific risks in single sector. For this reason, managers may wish to pursue a policy of diversification even when there is no benefit to shareholders (this is called the *agency problem*[6] – see Chapter 6 for more on this in the context of international investment). It is dangerous to assume that managers will always run companies to maximize returns for shareholders.

Asymmetric information and ineffective competition

Furthermore, the assumption that arbitrage results in the prices of assets being driven to their appropriate levels given the amount of risk is flawed because it is based on assumptions about markets which do not hold in real life. For example, investors differ in the amount of information they have so that some individuals are better able to assess likely returns and risks than others. Insider trading is an extreme example of this. In addition, there are barriers to entry and other discontinuities which mean that it is possible for investments to offer higher ex-ante returns than would be expected given the amount of risk to which they expose the investor.

Interested readers should visit our website at *www.costofcapital.net* for further illustrations of behavioral aspects of finance.

Key points from the chapter

This chapter has dealt with the fundamental concepts of risk and return. The key points it has covered are:

- Capital is defined as financial resources which must be committed to an enterprise or project with a delayed payback.

- There are two principal sources of capital: debt and equity. The promised cost of debt is simply the interest rate that must be paid on the loan or bond.

- Understanding and calculating the cost of equity capital is difficult. Equity investors expect to earn a return on their investment which at least matches the return they could reasonably expect from the next best alternative. The cost of equity is therefore an opportunity cost.

- Investors require a return even on a risk-free investment where the repayment of the principal is guaranteed. This is because of individuals' general preference for 'jam today,' which appears to be linked to factors such as expected higher future incomes and the increased probability of death.

- As individuals are also risk averse (given the choice, they prefer a given level of income with certainty rather than the same income with a degree of variability), investors require higher returns to compensate them for bearing risk in investments.

- However, modern portfolio theory tells us that there is an important distinction between systematic risks (i.e. those risk factors that tend to affect all investments simultaneously) and specific risks (i.e. those risks which are specific to a particular investment or group of investments).

- Because investors can 'diversify away' specific risks by holding a portfolio of different investments, the only risks to which they are exposed are systematic risks. Consequently, required returns on equity vary between investments according to the relative degree of systematic risks to which they expose the investor.

- Diversification at the company level does not in itself necessarily affect the cost of capital.

- Specific risks are nevertheless extremely important for all investors. They have a significant impact on the cash flows generated by an investment and hence on the success or failure of an investment. Ex-ante, investors will look for investments which they expect to achieve a satisfactory return, given the likely impact of all risks, specific as well as systematic, on probability-weighted cash flows.

Notes

1   For the time being we ignore the complexity that the interest rate is the 'promised' cost of debt, and is higher than the 'expected' cost of debt (which takes into account the risk of default). By convention this distinction is generally ignored, but it is discussed later in this chapter and in Chapter 5.

2   The authors have been told more than once in emerging markets that equity finance is cheaper than debt finance because in times of high inflation and economic difficulty the former does not have to be remunerated while the latter must always be paid.

3   Under the conventional approach to the return on debt, the same is not true of debt investments – see later in this chapter.

4   Standard deviation measures the dispersion of a set of values around the mean. For a variable x, which occurs N times, the standard deviation can be

calculated as: $\sqrt{\dfrac{\Sigma\,(x_i - \mu)^2}{N-1}}$

where x_i represents each individual value of x and μ is the mean of x.

5   This is only true when the yield being considered is the 'promised' (i.e. contractual) yield as opposed to the lower 'expected' yield (which takes into account the possibility of default). If the expected yield is considered, then risks are symmetric and debt providers benefit from diversification in the same way as equity providers. However, as we shall see in Chapter 5, it is conventional practice to consider the promised yield rather than the expected yield on debt, and this includes an element to compensate the debt provider for the risk of default due to risk factors specific to the borrower.

6   See Jensen and Meckling (1976) 'Theory of the Firm: Managerial Behaviour', *Journal of Financial Economics*.

2

CAPM @ WORK

This chapter is about using the Capital Asset Pricing Model (CAPM) to calculate the cost of equity capital. It is the first chapter in our 'field guide' section of the book and so dives straight into the mechanics of the CAPM in order to get practitioners' hands dirty.

We have found the CAPM to be the most widely used framework for calculating the cost of equity capital. The CAPM relies on a number of empirical inputs. These include the risk-free rate and beta. The risk-free rate can be estimated in real or nominal terms, using a variety of financial instruments and terms to maturity. The government security most commonly used is a long dated ordinary bond, although alternative instruments may be a better measure in certain circumstances.

Beta is a more complex variable to estimate. A number of data providers supply information on beta, but the practitioner must tread carefully. Bloomberg is a useful source because it allows flexibility to be applied in choosing how to calculate beta.

Introduction

In Chapter 1, we introduced the concepts of specific and systematic risk, and explained how these two types of risk are very different. We also discussed perhaps the most important proposition in financial theory: namely, that an equity investor can eliminate his or her exposure to specific risk by holding a diverse portfolio of equity investments. The consequence of this is that the only risk that equity investors will require a return for bearing is *systematic* risk, because *specific* risk can be diversified away.

The most commonly used model for assessing systematic risk and calculating the cost of equity capital is the Capital Asset Pricing Model (CAPM). This model is recognized by both the academic and commercial communities and has a strong pedigree. The CAPM is also used by investment analysts, utility regulators, corporate planners, and even government officials.

The formula for the model is reproduced below:

$$K_e = R_f + \beta_e * EMRP$$

$$
\begin{array}{lll}
\text{where} & K_e & = & \text{Cost of equity} \\
& R_f & = & \text{Risk-free rate} \\
& \beta_e & = & \text{Equity beta of investment} \\
& EMRP & = & \text{Equity market risk premium}
\end{array}
$$

The CAPM derives the cost of equity by adding to the risk-free rate an additional premium for risk. This risk premium is itself a product of an EMRP (a measure of the reward required by investors for investing in an equity of average risk) and the investment's beta (a measure of the relative systematic risk of the particular equity investment being considered).

> The CAPM derives the cost of equity by adding to the risk-free rate an additional premium for risk.

The CAPM therefore implies that the cost of equity will vary between different investments to the extent that investments exhibit differing degrees of systematic risk.

We outline below some of the pitfalls and difficulties associated with using the CAPM, and also highlight some of the practical techniques that can be used to make calculation of the cost of equity capital as painless as possible. We examine a number of issues associated with the determination of the risk-free rate, beta estimation, and unlevering and relevering formulae. Inevitably, calculation of the cost of equity would not be complete without discussion of the Equity Market Risk Premium (EMRP), which is left until Chapter 3 given the extensive nature of the debate.

Of course, there are other models that can be used to calculate the cost of equity capital, and these are discussed and considered at greater length in Chapter 4, 'CAPM is dead: long live CAPM.' However, the CAPM is probably the most practical and certainly the most commonly used model (at the time of going to press), and so it is appropriate for this chapter to focus on this model alone.

> CAPM is probably the most practical and certainly the most commonly used model.

Risk-free rate

The first component of the CAPM – the risk-free rate – represents the return an investor can achieve on the least risky asset in the market. This is usually made up of two distinct components:

- *The underlying real rate of interest* (or rate of time preference) – representing the return required by investors in order to be persuaded to lend today and defer consumption until tomorrow (a concept explained previously in Chapter 1).
- *Expected inflation* – representing compensation for expected depreciation in purchasing power during the period over which funds are lent.

A risk-free rate comprising both components is generally referred to as a *nominal* risk-free rate; one that is comprised solely of the first component (time preference) is a *real* risk-free return. Unsurprisingly, given the additional component for expected inflation, nominal risk-free rates tend to be higher than real risk-free rates.

The distinction between real and nominal risk-free rates and calculations is an important issue and one that is often a source of confusion. Sometimes an apparent discrepancy between two rate of return or cost of capital numbers can be explained in terms of one rate being quoted in *nominal* terms and the other being quoted as a *real* figure.

This can be better explained by considering the well-known Fisher equation. This is set out below:

$$(1 + r) = (1 + i) * (1 + p)$$

where   r   =   Nominal risk-free rate of interest
             i   =   Real risk-free rate of interest
            p   =   Projected rate of inflation

This relationship provides a quick and convenient means of converting nominal rates of return into real figures or inflating real rates to determine their equivalent nominal value.

So, for example, if the nominal risk-free rate of interest in a country is 6%, and projected inflation is 3%, this implies that the underlying real risk-free rate of interest is about 2.9%. This calculation is set out below:

$$(1 + 0.06) / (1 + 0.03) = \underline{1.029}$$

Similarly, a real return of about 2.9% can easily be converted into a nominal rate, as set out below:

$$(1 + 0.029)*(1 + 0.03) = \underline{1.06}$$

The fixed income world

At this point it becomes necessary to dive into the world of fixed income markets and fixed income securities in order to make progress towards the actual estimation of the risk-free rate. This is because we ultimately need to pick a very low risk, fixed income instrument as a proxy for the risk-free rate.

Because the fixed income world is heavily populated with jargon – for example, consider the term 'securities' in the last paragraph – we have constructed a 'jargon busting' schedule in Table 2.1 to help the reader make sense of some of the technical terms in use.

TABLE 2.1
Fixed income jargon busting schedule

Jargon	Busted translation
Security	A general term for the different forms of finance raised by companies and governments in the capital markets. The obligation to repay may be secured on assets or income streams of the borrowers, or may not.
Bond	A type of *security* taking the form of an IOU issued to lenders in return for a loan.
Redemption date or maturity	The point at which the issuer of a *bond* agrees to repay the loan in the future.
Par value	The face value of a *bond* when issued. For example, in the UK, these are usually expressed in terms of units of £100.
Coupon payments	The rate of interest on a *bond* (usually expressed as a percentage of the *par value*). The term coupon appeared because the very first bonds actually required investors to detach the paper coupons attached to the *bond* and surrender them in return for the *fixed interest* payments on the *bond*.
Redemption yield	The rate of return on a *bond* held to *maturity*. This can be different from the rate of interest (*coupon payments*) on a *bond,* because it is a function of both the *coupon payments* received on the bond and any difference between the current price of the bond and the *par value* that will be returned on *redemption*.
T-bills	Shorthand for Treasury bills. The term usually refers to *securities* issued by governments with *maturities* of less than one year.
US Treasuries	*Bonds* issued by the US government with *maturities* greater than one year.
Gilts	A generic term for *bonds* issued by the UK government, with *maturities* greater than one year.

Choice of financial instrument

With Table 2.1 at our side we are now ready to consider which fixed income instrument we should use as a proxy for the risk-free rate. Various securities are available in developed markets, but in practice, government-backed securities are usually chosen, as this is likely to minimize the likelihood of default on the instrument.

That said, while government securities are generally considered to be risk-free, it has been reported that only three countries have not defaulted on their debt in the last three hundred years – Sweden, Switzerland, and the UK. Even the US defaulted on its domestic debt after declaring independence in 1776.

In recent years, default has been largely confined to volatile emerging economies such as Mexico in 1994, Russia in 1998, and Argentina in 2002. Although there are some notable exceptions (in particular, some of the more recent members such as Poland and Mexico), the majority of OECD countries[1] are usually regarded as issuing risk-free securities. This makes the yields on their bonds reasonably suitable for use as a proxy for the risk-free instrument.

Once the green light has been given in respect of a government's credit worthiness, the practitioner faces a choice of which of the available government instruments to use to benchmark the risk-free rate. The options include: Treasury bills, index-linked government bonds, and ordinary government bonds.

These three options are considered, in turn, below:

- *Treasury bills* (or T-bills) are usually rejected as unsuitable due to the short maturity of these instruments (most T-bills have a maturity of between one and 12 months). This is a problem in all but the most unusual of circumstances – as explained more fully in the 'choice of maturity' section later in this chapter.

- *Index-linked bonds* provide a much better alternative. Not only do these have a longer period to maturity, but they are designed to provide investors with a real return, as the coupon and principal payments are typically indexed to some measure of consumer or retail price inflation. As investors will not require an additional return for any expected depreciation in purchasing power these instruments therefore provide investors with a real return. Consequently, some commentators regard index-linked bonds as the best proxy for the risk-free rate, as they are relatively free of both default risk and inflation risk (hence, the relatively low return). There is, however, a practical problem associated with using real measures of the risk-free rate: only a handful of countries issue index-linked securities. These include

Australia, France, Sweden, the UK, and recently the US and Greece. It is therefore usual to adopt the next best proxy available in the market. This is provided by ordinary, nominal (non index-linked), government bonds.

■ *Ordinary government bonds* are the securities used by most valuation practitioners when estimating the cost of capital. This is a direct consequence of their relatively common issuance and widespread availability. Some examples of ordinary government bonds are set out in Table 2.2.

TABLE 2.2
Sample of ordinary government bonds

	US Treasury	France	South Africa	Czech Republic	Japan
Coupon frequency	Semi-annual	Annual	Semi-annual	Annual	Semi-annual
Longest dated issue	30 years	50 years	26 years	7 years	30 years

A further advantage of ordinary government bonds is that most cost of capital and valuation work is conducted in nominal terms, and these securities provide a ready measure of the nominal risk-free rate. This matter is discussed more fully later in this chapter, but the astute reader will have noticed that this decision involves an implicit tradeoff between the convenience of having the risk-free rate expressed in a fashion consistent with its likely application, and the desire to measure a risk-free rate that is as free from risk (including inflation risk) as possible.

Measuring and observing the risk-free rate in the market

The return an investor receives on the risk-free instrument is given by the yield to redemption on that instrument (assuming that it is held to redemption). This takes into account the pattern of coupon payments, the bond's term to maturity and the difference between the current price of the bond and the par value that will be returned at redemption.

Consider, for example, the UK government bond known as Treasury 8pc. This was issued by the UK government in 1992, and paid a coupon of 8% (UK interest rates in 1992 were around 8%). The bond was redeemed in 2003.

Given the low interest rate environment in the UK, in the early years of the twenty-first century, the coupon payments on this bond were extremely attractive – investors received the 8% coupon payments at a time when interest rates in general were around 4%. This is why the price of this bond at Spring 2001 stood at around £106.

However, if this bond was purchased and held to redemption in 2003, an investor buying into the bond (and the 8% coupons) would have suffered a loss on the original price paid. This is because – on redemption – the investor would have received back the par value of the bond (£100), but would have paid around £106 for the opportunity to receive the 8% coupons at a time when any new bonds issued in the market were likely to have coupons in the region of 4%.

So, coupon payments and yields to redemption are unlikely to ever match up as a glance as Table 2.3 illustrates.

TABLE 2.3
Comparison of coupon rates and redemption yields, November 2002

UK government bond	Issue date	Coupon rate (%)	Redemption yield (%)
Treasury 8pc '03	1992	8.0	3.7
Treasury 10pc '04	1985	10.0	3.9
Exchequer 10½pc '05	1985	10.5	4.3
Treasury 6¼pc '10	1994	6.25	4.4
Treasury 4¼pc '32	2000	4.25	4.2

Real versus nominal yields

It is important to recognise that historic redemption yields for *ordinary* and *index-linked* government bonds are very different in terms of both their magnitude and volatility. The redemption yields on ordinary government bonds are much higher and more volatile than those on index-linked issues.

As we have highlighted before, nominal yields on ordinary government bonds include a component to compensate investors for expected loss of value due to inflation between purchase and redemption (whereas index-linked bonds do not). It is to be expected that nominal yields will therefore both be higher and vary over time specifically because of changes in inflationary expectations and macroeconomic conditions. This is illustrated by Figure 2.1, which shows how the historic nominal yield on benchmark UK 5-year gilts has varied between 1987 and 2001.

Over this period nominal returns (as given by the vertical axis) varied between 4% and 12%, with a general downward trend. It is likely that the main reason for this was that UK inflationary expectations were much lower in 2001 than they were ten years earlier. Some support for this view is given in Table

2.4, which shows how actual UK inflation fell over time. One could speculate that this in itself would have had a fairly direct impact on inflation expectations.

TABLE 2.4
UK retail price inflation (%), 1988–2001

'88	'89	'90	'91	'92	'93	'94	'95	'96	'97	'98	'99	'00	'01
4.9	7.8	9.5	5.9	3.7	1.6	2.5	3.4	2.5	3.1	3.4	1.6	2.9	1.8

Source: Thomson DataStream

Real yields, on the other hand, are less volatile because, in principle, they are not affected by relative changes in inflation and inflationary expectations. That said, it is possible for society's underlying rate of time preference to change and for there to be some residual volatility. Figure 2.2 shows how the average yield on five-year UK index-linked government bonds varied over the period 1982–98.

FIGURE 2.1
Yield to redemption (%) on UK benchmark five-year nominal gilt

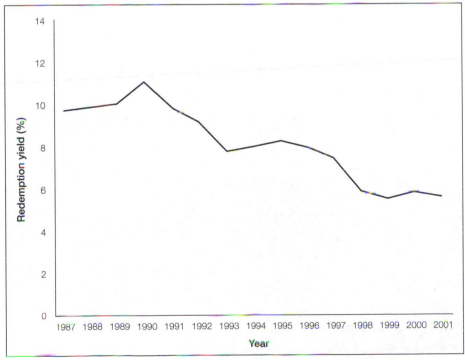

Source: Thomson DataStream

FIGURE 2.2

Yield to redemption (%) on UK benchmark five-year index-linked gilt

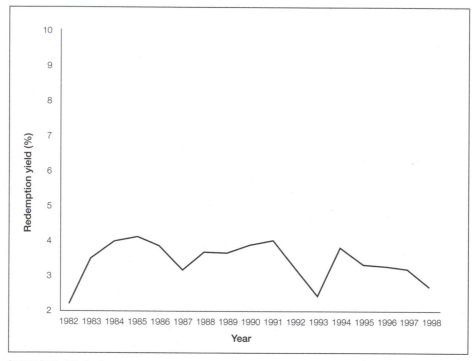

Source: Bank of England

FIGURE 2.3

US government nominal yield curve, October 2001

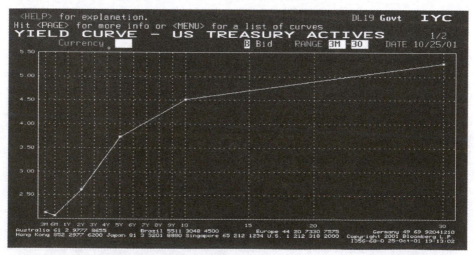

Source: Reprinted with permission from Bloomberg L.P.

Taken together Figures 2.1 and 2.2 confirm that:

- Real yields are much lower than nominal yields.

- Real yields are less volatile than nominal yields – although this volatility could hardly be described as insignificant.

Yield curves

Both nominal and real risk-free rates vary with maturity. This variation is commonly known as the yield curve, and can be plotted on a graph by joining up the redemption yields of risk-free securities of different maturities. For example, in the US, the nominal benchmark maturities are typically 2-, 5-, 10- and 30-year issues, as can be seen from the October 2001 nominal yield curve set out at Figure 2.3.

In nearly all cases, yield curves slope upwards (see also for comparison the Canadian October 2001 nominal yield curve in Figure 2.4). This is because investors are likely to regard the future as being more uncertain than the very near term (applies to both real and nominal yield curves) and because of the potential for inflation to increase at a later stage (only applies to the nominal yield curve).

FIGURE 2.4

Canadian government nominal yield curve, October 2001

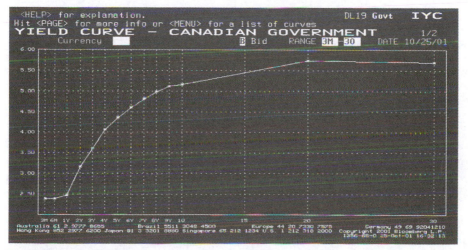

Source: Reprinted with permission from Bloomberg L.P.

Conversely, in very unusual circumstances – for example, very high inflation situations (more on this later in this chapter) – it is possible for a nominal yield

> In very high inflation situations redemption yields on short dated instruments are likely to be higher than redemption yields on longer dated issues.

curve to slope downwards. In the technical jargon, this is known as 'yield curve inversion.' It occurs when inflation is very high in the immediate short term, but is expected to fall in the medium to longer term as authorities take action to bring it under control. This means that redemption yields on short dated instruments are likely to be higher than redemption yields on longer dated issues. An example of yield curve inversion (Hungary, October 2001) is set out at Figure 2.5.

Choice of maturity

So what's the point of this digression into the world of yield curves and fixed income analytics? Getting back to the original issue, the reason is that we need to determine the maturity of instrument that should be used to assess the risk-free rate in the CAPM. As the diagrams illustrate, the maturity of the instrument chosen can have a significant impact on the risk-free rate thus calculated. This is particularly the case where the markets appear to believe that the rate of inflation will fall in the future and hence, as in Hungary in Figure 2.5, the yield curve is steeply inverted.

FIGURE 2.5
Hungarian government yield curve, October 2001

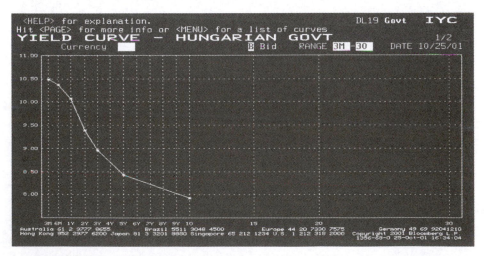

Source: Reprinted with permission from Bloomberg L.P.

The choice of maturity actually depends on the circumstances in question. A common approach is that the maturity of the risk-free instrument should match the profile of the cash flows in question. However, this is easy to say, but not necessarily so straightforward or appropriate in practice. For a discussion of these issues see Chapter 8, 'Using the cost of capital in business valuations.'

High inflation countries, and the real versus nominal debate

A challenge faces the practitioner in the context of high inflation countries. There is often a debate regarding the relative merits of real and nominal figures.

In principle, one should be indifferent to the manner in which the risk-free rate is specified, as long as it is consistent with the manner in which the cash flows have been estimated. However, the reality is not as simple as the principle suggests, with practitioners split between the relative merits of the two approaches.

Those who favor the real technique often make the following points:

■ Real figures have meaning – they give a guide to resource use – while nominal figures can be misleading. People can get excited by big cash figures in later years which simply represent cumulative inflation; real figures are simpler to model, and the results more easy to comprehend.

■ Revenues, costs, and interest are generally based on forecasts in real terms. To see this point, one should consider how these variables would be calculated nominally – typically, the answer is that forecasters take a view of their likely level in real terms and then adjust upwards for expected inflation.

Conversely, those who favor the nominal technique often suggest that:

■ People wish to 'see inflation in the modeling'; they are uncomfortable with the concept of real figures.

■ There are problems with modeling Income Statements and Balance Sheets in real terms because of difficulties with calculating tax charges, depreciation, and working capital charges. These problems arise because tax is generally paid on nominal profits, depreciation is usually calculated on nominal book asset values, and so on.

■ In order to resolve the problems above, it is necessary to express variables in nominal terms and then deflate by forecast inflation to derive the real figures required. It is therefore simpler to model all the figures in nominal terms.

In reality, there is no 'right' answer with regard to whether one of the techniques is superior to the other. Broadly speaking, nominal figures are more likely to be easier to use in the context of valuations where there is a requirement to model tax, depreciation, and changes in working capital. In addition, where the practitioner requires the cash flow valuation to link with Income Statement and Balance Sheet projections, the nominal model is likely to be the most appropriate – although it must be stressed that this is purely presentational and should not affect the underlying valuation.

On the other hand, there are also situations where a real model may be more sensible – for example, in a hyperinflationary environment, or where a model is projected over very long timescales (such as the appraisal of projects in the nuclear industry). These situations require that variables such as tax, depreciation, and changes in working capital be modeled in nominal terms and then deflated by forecast inflation.

In summary, selection of real or nominal risk-free rates is largely driven by the nature of the circumstance for which the calculations are required.

Beta

The second component of the CAPM is beta (or, more precisely, the equity beta – more on this below. For the time being, when we refer to beta we mean the equity beta). Beta is the factor in CAPM by which the Equity Market Risk Premium (EMRP) is multiplied to reflect the risk associated with a particular equity. This statement by itself does not, however, shed much light on what beta is actually about. To understand beta more fully, we need to return to the principles set out in Chapter 1, 'Risk and return revisited.'

> Shareholders face two types of risk: *market* (or *systematic*) risk and *specific* risk.

In Chapter 1, we saw that shareholders face two types of risk: *market* (or *systematic*) risk and *specific* risk. Specific risks are associated with events affecting cash flows that are specific to the company in question. An example of this is the possibility of a fire at a company's head office. Market risks on the other hand, are risks that are correlated with the stock market or general economy, such as the possibility of a rise in interest rates. Market risk means that on a day when the stock market falls (for example, because of a rise in interest rates), all stocks are systematically affected by the same risk, albeit to a greater or lesser extent.

The distinction between the two fundamental types of risk is extremely important and lies at the heart of modern portfolio theory. This is because equity investors do not need to bear specific risks, which – due to their random nature – offset each other and can be eliminated by holding a portfolio of diversified investments (this is explained and empirically validated in Chapter 1).

> Equity investors do not need to bear specific risks, which – due to their random nature – offset each other and can be eliminated by holding a portfolio of diversified investments. Market risks, on the other hand, cannot be eliminated by diversification.

Market risks, on the other hand, cannot be eliminated by diversification. They represent the fundamental risks that shareholders have to bear, because they affect all stocks to a greater or lesser extent and so are persistent at the level of the investor's portfolio. It is the level of this market risk that beta seeks to measure.

Calculating beta

In most circumstances where a practitioner wishes to calculate the cost of equity for a business the relevant measure is likely to be a forward looking one. For example, in performing a business valuation or investment appraisal the cost of equity or cost of capital will be applied as a discount rate to forecast *future* cash flows. Thus, for consistency, the cost of equity should also be calculated on a forward-looking basis.

As we have described above, the risk-free rate is typically calculated by examining the yield on government bonds with suitable future maturity dates. In principle we should also choose a forward-looking measure of the business's beta to calculate the cost of equity using the CAPM.

In practice, the best way to estimate the beta of a firm is to calculate the *historical* covariance[2] between the returns on the firm's equity and the returns from the stock market as a whole, and use this as a proxy for the *future* beta. This is set out in the following formula:

$$\beta_e = \frac{\text{Cov}(R_i, R_m)}{\sigma^2(R_m)}$$

where $\text{Cov}(R_i, R_m)$ = Covariance between returns on stock i and the returns on the market index (m)

$\sigma^2(R_m)$ = Variance of the market index (m)

To derive beta an ordinary least squares regression[3] is performed, measuring the observed, historic relationship between the change in a company's share price plus the dividend income received, and the change in the value of the stock market. In practice, the former is usually abbreviated to just the change in a company's share price, since academic research on this subject has shown that the incorporation of dividends in the regression makes little difference. Most data providers calculate beta on this latter basis.

Using the historic beta as a guide to the future

An historic beta for a firm calculated on this basis is generally used as a proxy for the firm's beta in the future. This is a pragmatic approach – only historic information is available to perform the regression analysis, and in the absence of such analysis it is difficult to quantify what the level of beta for a business should be.

Nevertheless it is important that the practitioner should be aware that the past value of beta for a business may not be a good guide to its future value, and in most situations it is the future value that is needed, not the historic value. If there is any reason to believe that the nature of the business in the future will be different from that in the past, then the historic calculations may be unreliable.

Below we examine those characteristics of businesses that influence the level of beta. If for a particular business such characteristics are likely to be different in the future than they have been in the past, caution needs to be exercised in using the historically calculated beta. It is for this reason that it is important that practitioners should understand the drivers of beta – only by understanding these can judgment be applied in interpreting historic data as a guide to the future. Simply accepting the historic betas provided by data-providers at face value can lead to errors in forward looking valuation and investment appraisal applications.

Reasons for differences in beta values

Astute readers will have spotted that the average beta in the market must, by definition, be one. This is because betas are measured relative to the market index and can be lower or higher than the average beta for that index. Put another way, the average beta must be representative of the index itself which, if regressed on itself, would imply a beta of one. As a consequence, firms that expose their equity investors to greater systematic risks than the average firm in the market have betas in excess of one; those that expose their equity investors to lower systematic risks have betas below one.

A number of factors drive betas. These include:

- cyclicality of revenues
- operational leverage
- financial leverage.

Cyclicality of revenues

Beta measures the historic observed correlation of changes in the returns on a firm's equity with changes in the returns on the market as a whole. As a consequence, while many people intuitively associate beta with the overall volatility of a business – as measured by the volatility of earnings – this is not what beta actually measures. If much of the overall volatility of a business is not correlated with the market as a whole then beta will not be large. This is as it should be since, as we saw in Chapter 1, much of this volatility may be diversifable at the level of the investor's portfolio, and beta only measures volatility that is undiversifiable.

Take Figure 2.6, which highlights a Bloomberg beta regression for Manchester United Plc. This is a UK company listed on the London Stock Exchange whose principal business is a top soccer club with associated sales of media rights and merchandising.

Manchester United's share price does fluctuate. This is because its earnings are heavily influenced by the soccer team's success with match results. Success (or otherwise) on the pitch determines the number and profile of the games played, affecting crowd attendance, sponsorship income, television rights values, and ancillary income. Its beta, however, is relatively low (0.52 on an adjusted basis and 0.27 on a raw basis – we'll explain what is meant by this later).

This is not a paradox. Match results and other soccer specific factors are unlikely to be correlated with the market. What really matters to equity investors who hold portfolios of equities is the degree to which Manchester United's cash flows are affected by factors systematic to all companies. These factors might include changes in GDP, interest rates, inflation, and so on (see Chapter 1 for further examples of systematic risk and the distinction between it and specific risk). For Manchester United, these factors are of little importance relative to specific factors such as match results.

FIGURE 2.6
Historic five-year monthly beta for Manchester United Plc

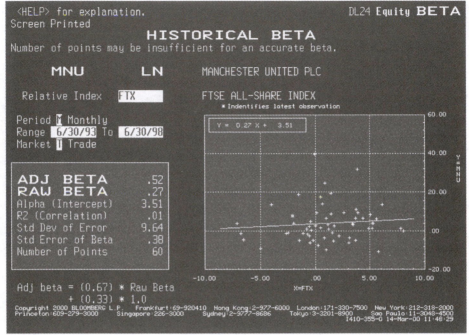

Source: Reprinted with permission from Bloomberg L.P.

In statistical terms, the 0.01 'R squared'[4] of the regression tells us that systematic risk (i.e. factors linked to movements in the stock market as a whole) makes up around 1% of the total risk of Manchester United's business. Specific risk (i.e. nonmarket related factors) accounts for the residual 99%. This is because, by definition, the regression estimates a beta for systematic risk, but this appears to explain only 1% of overall share price volatility.

At the other end of the spectrum, cyclical companies – whose revenues and earnings are strongly dependent on the state of the economic cycle – can have higher betas despite exhibiting similar or lower overall share price volatility than companies such as Manchester United.

An example of a high beta company is Invensys – see Figure 2.7. Invensys is a UK-based engineering company that has share price volatility not dissimilar to that of Manchester United, but a much higher beta (1.95 on an adjusted basis).

Invensys would appear to be a business where the systematic risks are perceived by equity investors as significant, which probably also explains why the R squared of the regression is high – the regression suggests that around 39% of the total risk of the business is systematic risk and the residual 61% is specific.

FIGURE 2.7

Historic five-year monthly beta for Invensys

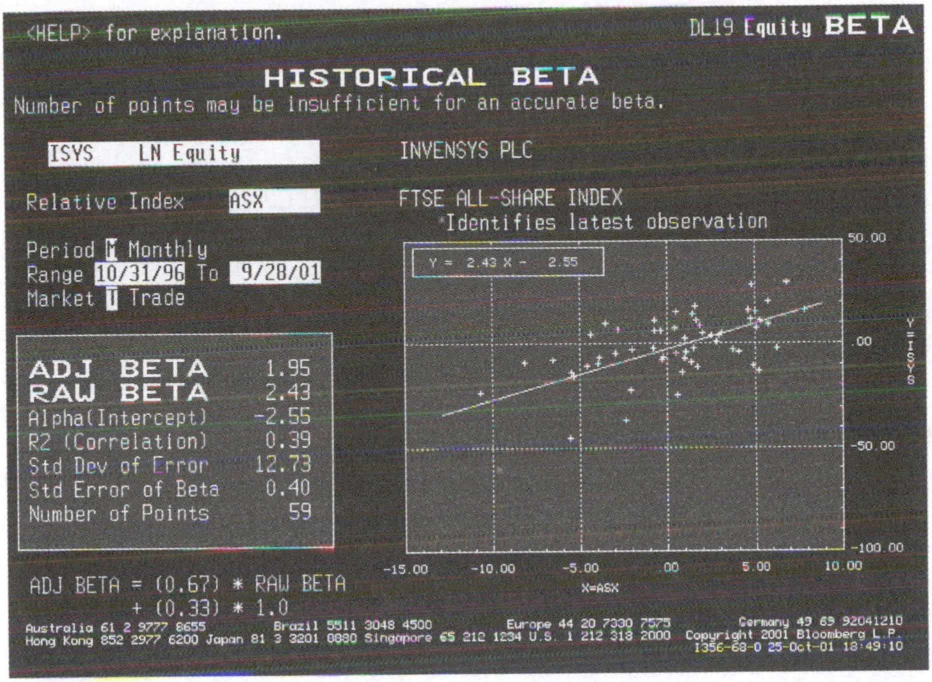

```
<HELP> for explanation.                              DL19 Equity BETA

                   HISTORICAL BETA
  Number of points may be insufficient for an accurate beta.

    ISYS    LN Equity           INVENSYS PLC

  Relative Index    ASX         FTSE ALL-SHARE INDEX
                                "Identifies latest observation
  Period M Monthly                                              50.00
  Range 10/31/96 To  9/28/01      Y = 2.43 X -  2.55
  Market T Trade

  ADJ BETA      1.95                                            .00
  RAW BETA      2.43
  Alpha(Intercept)  -2.55
  R2 (Correlation)   0.39
  Std Dev of Error  12.73                                      -50.00
  Std Error of Beta  0.40
  Number of Points    59
                                                              -100.00
              -15.00  -10.00   -5.00   .00    5.00   10.00
  ADJ BETA = (0.67) * RAW BETA            X=ASX
          + (0.33) * 1.0
  Australia 61 2 9777 8655     Brazil 5511 3048 4500    Europe 44 20 7330 7575    Germany 49 69 92041210
  Hong Kong 852 2977 6200 Japan 81 3 3201 8900 Singapore 65 212 1234 U.S. 1 212 318 2000 Copyright 2001 Bloomberg L.P.
                                                                       1356-68-0 25-Oct-01 18:49:10
```

Source: Reprinted with permission from Bloomberg L.P.

Operational leverage

Operational leverage is usually defined as the degree of fixed cost as a proportion of total cost in a business, and its level has an impact on the systematic risk to which equity investors in a firm are exposed.

This is because fixed costs represent cash outflows that occur regardless of the level of revenue. Variable costs, on the other hand, depend on output and hence fluctuate with the level of revenue.

The distinction between the two types of cost is important. Fixed costs magnify the effect of underlying systematic risk, because if revenues were to fall due to systematic factors the fixed costs of the business would still have to be met out of the cash generated. Variable costs, on the other hand, would also fall as a consequence of lower production volumes as revenues fall. It should therefore be clear that variable costs effectively provide a cushion to revenue cyclicality, whereas fixed costs 'gear up' revenue cyclicality, and increase the systematic risk of free cash flows.

> Fixed costs represent cash outflows that occur regardless of the level of revenue. Variable costs, on the other hand, depend on output and hence fluctuate with the level of revenue.

A numerical example of this effect is given in Chapter 10, 'Premia and discounts.' The key finding is that operational leverage increases a company's equity beta, all other things being equal.

Financial leverage

Taken together, cyclicality of revenues and operational leverage determine the operational risk associated with an equity investment. But equity investors face a further risk where part of a business is funded by debt. Financial leverage (the proportion of total business value financed by debt) 'gears up' the systematic risk of the free cash flows distributable to equity providers because debt service payments do not vary with the state of revenues and have to be met out of cash generated. This is referred to as *financial* risk (as opposed to *operational* risk), because it occurs at a sub-operational level on the cash flow statement.

Because debt service has a priority call on earnings over payments to equity investors, financial risk is increased whenever a business takes the decision to increase financial leverage.

Equity and asset betas

Financial risk also accounts for the distinction between equity betas and asset betas, to which we referred briefly above.

Betas provided by data-providers such as Datastream and Bloomberg are derived directly from historical market information on *equities* and are therefore known as *equity betas*. They reflect the risk equity providers have actually borne in the past in investing in specific equities, taking into account the effects of financial leverage as well as operational risk.

Asset betas, on the other hand, are generally unobservable. They reflect only the operational risk of the underlying business assets. Asset betas have to be calculated from equity betas by adjusting for the gearing of the company in question.

So, to be absolutely clear, equity betas include financial risk, whereas asset betas do not. This is summarized in Table 2.5.

TABLE 2.5
Equity versus asset betas

	Operational risk	Financial risk
Equity beta (β_e)	✓	✓
Asset beta (β_a)	✓	✗

This is an important concept, and one worth reiterating. While financial leverage (or gearing) may not affect the underlying systematic risk associated with a firm's assets, it does increase the risk borne by the firm's equity holders.

Put simply, more debt means more risk to shareholders because debt service commitments have to be honored before shareholders' claims on the firm can be considered. As a consequence, increasing the proportion of debt in a company's capital structure increases that company's equity (or levered) beta, and hence the return required by the shareholders. Whether this would lead to an increase in the overall cost of capital for the business is an interesting issue but is not considered here – we will return to this in Chapter 5.

The conventional relationship[5] between asset betas and equity betas is set out in the formula below:

$$\beta_a = \frac{\beta_e}{\left[1 + \frac{D}{E}\right]}$$

where $\frac{D}{E}$ is the ratio of the market value of debt to the market value of equity.

So, for example, for a company with an observed equity (levered) beta of 0.72 and 20% debt funding – the formula implies an asset (unlevered) beta of 0.58.

This calculation is set out below:

$$\beta_e = 0.72$$

Capital structure $= $ 20% debt; 80% equity

$$\beta_a = \frac{0.72}{\left[1 + \frac{0.2}{0.8}\right]} = \frac{0.72}{1 + 0.25}$$

$$\beta_a = \underline{0.58}$$

This is an important result, and allows us to draw the following conclusions about the company:

■ In terms of the overall equity market, the company (equity beta: 0.72) exposes equity investors to less nondiversifiable risk than the average listed company (equity beta: 1.0, by definition).

- Part (0.14) of this equity beta can be attributed to the financial risk from the gearing structure of the company (capital structure: 20% debt, 80% equity).

- The underlying (systematic) operating risk of the company – attributable to the cash flow cyclicality and operational leverage of the business – is represented by the asset beta of 0.58.

- It is difficult to tell whether this 0.58 asset beta is higher or lower than the average asset beta in the market, because the average asset beta can only be determined by unlevering every firm's equity beta in line with the most up-to-date estimates of gearing available.

Sector asset betas

It should be clear by now that equity and asset betas will vary across different sectors because of differences in revenue cyclicality, fixed costs, or even gearing. To see this point more fully, consider Table 2.6. This shows how asset and equity betas vary across the companies in the UK FTSE 350[6] aggregated by sector.

TABLE 2.6
Equity and asset betas across FTSE 350

Industry	Asset	Equity	Gearing (%)
Housebuilders	1.15	1.24	10.5
Advertising	1.08	1.14	6.2
Travel	1.00	1.12	14.3
IT	0.98	0.98	1.0
Construction	0.95	1.16	24.4
Telecommunications	0.94	1.00	7.9
Retail	0.90	1.01	14.4
Oil	0.73	1.00	34.9
Airline	0.72	1.57	63.0
Hotel	0.71	1.04	40.3
Electricity	0.54	0.71	32.1
Bank	0.51	1.27	68.2
Tobacco	0.49	0.69	36.0
Water	0.33	0.54	47.2
Average	*0.79*	*1.01*	*27.0*

A number of conclusions can be drawn from Table 2.6 – not least that the average asset beta for the FTSE 350 was 0.79 at the time of the analysis, and the average equity beta was near to 1.0.[7] However, the most value in Table 2.6 comes from the ability to make comparisons between the fundamental operating risks of different sectors through the comparison of different sector asset betas.

For example, housebuilders with their highly cyclical revenues and high fixed costs have much higher asset betas than tobacco companies – whose revenues are more stable and costs less fixed. Equivalent conclusions can be drawn in respect of other sectors. Advertising businesses appear to be more systematically risky than telecommunications companies which, in turn, appear to be more systematically risky than water companies.

Measuring beta: the practical difficulties

We have covered a lot of ground, and it would be easy to believe that we now know everything we need to know about calculating beta. Surely we can estimate equity and asset betas with confidence, as the input historic equity betas in Table 2.6 are readily available and beyond argument? Unfortunately, measuring historic equity betas is not as straightforward as it seems.

Imagine for a moment you are a traffic cop in possession of a speed gun trying to evaluate the speed of a particular passing car. Sounds a simple task: you just point the gun, touch the trigger, and 'bang,' the speed appears on the dial in front of you.

Imagine, now, that the gun assesses speed in six different ways (each of which gives valid but different results); your police colleague tells you that the gun isn't always accurate (it has a tolerance of +/– 20%); and, most importantly, the car you want to evaluate isn't actually traveling along your stretch of road today! Your colleague suggests you benchmark its speed based on a selection of other cars going along the stretch that are in some ways similar to the vehicle earmarked.

Historic beta estimation presents similar challenges. These include:

- the choice of period over which to measure beta;
- the frequency and number of observations used;
- whether Bayesian adjustment techniques are beneficial or not;
- the choice of data provider;
- whether there is value in comparator or sector analysis;

■ the consideration of other models of estimating beta, such as the divisional approach and the 'spanning method'.

These are considered in turn below.[8]

Choice of period for measurement

The choice of period for historical beta measurement involves a difficult tradeoff, which needs to balance two conflicting objectives. On the one hand, it is desirable to have as many observations as possible in order to maximize confidence in the statistical reliability of the beta measured. This is measured by the standard error[9] of the beta: the lower the standard error of the beta the greater the confidence we can have in the estimate. Figure 2.8 illustrates the standard error of betas across 60 German industrial companies as a function of the number of observations available for regression.

FIGURE 2.8
Mean standard error of betas across 60 German industrial companies

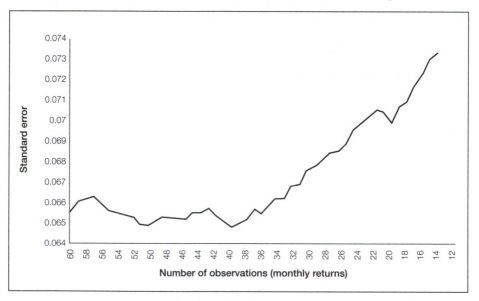

As can be seen, the average standard error falls as the number of observations increases, bottoming out at around the 40 observations point. As we are using monthly data, this corresponds to approximately three years of data. So this would suggest that we need at least three years of monthly data.

FIGURE 2.9
Equity beta of Hoechst over time

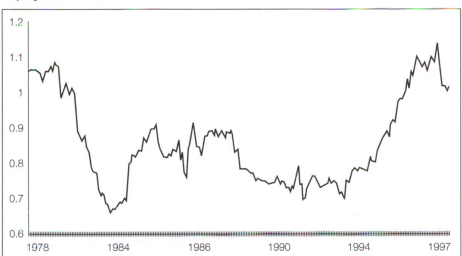

On the other hand, it is important to recognize that corporate risk profiles do change, as can be seen from Figure 2.9. This details how the beta for the German pharmaceutical company Hoechst has changed in recent times.

So, over a three-year period beta can change significantly. Choosing a long period to improve accuracy may therefore come at the expense of using historic information that is out of date.

In practice, this tradeoff is best resolved by selecting a period that is long enough to capture sufficient observations to minimize standard errors, but not so long that it is likely that the corporate risk profile will have changed fundamentally. Empirical research suggests that five to seven years probably gives the best results for beta estimation; in practice, it is common to use five years as the default duration.

Frequency and number of observations used

If five years of stock market information is typically considered appropriate for the purposes of beta estimation, the remaining problem that needs to be addressed is whether the share price and stock market index information used in regressions should be of a monthly, weekly, or daily nature. Generally speaking, regressions using monthly information have lower standard errors than regressions using either weekly or daily data. This is probably because monthly observations are less likely to suffer from 'noise'[10] than weekly or daily observations. They are also less likely to introduce measurement problems associated with thin trading.[11]

Table 2.7 compares the standard error and the R squared of Boeing's beta calculated from 60 observations of monthly, weekly, and daily data:

TABLE 2.7
Boeing's beta

	Beta	R squared	Standard error
Monthly	0.94	0.26	0.21
Weekly	1.05	0.21	0.27
Daily	0.37	0.03	0.26

It is clear that the monthly beta has the highest R squared and the lowest standard error of the three different measures. In other words, it appears to be the most statistically reliable of the three betas measured. This is, of course, not always the case, and in other circumstances use of weekly and even daily data can be of merit.

Bayesian adjustment

As we have seen, betas are typically measured from a regression of share prices against stock market indices and – as is the case with the results from any regressions using a limited number of observations – there is likely to be error in the estimate obtained. Bayesian adjustment techniques can be used to offset this problem. In essence, these weight raw beta estimates (derived from regression analysis) towards one in order to compensate for errors in the estimation process.

The rationale for Bayesian adjustments is that regressions to estimate beta provide only one out of two potential sources of information about what the underlying beta might actually be. The second potential source of information is that the practitioner knows that the average firm in the market has a beta of one.

While it might seem implausible that this additional information has any commercial value, statistical analysis shows that weighting observed raw betas towards one improves the quality of the subsequent estimates (these are often called *adjusted* or *Bayesian* betas).

A typical formula for this is set out below:

$$\beta_{adjusted} = \beta_{raw} * P + 1.0 (1 - P)$$

$$\text{where} \quad P = \text{measure of estimation error}$$
$$1.0 = \text{beta of the market portfolio}$$

This statistical idea has been tested empirically by Marshall Blume. Blume calculated betas for 415 different companies, and then formed portfolios of securities ranked by beta; the first portfolio consisted of securities with the smallest estimates of beta, the second the next smallest estimates until the portfolio with the largest betas had been determined. Blume then assessed the stability of these portfolios by regressing betas of the portfolios in one period on the values estimated in a previous period. He found that the portfolios that were made up of securities with betas closer to one were more stable than those portfolios constituted of stocks with betas at the extremes. In other words, there appeared to be greater measurement error associated with betas of extreme values. Blume's conclusion was that some form of adjustment towards one would be beneficial.

Many data providers – for example, Bloomberg and Merrill Lynch – adjust betas using a formula based on Blume's Bayesian adjustment. Both these providers weight the raw stock market beta by a factor of 0.66 (i.e. in terms of the formula P = 0.66) and the market portfolio value (1.0) by 0.33. The Blume analysis is, however, quite outdated (much of the share price information relates to the period 1926 to 1961). In addition, the adjustment formula used by many providers is based (rather arbitrarily) on only one of the many regression results in his paper. These concerns prompted us to replicate Blume's analysis for 250 British stocks over a sample period from 1964 to 1999. The result of our analysis was clear: some form of adjustment still appears beneficial.

Further details of this work can be found at our website *www.costofcapital.net*.

So, whose beta do you believe?

The practitioner is not stuck for choice when it comes to selecting a source for the provision of betas. A number of options exist, including:

- Datastream – *www.datastream.com*
- Value Line – *www.valueline.com*
- London Business School (Risk Measurement Service) – *www.london.edu*
- Barra – *www.barra.com*
- Bloomberg – *www.Bloomberg.com*

These providers tend to calculate betas in slightly different ways, as Table 2.8 reveals.

TABLE 2.8
Data-providers for beta

Source	Period	Frequency of observations	Technique	Bayesian adjustment
Datastream	5 years	Monthly	Log regression	Yes
Value Line	5 years	Weekly	Linear regression	No
LBS	5 years	Monthly	Linear regression	Yes
BARRA	5 years	Monthly	Linear regression	No
Bloomberg	Any (but 2-year default)	Any (but weekly default)	Linear regression	Yes or No

Bionic betas: a valuable enhancement?

In principle, as we have seen, betas should be forward looking but, of course, in reality it is only really possible to calculate certain betas historically.

Certain betas provided by Barra are sometimes described as 'bionic.' This means they have been adjusted to take account of fundamental accounting and financial factors for the firm in question. These factors include size, yield, price/earnings ratios, and so on. Barra considers this practice to be beneficial and believes, among other things, that it helps address the potential difficulties caused by relying on betas calculated from historic data to proxy for forward looking betas. However, as the adjustments that are made are not disclosed it is difficult for independent practitioners to evaluate the contention that bionic betas increase predictability and confidence. Bionic betas have not been widely adopted by the mainstream financial community.

Comparator analysis: finding a peer

One practical solution to the problem of errors in beta estimation is provided by comparator analysis. This seeks to average betas across a selection of peer-group or comparator companies, because the standard error of the peer-group beta is likely to be considerably less than the standard error of each of the individual companies. It is also a useful technique for estimating betas for companies that are not quoted or listed on any stock market.

For comparator work, it is usually necessary to strip out the effects of different levels of corporate leverage to make meaningful comparisons between companies. This is because different businesses in the same sector can have different levels of leverage. In these circumstances, because asset (unlevered) betas are not directly observable, it becomes important to convert equity (or levered) betas into asset betas.

TABLE 2.9
Comparator analysis in the telecommunications sector

	Company	Equity beta	Debt/ Equity (%)	Asset beta	Sector arithmetic average asset beta
Telephone integrated carriers	BT Group	1.48	85.8%	0.80	
	SBC Communications	0.89	18.7%	0.75	
	Cable & Wireless	1.46	42.0%	1.03	
	Koninklijke KPN	1.75	107.5%	0.84	
	France Telecom	1.75	142.2%	0.72	
	Telefonica	1.16	45.1%	0.80	
	Portugal Telecom SGPS	1.05	54.7%	0.68	
	Deutsche Telekom	1.41	77.1%	0.80	
					0.80
Telephone fixed long-distance operators	AT & T Corp	1.05	153.6%	0.41	
	Sprint	1.16	22.4%	0.95	
					0.68
Fixed local loop operators	Verizon Communications	0.96	42.2%	0.68	
					0.68
Mobile operators	Vodafone Group	1.00	13.2%	0.88	
	Tim	1.09	2.2%	1.07	
	Orange	1.23	17.7%	1.04	
	Cosmote Mobile Communications	0.82	9.9%	0.75	
	Telefonica Moviles	0.95	8.0%	0.88	
					0.92
Equipment manufacturers	Motorola	1.24	28.5%	0.97	
	Nokia	1.46	0.7%	1.45	
	Ericsson	1.28	8.2%	1.18	
	Alcatel	2.10	41.8%	1.48	
					1.27

An example of this sort of comparator analysis – for the global telecommunications sector in 2004 – is set out in Table 2.9. This splits the sector into five distinct business types: integrated carriers, fixed long distance operators, fixed local loop operators, mobile operators, and equipment manufacturers.

The analysis shows that the different businesses have different degrees of systematic (nondiversifiable) risk. For example, equipment manufacturers have greater exposure to systematic risk than the local loop businesses. This may be because the cyclicality of revenues in equipment manufacture is far greater than that in the local loop (where demand for services may be fairly constant).

Divisional benchmarking

Divisional benchmarking has become increasingly important in recent years as one of the key tools for shareholder value analysis and value based management. The difficulty with using comparator analysis for divisional benchmarking purposes is that good comparator analysis requires the existence of 'pure-play' listed analogs, which are not always available. For example, in the oil industry, which is highly integrated, businesses can often be split into several different operating divisions, such as:

- exploration and production (E&P);
- refining;
- transportation;
- retail.

The difficulty with this split is that while it may be possible to obtain 'pure play,' market quoted comparators for some of these divisions (for example, E&P) – giving a readily available source of information to calculate beta – the same is not necessarily true for all of the other divisions (for example, retail). This has prompted the phenomenon of the 'synthetic beta' – that is, a beta calculated by some other method than simple observation of a comparable market quoted business.

Synthetic betas

A number of approaches exist that purport to estimate synthetic betas, whether to benchmark divisions of quoted companies or unquoted businesses where there is a lack of readily comparable quoted companies. These include:

- multicompany regression techniques;
- the questionnaire approach;
- the 'spanning' model.

The first technique – which has been developed by Michael Ehrhardt in the US – attempts to use multicompany regression analysis to 'purify' comparators that are not 'pure play.' In essence, this method assumes that the overall market beta of a company is the weighted average of component divisional betas, which should be similar for each company.

Given sufficient data, the betas of the individual divisions can be estimated by performing a regression analysis. This involves estimating the relationship between the historic company betas observed in the market and the (unknown) divisional betas, given observed information on the different proportions of each company's business accounted for by the different divisions.

The second approach uses a questionnaire (perhaps sent to corporate managers and analysts) aimed at identifying the key risks in a business and their likely impact on beta.

The questionnaire approach assumes that all respondents are able to differentiate satisfactorily between specific and systematic risks, and have the additional ability to assess the quantitative impact of systematic risk factors on beta. These are two extremely strong assumptions. We have seen this approach used only once in practice, and do not expect to see it used frequently in the future.

The final approach is known as the 'spanning model.' It has slightly more intellectual credibility, but appears extremely difficult to implement in practice.

The spanning approach recognizes that the cyclicality of a firm's cash flows is likely to be the key driver of market risk and hence a firm's beta. The difficulty with this approach is that in order to measure cyclicality it appears necessary to correlate the volatility of a firm's cash flows against a market benchmark.

We are not aware of any practical application of the spanning model, although it remains an intriguing and conceptually useful theoretical approach.

Key points from the chapter

This chapter has dealt with practical issues in calculating the risk-free rate and beta – two of the fundamental components of the CAPM. We leave to later chapters the EMRP and financial leverage, the other key issues in the practical application of the CAPM.

The main conclusions from this chapter are:

Risk-free rate

- The risk-free rate is usually proxied by the yield on a government security.
- The risk-free rate can be stated in either real or nominal terms.
- Use of the Fisher equation enables the practitioner to toggle between real and nominal figures.
- It is important to have consistency between the risk-free rate and any cash flows to be discounted – for example, matching the period to maturity, and using the appropriate real or nominal number.

Beta

- Beta is a measure of the relative nondiversifiable risks associated with a company's equity.
- Beta is naturally measured historically, even though it is usually desirable to have forward looking estimates.
- Equity betas include the financial risk associated with gearing, whereas asset betas do not.
- The average company in the market has an *equity* beta of one.
- There are many different sources for the provision of beta estimates. These include Bloomberg, Barra, Datastream, and Merrill Lynch. They differ from each other in several ways, for example, in terms of the frequency and duration of data used to calculate beta, and whether or not they apply a Bayesian adjustment to the raw beta.
- Beta can be estimated for nonquoted companies using comparator analysis. Synthetic techniques are also available.

Notes

1 The OECD countries are currently Australia, Austria, Belgium, Canada, Czech Republic, Denmark, Finland, France, Germany, Hungary, Iceland, Republic of Ireland, Italy, Japan, Republic of Korea, Luxembourg, Mexico, Netherlands, New Zealand, Norway, Poland, Portugal, Spain, Sweden, Switzerland, Turkey, UK, and the US.

2 Covariance measures the extent to which a pair of variables move together. For the pair of variables, x and y, which occur N times, the covariance can be calculated as:

$$\frac{\Sigma(x_i - \mu_x)(y_i - \mu_y)}{N-1}$$

where x_i and y_i represent the individual values taken by x and y, while μ_x is the mean of x and μ_y is the mean of y.

3 This is a statistical technique whereby one variable 'is regressed' on another to establish the extent of any relationship. The relationship is expressed by convention in the form $y = \alpha + \beta x$ where y is a variable whose magnitude can be partly explained by movements in x. α is a constant, and β is a parameter reflecting how y reacts to a change in x. In the case of the CAPM, y is the returns on a particular company and x is the returns in the stock market, and so β reflects the relationship between these two variables. It is because of the conventional expression of the regression equation that β is called β!

4 R squared is a measure of the explanatory power of a regression – the proportion of the observed movement in variable y that can be explained by observed movements in variable x.

5 Other formulae exist. This is discussed further in Chapter 8.

6 An index comprising the top 350 UK companies by market capitalization.

7 There are two reasons why this is not exactly 1.0. The first is that individual company betas used as the basis for the table have been calculated with reference to the FTSE All Share Index, not the FTSE 350. Second, we have taken a straight average of the equity betas rather than a market capitalization weighted average.

8 These are the difficulties in measuring *historic* betas. But remember, as we saw earlier, generally we are interested in historic betas as a guide to the future. So even if a practitioner is confident in his or her ability to calculate historic betas, thought needs to be given to their application where future betas are needed.

9 Standard error reflects the error in measuring the actual mean of a variable, which occurs if only a sample, rather than the entire population, of the variable is examined. The standard deviation of the sample means around the actual mean is the standard error. Standard errors increase with the standard deviation of the

variable under examination and decrease with the size of the sample. For a variable x with deviation σ and sample size n the standard error can be calculated as:

$$\frac{\sigma}{\sqrt{n}}$$

10 Monthly regressions are likely to be more representative of underlying systematic risk than daily share price regressions. This is because daily share price regressions may be influenced by short-term price movements that have little to do with systematic risk – this is known as regression 'noise' because it obscures the relationship we are trying to measure.

11 Situations where a stock is not widely traded ('thin trading') can cause a problem because if the correlation of two variables is measured and one is moving more often than the other simply because of trading conditions there may be bias in the result obtained.

3

THE GREAT EMRP DEBATE

The Equity Market Risk Premium (EMRP) is a simple concept. It represents the additional expected return investors require to invest funds into equities rather than risk-free instruments. However, quantification of the EMRP is highly dependent on the measurement approach adopted and, as a consequence, it is one of the most controversial subjects in financial literature.

There are two basic techniques: the historic approach and the forward-looking approach. Proponents of each camp will argue their case but, in reality, neither is demonstrably correct and the issue remains an unresolved debate of considerable practical importance.

Introduction

Chapter 2, 'CAPM @ work,' dealt with the risk-free rate and beta, but did not deal with the third and most contentious component in determining the cost of equity – the Equity Market Risk Premium (EMRP).

EMRP is probably the most significant number in cost of capital analysis.

This is probably the most significant number in cost of capital analysis. Views on the likely magnitude of this variable determine asset allocation strategies and corporate acquisitions, and can even influence public sector policy through capital budgeting techniques.

What is this fundamental concept? It is the additional *expected* return that an investor demands for putting his or her money into equities of average risk, rather than a risk-free instrument. It can be expressed mathematically as:

$$EMRP = (R_m - R_f)$$

where R_m = the expected return on a fully diversified (market) portfolio of securities

R_f = the expected return on a risk-free security, proxied by the return on a government bond (as we have seen in Chapter 2).

There are two approaches that can be used to determine the level of the EMRP. They are:

- the historic (or ex-post) approach

- the forward-looking (or ex-ante) approach.

We examine the advantages and drawbacks of both techniques, provide a guide to their strengths and weaknesses and give a flavor of the results obtained.[1]

The historic approach

The most documented and frequently discussed approach to determining the magnitude of the EMRP is to use historic information to calculate the additional returns that equities have *actually* achieved over a number of years in the past. This is of interest in considering the EMRP, because what was actually achieved in the past should, in principle, reflect the additional returns required.

> The most documented and frequently discussed approach to determining the magnitude of the EMRP is to use historic information to calculate the additional returns that equities have *actually* achieved over a number of years in the past.

To understand why this is the case, recall the material on arbitrage in Chapter 1. If actual achieved returns were above those required, one would have expected equity investors to be attracted to invest more money in equities, driving up share prices, and reducing returns. Similarly, lower than required returns would lead to less equity investment, driving share prices down and returns up. Arbitrage should ensure that – in well functioning capital markets – required and achieved returns should be equivalent.

Consequently, the key issue in examining the historic achieved EMRP as a guide to what EMRP investors expect when they invest in equities today is whether the past provides a good indicator of how the market will behave in the future. In part, this depends on whether investor expectations are influenced by the historic performance of the market. It also depends on whether market conditions and investor expectations going forward differ to those observed historically.

Arithmetic versus geometric means

Historic returns achieved by a diversified market portfolio of equities (R_m in the EMRP formula above) are best proxied by the returns achieved from the stock market itself. Historic returns on government bonds (as a proxy for the risk-free rate) can then be subtracted to give an estimate of the historic EMRP.

> Arithmetic means suggest higher historic EMRPs than geometric means.

But how should these historic returns be calculated? This is an important issue, because it is possible to measure returns using either an arithmetic mean or a geometric mean. The resulting EMRP will differ depending on the type of mean that is adopted.

Arithmetic means suggest higher historic EMRPs than geometric means. This is because an arithmetic mean simply averages the individual annual returns over the period being considered, whereas a geometric mean calculates the annual compound growth in returns over the period. Example 3.1 illustrates the distinction between the arithmetic mean and the geometric mean.

Example 3.1 Two ways of measuring returns

Consider an investor who starts out with $1, and invests this dollar in the stock market. At the end of the year, suppose the market has risen by 20%, meaning that the dollar is now worth $1.20. In the following year, the investment is subsequently left in the stock market, which falls by 12.5%. The $1.20 is now only worth $1.05. What is the average return?

Arithmetically, the return is (20% + –12.5%)/2 = <u>3.75%</u>

Geometrically, the return is <u>2.5%</u> (the geometric mean of the return for the two-year period, which is calculated by taking the square root of the ratio of the final value, $1.05, to the starting value, $1.00).

$$\sqrt{1.05} - 1 = \underline{\underline{2.5\%}}$$

From the point of view of calculating returns actually achieved by investors historically, which is likely to be the more appropriate measure? The geometric mean for a period gives a measure of the average annual return achieved by an investor who held equities for the whole period. The arithmetic mean provides a measure of the average returns earned by investors holding equities for sub-periods within the period being considered. So the geometric average arguably provides the best guide on actual returns achieved in the past if one believes it is realistic to look at returns for any period being considered (a two-year period in Example 3.1) on the basis that investors could be assumed to have engaged in a buy and hold strategy during that period. This seems somewhat unrealistic. For example, in calculating equity returns for a 70-year data set this implies a holding period of 70 years. If, however, one believes it is more realistic to look at average returns on the basis that within any period different investors will have moved into and out of equities over time, then the arithmetic mean may have more relevance.

This point is illustrated further in Example 3.2.

Example 3.2 Arithmetic versus geometric means revisited

Consider the same investor with $1. Let us assume that there is an equal probability of the stock market rising by 20% each year as there is of its falling by 12.5% (the outcomes highlighted in the earlier example). Over two years, this situation can be modeled using probability analysis as follows:

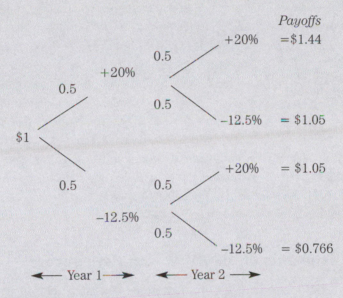

What is the expected return from making the $1 investment? It is:

$$(\$1.44 + \$1.05 + \$1.05 + \$0.766)/4 = \$1.0765$$

This equates to a compound (geometric average) return of 3.75% each year.

$$\sqrt{1.0765} - 1 = \underline{3.75\%}$$

This is the *arithmetic* mean of the returns as calculated in Example 3.1.

This analysis shows that taking the arithmetic mean is equivalent to taking each annual outcome actually observed in the period being examined, assigning an equal probability to each, and calculating the expected outcome on the basis of all the possible permutations of these outcomes. The arithmetic mean is then the average compound (geometric) return for this expected outcome.

This demonstrates that the arithmetic mean effectively assumes that, when considering a historic period, each of the individual annual returns observed in that period gives an equally valid insight into the range of possible variation in returns to which an equity investor was exposed.

On a related point, it is also possible to argue that even if investors do not move into and out of equities over time, investors are actually making subconscious investment decisions to hold onto their portfolio of shares in the market every instant of every day. They may therefore be concerned by short-term share price volatility, and consider this to be the relevant measure of risk.

'Investment myopia' is sometimes used to justify a preference for the arithmetic mean rather than the geometric.

This is known as 'investment myopia,' and is sometimes used to justify a preference for the arithmetic mean rather than the geometric. In this context, holding periods may be a misleading guide to the manner in which equity investors take decisions.

So, which estimate should you use? The choice between geometric and arithmetic means would appear to depend on subjective views that are formed in respect of how investors behave, the psychology underlying how they assess risk and also the behaviour of the stock market. Practitioners should not expect an early resolution to this debate.

Historic estimates of the EMRP – the evidence

The historic EMRP also depends on the number of past years over which it has been calculated. This can result in considerable variation in the absolute level of the EMRP itself, as can be seen from Table 3.1, which shows equity, bond, and bill returns data for the UK based on work by Barclays Capital (formerly known as BZW).

The implicit EMRP in Table 3.1 varies from 4.6% (on a bond basis using a geometric calculation technique between 1963 and 1996) to 8.4% (on a bill basis using an arithmetic calculation technique between 1919 and 1996).

Long-term stock and bond prices are usually only available in countries with substantial track records of equity and bond ownership. In practice, this has meant that the historic approach has – for many years – been largely confined to the US and UK markets, although a recent study by Dimson, Marsh, and Staunton[1] has widened the geographic catchment area to include countries such as Denmark, Italy, and Australia. This work is summarized in Figure 3.1.

That the results vary between geometric and arithmetic calculation techniques is unsurprising but, interestingly, there is also significant variation between countries, despite the fact that the period over which the EMRP is measured in

TABLE 3.1
UK stocks, bonds, and bills

	1919–96	1946–96	1963–96
Arithmetic average returns			
Equities	10.1	9.1	9.4
Bonds	3.0	0.9	2.7
Treasury bills	1.7	0.9	1.8
Ex-post EMRP			
Relative to bonds	7.1	8.2	6.7
Relative to bills	8.4	8.2	7.6
Geometric average returns			
Equities	7.8	6.7	6.5
Bonds	2.1	0.2	1.9
Treasury bills	1.5	0.8	1.7
Ex-post EMRP			
Relative to bonds	5.7	6.5	4.6
Relative to bills	6.3	5.9	4.8

Sources: Barclays Capital (1997), *The BZW Equity Gilt Study (now Barclays Capital)*; and Jenkinson (1998), *The Equity Risk Premium: Another Look at History*, The Utilities Journal, OXERA

this study is uniformly taken as between 1900 and 2000. It may be the case that there is a degree of capital market segmentation between these countries, and Dimson, Marsh, and Staunton have observed genuine differences in EMRPs.

In the US, data going back to 1926 published by Ibbotson Associates is widely used. Good stock market data is, however, available going back to 1871, with less reliable data available from various sources going back to the end of the eighteenth century. Data for government bonds is also available for these periods.

Table 3.2 presents the realized average annual premia of US stock market returns (relative to the returns on US long-term Treasury securities) for alternative periods through to 1997.

Table 3.2 confirms that historic estimates of the EMRP are clearly sensitive to the period chosen for measuring the average – as well as the choice of average (arithmetic or geometric) used.

Likewise, if one takes the same Ibbotson data and looks at the return in different decades, the figures are even more unstable. This is illustrated in Table 3.3 (arithmetic mean only).

It is interesting to note that if the Ibbotson data is broken into two equal 36-year subperiods – the first covering the period 1926–61, and the second

FIGURE 3.1

Historic equity market premia* in different territories 1900–2000

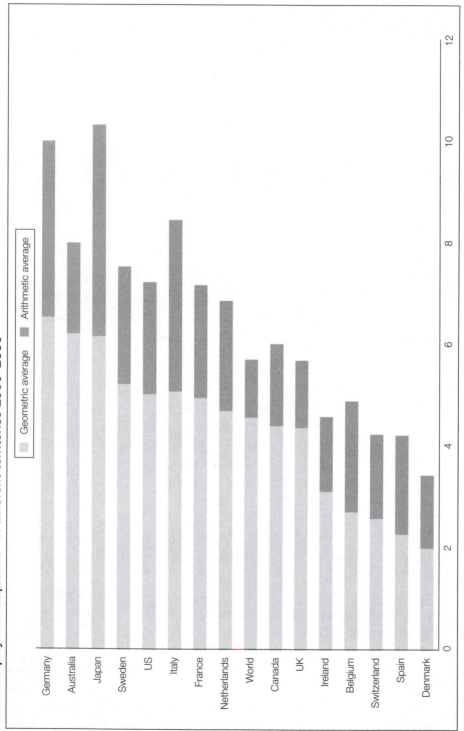

Source: Dimson, Marsh, and Staunton (2002) *Triumph of the Optimists*

* Measured relative to bonds. Note that the arithmetic average in this figure is illustrated cumulatively, so that the arithmetic average for Germany should be read as around 10% with the geometric average approaching 7%.

TABLE 3.2
US equity premia over time

Period	Arithmetic	Geometric
20 years (since 1978)	8.5%	7.8%
30 years (since 1968)	5.2%	4.0%
40 years (since 1958)	6.3%	5.2%
50 years (since 1948)	8.1%	6.9%
60 years (since 1938)	8.2%	7.0%
72 years (since 1926)	7.8%	5.8%
156 years (since 1872)	6.2%	4.6%
200 years (since 1798)	5.2%	3.8%

Source: Ibbotson Associates and Standard & Poor's

covering 1962–97 – the implicit historic equity premia for the two periods are quite different. Many commentators feel that the EMRP may have fallen in more recent times, and this appears consistent with Table 3.4.

TABLE 3.3
US equity premia by decade (arithmetic)

Period	Percentage (%)
1930s	2.3
1940s	8.0
1950s	17.9
1960s	4.2
1970s	0.3
1980s	7.9
1990s	12.1

Source: Ibbotson Associates

TABLE 3.4
US equity premia in two periods of the twentieth century

	1926–61	1962–97
Equity premia over Treasury bond returns		
Arithmetic average	10.4%	5.2%
Geometric average	7.6%	4.0%

Source: Ibbotson Associates

Explanations are required, and some have been provided. For example, the 1962–97 period was characterized by more stable stock markets and more volatile bond markets compared to the earlier period. This would lead to an increase in fixed income returns and a narrowing of the gap between the expected return on equities and the expected return on bonds.

Separately, it is also true that the 1962–97 period saw a substantial increase in pension fund and other long-term institutional investment in the market. All other things equal, an increase in the supply of capital should lead to a reduction in the EMRP, the price of equity capital.

Other issues in using historic data to calculate the EMRP

Besides the problems associated with identifying the appropriate period of measurement, choosing between the arithmetic and geometric means, and choosing which instruments to use as a proxy for the risk-free rate, there are two additional difficulties associated with the historic approach:

- First, historic data may overstate contemporary expected returns, given opportunities in the modern marketplace for international diversification.

- Second, historic data may be adversely affected by survivor bias.

International diversification

As we shall see later in Chapter 6, 'International WACC and country risk', international diversification reduces the volatility of equity investors' portfolios. In principle, this reduced volatility should lower the required return on the average asset in the portfolio, thereby lowering the expected return on equities generally. This suggests a lower EMRP on a forward-looking basis than is indicated by historic data from periods where opportunities for international investment were more limited.

> Some commentators have suggested that the increased globalization of financial markets has lowered the contemporary EMRP to around two-thirds of the post-1926 average realized premium.

Some commentators have suggested that the increased globalization of financial markets has lowered the contemporary EMRP to around two-thirds of the post-1926 average realized premium.

Survivor bias

Historic information may also be distorted by survivor bias. That is to say, observed historic returns reflect the returns from those companies that have continued to trade in their markets – they do not necessarily capture the zero or negative returns associated with those companies that have failed or exited the market.

Investors bear the risk of success and failure, and will form expectations given their assessment of the probability of each. However, without adjustment for survivor bias, measuring achieved premia historically may overstate future expectations. Adjusting for survivor bias is a relatively new development, but it is worth noting that Dimson, Marsh, and Staunton have made some adjustment for it in their recently published work.[2]

Forward-looking approaches

As the name would suggest, forward-looking approaches estimate the EMRP on the basis of market forecasts rather than historic returns. They subtract the risk-free rate from forecasts of returns expected from investing in the stock market.

Forecasts of stock returns can be gathered from a variety of sources, but there are two basic techniques:

- **'Bottom-up'** studies – which forecast rates of return (weighted by market value) for a large number of individual companies.
- **'Top-down'** reviews – which survey aggregate investor expectations about returns from investing in the market as a whole.

Bottom-up models

Bottom-up models typically work by projecting future company dividends, and then calculating the internal rate of return (IRR) that sets the current market capitalization equal to the present value of future expected dividends. A similar procedure can be applied to all companies in aggregate, to obtain a measure of the expected growth rate of the market.

In the US, **Merrill Lynch** (*www.MerrillLynch.com*) publishes 'bottom up' expected returns on the Standard & Poor's 500, derived by averaging expected return estimates for stocks in the Standard & Poor's 500. Merrill uses a multi-stage Dividend Discount Model (DDM) to calculate expected returns for several hundred companies, using projections made by its own securities analysts (see Chapter 4 for more about the DDM). The results are published monthly. Merrill Lynch uses the term 'implied return' to describe the DDM expected return.

A number of consulting firms are reported to be using the Merrill Lynch DDM estimates to develop discount rates, including Merrill Lynch's own investment banking group, and Corporate Performance Systems (CPS) – formerly known as Alcar.

Three potential problems arise when using data from organizations like Merrill Lynch. First, what we really want is investors' expectations, and not those of security analysts. This may not be a real issue, however, as several studies have proved beyond much doubt that investors, on average, form their own expectations on the basis of professional analysts' forecasts. The second problem is that there are many professional forecasters besides Merrill Lynch, and, at any given time, their forecasts of future market returns are generally somewhat different. However, generally these forecasts do not vary substantially. Third, and last, there is some evidence to suggest analysts' forecasts of expected earnings or dividend growth may overstate outturn actual earnings or dividend growth. All other things equal, if there is upward bias in analysts projections used in the bottom-up model then the implicit EMRP that is derived may also be on the high side.

In recent years, the Merrill Lynch expected return estimates have indicated an EMRP in the region of 4% to 5%.

Again, with reference to the US market, it is possible to use **Value Line** projections (*www.valueline.com*) to produce an estimate of expected returns. Value Line analysts routinely make 'high' and 'low' projections of price appreciation over a three- to five-year horizon for over 1,500 companies.

Value Line uses these price projections to calculate estimates of total returns, making adjustments for expected dividend income. The high and low total return estimates are published each week in the *Value Line Investment Survey*, and midpoint total return estimates are published in the *Value/Screen* software database. There is some evidence that Value Line analysts, in common with other analysts, tend to have an upward bias in their estimates of corporate earnings per share: that is, the short-run forecasts tend to be on the high side. Whether this leads to a bias in total return estimates over a three- to five-year horizon is an open question.

The Value Line projected market risk premia are somewhat more volatile than those from the Merrill Lynch DDM model. In recent years they have generally ranged from 2% to 6%.

Top-down approaches

Perhaps the most fundamental 'top-down' approach uses a combination of the dividend yield model and long-term GDP growth rates to estimate expected returns.

The model takes the aggregate current dividend yield of the market and adds to this long-term GDP growth as a proxy for the growth of corporate dividends. The rationale for using GDP growth as a proxy for the growth of dividends is that it is a reasonable assumption that the share of profits in GDP will remain constant in the future. Thus, GDP growth can be seen as a satisfactory proxy for the growth of corporate dividends.

As an example, if the aggregate dividend yield in the market was 3%, and long-term real GDP growth was 2.5%, the model would imply future equity returns of around 5.5% (in real terms). Given a prevailing real risk-free rate of interest of 2%, this would imply an EMRP of 3.5%.

This dividend yield technique is, however, only one of many 'top-down' approaches. Other top-down approaches generally take the form of surveys of the investment community, requesting investors' views of required returns. In recent years, these surveys have become increasingly fashionable and their coverage more prolific, although (unsurprisingly) they are far more commonplace in the US than in other countries.

For example, **Greenwich Associates** (*www.Greenwichassociates.com*) has published the results of an annual survey of pension plan officers regarding expected returns on the Standard & Poor's 500 for a five-year holding period. The Greenwich Associates survey has generally indicated an EMRP in a 2%–3% range. The survey covered a large number of respondents (several hundred), but it was limited to the expectations of pension plan officers.

Separately, one US survey of over one hundred financial economists at leading universities found that – for long-term investments – one quarter of the respondents recommended using an EMRP of 5% or less, another quarter recommended 7.1% or more, and the median recommendation was 6.0%.

Another survey of corporations and financial advisory firms found a variety of practices among the respondents. Corporate respondents commonly reported using EMRP estimates in a 4%–6% range, while financial advisors reported using estimates more often in the 7%–7.8% range (consistent with Ibbotson Associates' 1926–present day arithmetic average).

So, what are we to make of this? Probably the key conclusion is that the answer you get from such a survey depends on the person you ask. Pension fund managers tend to suggest low values for the EMRP. One can speculate that this is because their performance will be judged on the basis of the return they actually secure for their pensioners, and they want to manage expectations down. Personal financial advisors, however, tend to quote high figures. Are we being too cynical if we suggest that this is because they want to attract clients to invest?

> The key conclusion is that the answer you get from such a survey depends on the person you ask. Pension fund managers tend to suggest low values for the EMRP. Personal financial advisors, however, tend to quote high figures.

Academics seem to respond with a wide range of different figures – probably because they hold different views on the various theories for calculating the EMRP, and do not necessarily need to justify their views, or take financial decisions dependent on them. Which leaves corporate organizations somewhere in the middle. Their main vested interest in the EMRP seems to be to get it right, so perhaps their views should be given the most weight.

Practitioners' reference books and academic textbooks

A number of authors have expressed their own views on the level of the EMRP in a variety of texts. These include:

- *Graham and Dodd's Security Analysis*, fifth edition (1988), by Sidney Cottle *et al.* The authors use an 'equity risk premium' of 2.75% over the yield on Aaa industrial bonds for valuing the aggregate Standard & Poor's 500 index. This translates into a premium of about 3% over long-term Treasuries.

- *The SBBI Yearbook* series by Ibbotson Associates is generally regarded as an authoritative source of historical US market data for broad asset classes. In addition to supplying data, Ibbotson also makes recommendations on how the data can be used. Ibbotson recommends the arithmetic average since 1926. Measured relative to long-term government bonds this premium is presently 7%.

- *Shannon Pratt's Valuing a Business* is often seen in a valuation practitioner's office. The second edition (1989) suggests that investors might find guidance from historical averages (both arithmetic and geometric) over periods ranging from 20 to 60 years. Also, Pratt mentions the Merrill Lynch and Value Line data, but the book does not make any overall recommendation. The fourth edition, coauthored with Robert Reilly and Robert Schweis (2000), offers the arithmetic average from Ibbotson, suggesting 'this is a widely (but not universally) accepted procedure for estimating the equity risk premium.'

■ *McKinsey & Co, Copeland, Koller, and Murrin's Valuation: Measuring and Managing the Value of Companies*, third edition (2000), recommends a premium of 4.5% to 5%, based on a survivor bias adjusted arithmetic average of US data since 1926.

■ *James Van Horne's Financial Management and Policy*, eighth edition (1989). The author recommends using 'consensus estimates of security analysts, economists, and others who regularly follow the stock market,' and adds 'the *expected* return on the market portfolio has exceeded the risk-free rate by anywhere from 3 to 7 percent in recent years.'

■ *Richard Brealey and Stewart Myers' Principals of Corporate Finance*, seventh edition (2003). The authors use a premium of 8% in quoted examples, favoring use of the arithmetic average relative to government bills.

■ *Eugene Brigham and Louis Gapenski, Financial Management: Theory and Practice*, fifth edition (1988). According to the authors 'the risk premium of the average stock cannot be measured with great precision. However, empirical studies suggest that [the market risk premium] has generally ranged from 3 to 6 percent during the last 20 years.' The authors recommend the Merrill Lynch Dividend Discount Model as a good indicator.

■ *Jeremy Siegal's Stocks for the Long Run* (1994), has become a widely read text on strategies for long-term investments. Siegal comments that 'as real returns on fixed-income assets have risen in the last decade, the equity premium appears to be returning to the 2 percent to 3 percent norm that existed before the post-war surge.'

■ *Aswath Damodaran's Damodaran on Valuation: Security Analyses for Investment and Corporate Finance*, second edition (2002) is a text on security valuation. Damodaran recommends a premium of 5.5%, based on a long run geometric average in the US.

■ *Michael Ehrhardt's The Search for Value: Measuring the Company's Cost of Capital* (1994), is a text on rate of return estimation. Ehrhardt recommends a long-run arithmetic average, but recognizes that practitioners also use geometric averages and forward-looking methods.

■ *Bradford Cornell's The Equity Risk Premium* (1999), is a text devoted solely to the equity market risk premium. The author quotes the Ibbotson studies, but cautions that in the long run the equity market risk premium is likely to fall to 3.5% to 5.5% over Treasury bonds and 5.0% to 7.0% over Treasury bills.

Some tentative conclusions for developed markets

In our practical work in the field of cost of capital, we have examined a lot of evidence regarding the size of the EMRP in developed markets. We have encountered many different views on this issue from around the world. We have looked at the issue retrospectively, prospectively, top-down, bottom-up, geometrically, arithmetically, internationally, domestically, drunk, and sober. Table 3.5 attempts to characterize the position.

TABLE 3.5
Summary EMRPs

	Historic	Forward-looking
EMRP	4%–8%	2%–6%

While some commentators are prepared to take extreme positions based on the use of one technique versus another, in truth, the great EMRP controversy is still an unresolved debate. It may be necessary to balance the forward-looking approach, which often involves *ad hoc* estimation, against the historic approach, which can be more effectively quantified, but which does not necessarily provide a good guide to the future.

Furthermore, even within the broad range of views that exists, there is room to reconcile the geometric prospective view of the EMRP with the arithmetic retrospective view, as there is common ground around the 4% to 6% mark. Figures within this range may be acceptable to proponents of both the historic and forward-looking techniques. Compromise may be no bad thing.

Key points from the chapter

This chapter has dealt with the equity market risk premium (EMRP). The main conclusions are:

- There are two alternative approaches: the historic approach and forward-looking techniques.
- The historic approach relies on the past being the best indicator of how the market will behave in the future, supported by a belief that investors' expectations are influenced by the historic performance of the market, and

that future market conditions do not differ substantially from those in the past.

■ Depending on the time period selected, and whether an arithmetic or a geometric mean is adopted for calculation purposes, the historic approach produces figures in the range of 4% to 8% for the US, with similar or slightly lower results for the UK and other developed markets (according to the most recent research by Dimson, Staunton, and Marsh).

■ Forward-looking techniques can be categorized as either bottom-up or top-down and seek to determine the future returns today's investors expect when investing in the market.

■ Surveys of expectations can be obtained from firms in the US such as Merrill Lynch, Value Line, and Greenwich Associates. These tend to indicate premia in a range of 2% to 6%, and we would not expect radically different results in other developed markets.

Note

1   This chapter draws on work by Roger Grabowski and David King – see for example David W. King and Roger J. Grabowski (2000) *Equity Risk Premiums* in *The Handbook of Advanced Business Valuation*, McGraw-Hill.

2   Dimson, Marsh, and Staunton (2002) *Triumph of the Optimists*.

4

CAPM IS DEAD: LONG LIVE CAPM

The two previous chapters have dealt extensively with the CAPM as a framework for calculating the cost of equity.

The reason we have devoted so much space to explaining how to implement the CAPM is that we have found that it is far more commonly used than other approaches. But the CAPM is not universally accepted. For example, some academics are concerned that there is conflicting empirical evidence about the CAPM's ability to explain historical stock returns. Some business people doubt its relevance to the real world.

In this chapter we explore some of the other models that can be used to calculate the cost of equity, and highlight some of the advantages and drawbacks. But none of these models is universally accepted and there are often practical issues with data.

Moreover, there is a good reason for using the CAPM in preference to these other models. If the model is used by the majority of investors, the case for adopting the CAPM becomes self-fulfilling. In this case the CAPM is valid as long as it continues to be used.

Introduction

In this chapter we review CAPM and other competing models that are used today for calculating the cost of equity. We also review the underlying concepts that underpin the models.

We have categorized the main approaches to determining the cost of equity under two headings:

- *Explanatory models*. These take hypotheses (models) of equity investor behavior which are interpreted in formulae which are then populated with numbers estimated statistically from market data to calculate the cost of equity. They include CAPM, Arbitrage Pricing Theory (APT), and the Fama-French Three Factor model.

- *Deductive models*. These deduce what the cost of equity is by inferring from observed current share prices what discount rate equity investors appear to be applying. In contrast with explanatory models, this approach does not therefore involve understanding or modeling what determines the cost of equity. Examples of the deductive approach are the Dividend Discount Model (DDM) and the Stochastic/Option pricing approach.

A further practical approach that is described in more detail in Chapter 7 involves firms adopting a very simple, but arbitrary, hurdle rate such as 10%. This is not really based on any model – it is based on a conscious decision to simplify matters to such an extent that the same hurdle rate is used for all investments regardless of the degree of risk. There are drawbacks to this approach and these are outlined further in Chapter 7. The remainder of this chapter concentrates on explanatory and deductive models of the cost of equity.

Explanatory models of the cost of equity

Explanatory models of the cost of equity have as their starting point a hypothesis, or model, of equity investor behavior. The thinking is that if we can understand how equity investors go about making their investment decisions then we will be in good shape to anticipate their future decisions.

Most series of cash flows will have an expected variation, or volatility. Cash flows vary for two reasons – first, because of generic economic and market risk factors to which every business is exposed, and second, because of specific risk factors that relate to the operating environment of the particular project or company. Clearly, the cash flows of some companies or potential investments are much more volatile than others – one or other, or both, of these risk classes must be responsible.

> Cash flows vary for two reasons – first, because of generic economic and market risk factors to which every business is exposed, and second, because of specific risk factors that relate to the operating environment of the particular project or company.

As we saw in Chapter 1, modern portfolio theory suggests that the second type of risk, specific risk, can be 'diversified away,' so that in efficient capital markets portfolio equity investors are only exposed to market risk.

The explanatory models that we cover in this chapter are all based on the hypothesis that equity investors hold diversified portfolios of equity investments and therefore only require returns for market (systematic) risk. However, the models differ in the way in which they seek to model investor evaluation of systematic risk.

In order to be of practical use in calculating the cost of equity, the hypotheses regarding investor behavior need to be interpreted in formulae that can be used to calculate the cost of equity. The CAPM formula is an example of one of these formulae. Implementation of the models then requires the formulae to be populated with estimates for the different variables, generally derived through observation and statistical analysis of market data.

As we shall see below, the factors in the formulae differ slightly between the alternative approaches, reflecting the different hypotheses regarding equity investor behavior, and/or the different approaches to using available market data to quantify that behavior.

We consider three explanatory models below in turn. The Arbitrage Pricing Theory (APT) model and the Fama-French Three Factor model will follow, but to set the scene we start with the most important explanatory model of them all – the CAPM.

The Capital Asset Pricing Model

CAPM is used around the world and the authors have found awareness of it wherever the process of discounted cash flow valuation exists. Although we have seen it earlier, the formula for the model is reproduced below.

$$K_e = R_f + \beta_e * EMRP$$

where
K_e = Cost of equity
R_f = Risk-free rate
β_e = Equity beta of investment
EMRP = Equity market risk premium

CAPM is a very simple model for calculating cost of equity which attempts to explain a highly complex world. Like most models of the cost of equity, it attempts to predict the future returns required by investors largely through the examination of historic returns (beta is usually calculated using historic data, and the EMRP is often estimated with reference to past returns). This means that CAPM provides an approximation to the cost of equity, as it would be surprising if there were an exact relationship between the historic return on an investment and the rate of return required by an investor on a prospective investment at a particular point in time.

The CAPM assumptions

CAPM is formulated on the basis of a number of assumptions. These are set out below.

- Investors are risk-averse individuals seeking to maximize their wealth.
- Investors have homogeneous expectations.
- Investors can borrow or lend at the risk-free rate.
- All assets are liquid.

- Asset markets are frictionless and all investors have access to perfect information.

- There are no taxes, transaction costs, or other market imperfections.

Very few of these assumptions conform to reality, and so it should be clear that the CAPM is based on a set of assumptions that appear highly restrictive. Does this mean that the model is inappropriate in the context of everyday cost of capital analysis and investment decisions?

We don't think so. To reach such a conclusion would be premature without first considering evidence from empirical tests of the CAPM, and this is evaluated in the section below. We also recall Milton Friedman's well-known contention – that the test of a good model is not necessarily the examination of whether the assumptions made are realistic, rather it should be whether the model provides an accurate description of observed reality.

> The test of a good model is not necessarily the examination of whether the assumptions made are realistic, rather it should be whether the model provides an accurate description of observed reality.

On this basis, the CAPM scores rather well. If the model is used by the majority of investors to price risk in the market, the case for adopting the CAPM becomes self-fulfilling. But what does the evidence say?

Tests of CAPM

A number of studies have been carried out over the years since the CAPM was first put forward with the objective of testing whether CAPM holds over time. Typically, these involve forming portfolios of securities ranked by beta and testing over long periods of time whether actual returns can be explained by the different portfolio betas.

These tests have had varying results; some work may have supported CAPM while many other studies suggested that other factors, such as total capitalization of quoted companies, dividend yield, or ratio of book value to market value seem to be useful in explaining the relationship between stock pricing and returns in addition to beta. Later in this chapter, some of the models incorporating these other factors are tabulated and summarized.

Situations where CAPM is widely regarded as performing less well, based on published studies, include:

- small companies;
- companies with extreme book to market ratios;

- companies with relatively high dividend yields;
- highly leveraged companies.

So what should we conclude from this? The variability of the empirical support for CAPM might on the face of it seem to undermine its validity. However, there are two key issues that arise when considering whether the tests can be relied upon.

First, as we will see in Chapter 6, some academics argue that the data periods used in the empirical tests are of insufficient length to give decisive results (for example, see note 9 in Chapter 6). Second, other academics argue that the empirical tests are conceptually flawed because the datasets used are unable to capture true market portfolios; these should include all measures of investors' wealth including property portfolios, future earnings potential and pension expectations. This is the so-called 'Roll critique.'

> No clear evidence has yet been produced to either support or disprove the CAPM as explaining required returns, in the situations that have been studied.

What does emerge from the historical studies of quoted stocks in this area is that different researchers have found conflicting evidence that appears to both support and disprove a variety of theories. No clear evidence has yet been produced to either support or disprove the CAPM as explaining required returns, in the situations that have been studied.

Outside the world of CAPM

While the other theories and practices for calculating a required rate of return to apply to an equity investment situation are less commonly used than CAPM, it is nevertheless important for the practitioner to be aware of them. In practice, some may be used as a cross-check to a CAPM calculation, or to provide an alternative view, or may be considered to give more insight into investor perceptions in a particular industry or market.

Furthermore, even if a practitioner decides to use CAPM exclusively, it is possible that in the course of applying CAPM in business situations he or she will come across others using the alternative models. This can happen, for example, in transaction negotiations or regulatory applications where different parties may have conflicting views which can be supported by the use of different models. It is therefore important to have a working knowledge of the underpinnings and strengths and weaknesses of the main alternatives to CAPM.

We have seen that the evidence supporting the application of CAPM is not conclusive. The evidence for other models, at the time of writing, is not conclusive either. Data limitations, as discussed earlier in this book, contribute to the fact that this can never be an exact science.

Other explanatory models – Arbitrage Pricing Theory ('APT')

In CAPM, beta is generated by regressing the movements in the returns on a specific security against returns on the market as a whole. A beta of 1 means that the security is perfectly correlated with the market; a lower or higher beta means movements are less or more correlated.

There are a number of factors that can account for differences in the level of beta between different stocks, which are examined in Chapter 2. However, within CAPM itself all that matters is the level of the beta. This drives differences in the cost of equity since the other components of the CAPM formula (the risk-free rate and the EMRP) are common across all stocks. As long as we think we know what the beta of a stock is we can measure the cost of equity using the CAPM formula, and it doesn't matter greatly what factors have resulted in beta being at this particular level.

That summarizes the position for CAPM and beta. APT introduces a range of coefficients and terms which play a similar role in capturing risk to that which beta and the EMRP play for CAPM. However, these terms are for fundamental (economic) variables which are considered to be important in determining how sensitive a stock is to market risk factors. This potentially increases the power of APT in explaining differences in the cost of equity across different stocks.

The formulation for APT is set out below.

$$K_{ei} = R_f + (B_{i1}K_1) + (B_{i2}K_2) + \ldots\ldots + (B_{in}K_n)$$

where K_{ei} = Cost of equity of the security i

R_f = Risk-free rate

$K_1 \ldots K_n$ = Expected risk premium associated with each unit of risk factors 1 to n

$B_{i1} \ldots B_{in}$ = Sensitivity of the security i to each of the n risk factors

This looks extremely fearsome, but we can move straight to what it actually means and how it drives on the road. If you can use and interpret CAPM results, you can use and interpret APT. Table 4.1 gives examples of the factors used in APT.

TABLE 4.1
Examples of factors for APT

Risk factor	Measurement
Interest rate	The difference between long-term and short-term yields
Inflation	Changes in inflation forecasts
Business outlook	Change in forecasts for factors such as GNP (gross national product)

Individual data providers use different factors so if this method is to be applied effort has to be made to understand what goes into the 'black box,' so as to interpret what comes out.

Depending on the variables chosen, some studies suggest that these models may give a better explanation of investment returns in industries such as banking, oil and utilities than CAPM.

> The general consensus is that APT's complexity, lack of transparency, and reliance on particular US-based data-providers makes it unlikely to become a world standard capable of competing with CAPM in the near future.

However, the general consensus is that APT's complexity, lack of transparency, and reliance on particular US-based data-providers makes it unlikely to become a world standard capable of competing with CAPM in the near future. It is also historic, in that it contains an implicit assumption that the world of share prices will perform in the future as it has in the past. With phenomena such as e-business and globalization overtaking various industries, this may be wishful thinking.

Other explanatory models – the Fama-French Three Factor model

The Fama-French Three Factor model again is built on the same principle as CAPM and APT, but as well as a measure similar to beta adds factors reflecting the effects on cost of equity of company size and the ratio of book value/market value.

The formula for this model is set out below.

$$K_e = bi\,[EMRP] + si\,E(SMB) + hi\,E(HML)$$

where K_e = Cost of equity capital

EMRP   = Equity markket risk premium

bi   = Sensitivity of security i to EMRP

E(SMB) = The 'small minus big' premium; the extra

		return expected for small capitalization companies
si	=	Sensitivity of security i to E(SMB)
E(HML)	=	The 'high minus low' premium; the extra return expected for companies with high book to market ratios
hi	=	Sensitivity of security i to E(HML)

The risk-free rate and EMRP terms should be familiar to the reader by now from the CAPM. The additional terms are company-specific factors that could be regarded as contradicting modern portfolio theory. However, Fama and French have included these terms because they believe this improves the performance of the model in explaining observed historical returns.

The use of size adjustments is discussed in Chapter 10, 'Premia and discounts,' where the reasons why the cost of equity might be higher for smaller companies are examined. The inclusion of the ratio of book to market value implies that the cost of equity rises as a company's market capitalization falls. The rationale for this appears to be that equity investors will require a higher return as a firm gets closer to being in a state of financial distress.

In the real world, the Three Factor model is not widely used in its pure form and where we have seen it, it is often used in conjunction with data from proprietary providers. Practitioners may increase the cost of equity in a judgmental way to reflect effects such as greater perceived risk for a small company (the so-called 'size premium' or 'small stock premium' – see discussion in Chapter 10). We have rarely seen any separate adjustment made for book to market value in practice, although this does not imply that one should not be made.

A comparison of the output from explanatory models

To illustrate that cost of equity models built on the same basic principles as the CAPM can give a wide range of estimates, Table 4.2 sets out cost of equity calculations from the three alternative models. These are calculated as of the beginning of 1999 using US data sources and dollar interest rates. The three groups of companies include a collection of well-known miscellaneous large capitalization companies from various sectors, several integrated petroleum companies, and several large financial services companies.

TABLE 4.2
Illustrative cost of equity calculations from three explanatory models

	CAPM	APT*	Fama-French Three Factor
General			
AT&T Corp	10.02%	12.23%	14.74%
Bristol Myers Squib	10.32%	11.78%	8.87%
Coca-Cola	10.47%	10.68%	6.23%
General Motors Corp	9.87%	12.14%	19.78%
IBM	11.52%	10.88%	4.30%
McDonald's Corp	10.62%	11.96%	5.74%
Merck & Co	10.97%	13.37%	5.91%
Proctor & Gamble	10.12%	11.21%	7.13%
Walt Disney Company	10.62%	15.14%	13.10%
Average	10.50%	12.15%	9.53%
Integrated Petroleum			
Amoco	7.02%	8.40%	6.02%
Atlantic Richfield	8.92%	11.84%	14.94%
Chevron Corp	8.32%	10.86%	10.86%
Exxon	8.52%	11.52%	8.88%
Mobil	7.97%	10.13%	9.76%
Texaco	7.67%	12.09%	10.24%
Average	8.07%	10.81%	10.12%
Financial Services			
American Express	12.07%	13.98%	16.13%
Bank of New York	12.92%	16.38%	19.69%
Bank One	12.82%	15.45%	19.82%
BankAmerica	12.02%	15.45%	17.53%
Chase Manhattan	12.32%	12.12%	16.96%
Citigroup	14.07%	16.01%	18.39%
Morgan Stanley Dean	15.72%	16.46%	20.25%
Wells Fargo	11.57%	13.59%	18.99%
Average	12.94%	14.93%	18.47%

* BIRR proprietary APT model

Table 4.2 shows the variation by industry, by company within industry, and between models. For the three sectors covered, we see bigger ranges between results using the Fama-French model than, for example, CAPM (because the additional two factors allow for more differentiation); we also see quite significant divergence for APT in some sectors although less marked for oils. Clearly a straightforward averaging of results would be foolish. The wide variation in some cases merits an examination of the data and methodology to understand why the results are so different before adopting a particular model, or even a range, as the basis for estimating the cost of equity.

Deductive models of the cost of equity

Explanatory models such as CAPM, APT, and Fama-French use largely historic information combined with hypotheses about investor behavior and the nature of equity risk, to model likely future required returns. Deductive models provide an alternative approach. These models do not seek to explain the behavior of equity investors. Rather, they seek simply to infer from available market information what cost of equity is actually being applied by investors.

Dividend discount model (DDM) and related approaches

These seek to infer the cost of equity from the current share price, combined with forecasts of future movements in dividends and growth estimates of a company or of the market. Here's a simple example (Example 4.1).

> Deductive models provide an alternative approach. These models do not seek to explain the behavior of equity investors. Rather, they seek simply to infer from available market information what cost of equity is actually being applied by investors.

Example 4.1 Using the dividend discount model

The DDM seeks to explain the share price of a company by discounting the expected future stream of dividend payments at the cost of equity (K_e) for the business. This is done by first taking the most recent dividend paid and uplifting it to a current level by multiplying by a consensus annual growth rate. Having obtained the current dividend rate, the discounted value of the future ▶

stream is then calculated using the standard perpetuity formula – dividing the current dividend by the discount rate (cost of equity) less the growth rate.

$$\text{Share price} = \frac{\text{Dividend} \,(1 + \text{growth \%})}{K_e - \text{growth \%}}$$

Rearranging the formula gives us an expression for the cost of equity:

$$K_e = \frac{\text{Dividend} \,(1 + \text{growth \%})}{\text{Share price}} + \text{growth \%}$$

Suppose that a company has just paid a dividend of 73 cents per share, the current share price is $10 and the analysts' consensus forecast for average long-term growth in the dividend is 2.5%; this calculation would appear as:

$$K_e = \frac{0.73(1 + 0.025)}{10} + 0.025 = 10\%$$

This methodology is used by some analysts to generate cost of equity estimates from market data as discussed in Chapter 3. In its most simple form, as in Example 4.1, the DDM uses a constantly growing cash flow in perpetuity (a single-stage DCF approach). A more sophisticated approach is to use a formula which divides growth of dividend flows into various stages of assumed number of years (a multistage approach); instead of dividends, net cash flows to equity are often used on the assumption that investors eventually receive the benefit of these cash flows either through dividends or through the share price.

Therefore, in the real world, forecasts of investment returns and growth expectations can be used to build up a forward-looking picture of the cost of equity without many of the conceptual and practical difficulties associated with the CAPM-based methods. So does this mean we can forget about explanatory models with their conceptual difficulties, myriads of arcane assumptions and painstaking data gathering requirements? Of course not – the catch for the deductive approach is the art of forecasting dividends and growth; output from these approaches will only be as good as the forecasts going in, and there is a danger that these may have upward bias.

Ibbotson Associates use a DDM approach in their *Cost of Capital Quarterly* (*www.Ibbotson.com*) based on earnings per share projections, using a three-stage growth model.

In practice, the DDM approaches tend to be used more by investment analysts than by valuation practitioners. There seems to be a great divide between market-facing approaches, which look to the future, and the more traditional approaches which are rooted firmly in past investment performance. A stronger bridge between these two schools of thought must be helpful to the cost of capital debate and should build greater understanding of the relationship between valuation and market price.

Stochastic/option pricing models

A number of academics in the finance field have been developing approaches to estimating cost of capital based on traditional Black-Scholes option pricing methodology. These models use implied volatility, calculated from traded options data, to describe risk, instead of beta. Much of the work in this area is unpublished and, moreover, highly mathematical as far as the average finance professional is concerned.

The key feature is that it usually captures both systematic and unsystematic risk in the rate of return, so it is actually performing a different function to the CAPM and APT approaches.

Summary of choice of model

In this section, a number of other approaches to calculating equity cost of capital are put alongside CAPM (see Table 4.3). We have tabulated these so as to compare and contrast the approaches.

We have seen that empirically none of the models of the cost of equity has been accepted as consistently holding in practice or providing a 'best answer.'

But the CAPM is very commonly used, by businesses, investors, and share analysts, to calculate the cost of equity. This means that, notwithstanding all the conceptual and practical issues surrounding its validity and practicality, it is worth getting to grips with it. Because so many business decisions are made on the basis of the CAPM it follows that at least some share and asset prices are driven by the CAPM. Popularity can make the CAPM a self-fulfilling approach.

TABLE 4.3
Comparison of models for estimating cost of equity

Methodology	Specific risk	Market risk	Historic information	Prospective information	Can extrapolate benchmark returns	Practical issues	Proprietary data providers
CAPM	✗	✓β	✓	✓Ex-ante EMRP (if chosen) ✓Risk-free rate	✓Industry or comparable β	See Chapters 2, 3, and 6; widely used around the world and capable of being adapted for international situations; may work less well for some industries	See Chapters 2, 3, and 6.
Arbitrage pricing theory (APT)	✗	✓	✓	✓Risk-free rate	✗	Is only calculated for some specific companies; evidence to date suggests that it may provide a good alternative to CAPM for some industries	Advanced Portfolio Technologies Inc BIRR Portfolio Analysis Inc
Fama-French Three Factor model	✓Company size and book to market ratio	✓β	✓	✓Ex-ante EMRP (if chosen) ✓Risk-free rate	✓Industry and/or comparable factors	Developed in 1992 to address criticisms of CAPM and β as a predictor of returns – adds two additional factors; company size and book/market ratio. It can be argued that these factors do affect markets and therefore this model does not conflict with MPT.	Ibbotson Associates
Dividend discount model(s)	✓	✓Through share price	✗	✓Dividend forecast	✓Comparables and also returns on the market	Forecasting dividend growth and rates and payout; dealing with share buybacks	
Stochastic/ Option pricing models	✓	✓	✗	✓	✗	Can only be used if traded options in the shares exist; has been endorsed by Dean Paxson (MBS); Gerry Salkin (Imperial London); Max Ziff	Not known

Key points from the chapter

This chapter has moved us from the CAPM through to other frameworks that have been formulated.

- This chapter has looked at two broad classes of models: explanatory models and deductive models. Examples of explanatory models include the CAPM, APT and the Fama-French Three Factor model. Examples of the deductive approach are the DDM and Stochastic/Option pricing models.

- We have found that the CAPM is widely used and recognized around the world, despite a lack of concrete proof that it consistently explains share price returns. Situations where the CAPM is regarded as performing less well include: small companies, companies with extreme book to market rations, companies with relatively high dividend yields and highly leveraged companies.

- These anomalies have led to the development of multi-factor models such as APT and the Fama-French Three Factor model. APT is more of a theoretical tool, but the Fama-French Three Factor model is sometimes used in the real world. Many practitioners make adjustments to the standard CAPM for size as an alternative to the Fama-French approach.

- A comparison of the output from CAPM, APT and Fama-French shows that the models do not necessarily produce the same figures. Variability in costs of capital across different sectors is probably greatest using the Fama-French approach rather than APT or CAPM.

- The solution of the choice of model is to bear in mind the model that is most often used in the circumstances in which you are operating, and to seek to understand the data you will use and the results it will give.

5

THE COST OF DEBT AND OPTIMAL CAPITAL STRUCTURE

Generally far less attention has been paid to the cost of debt than the cost of equity when calculating the cost of capital. With a historically small share of overall company financing its importance has often been overlooked. Only in certain circumstances, such as leveraged buyouts and project finance has debt moved centre stage. This is beginning to change.

Lower interest rates and a greater appetite from investors for corporate bond issues mean that companies are looking more towards debt, particularly bond financing, as a core component of business capital. As debt becomes a bigger source of capital for companies, so it becomes more important for the practitioner to be able to estimate the cost of debt accurately.

A key question for businesses is how to assess the amount of debt that can be supported, and the optimal mix between debt and equity financing. The benefits of debt financing are becoming well understood, yet the disastrous consequences of excessive debt levels provide a chilling reminder of the dangers of gearing up too much.

Introduction

In Chapter 1 we saw that there are essentially two sources of capital for companies, equity and debt. The preceding chapters have considered the cost of equity and now we move on to the cost of debt. This will allow us to complete the second part of our weighted average cost of capital formula:

$$WACC = Ke * \frac{E}{V} + Kd * (1 - T) * \frac{D}{V}$$

In many ways the cost of debt is more transparent than the cost of equity. While the cost of equity is purely an opportunity cost concept, and is usually estimated using models of equity investor behavior, debt finance costs are visible in terms of promised interest payments and redemption yields on bonds. Even so, the calculation of the cost of debt is not entirely straightforward.

In this chapter we consider the definition of debt, how to calculate the cost of debt, the impact of debt finance on corporate taxation, and the optimal mix of debt and equity in company financing.

The characteristics of debt

Debt can take the form of bonds, loans, and overdrafts. These forms of finance have three key characteristics in common that classify them as debt. First, in each case the business in receipt of any of these types of finance is contractually committed to repayment of the original finance (principal) at some later date, together with additional payments in the meantime (interest payments in the case of a loan or overdraft, and coupon payments in the case of bonds).

Providers of debt finance face a significantly different risk profile by comparison with equity investors. The fact that interest costs are paid out of corporate incomes before taxation, and take priority over payments to equity investors, reduces the risk to which debt providers are exposed.

Secondly, payments by a company to honor its contractual obligations to the providers of such finance have a priority call on the company's resources over shareholder dividends. Thirdly, investors who provide these types of finance have no right to any other payments over and above these contractually committed payments. Providers of debt, unlike equity investors, do not benefit in the event that a business performs well.

Providers of debt finance therefore face a significantly different risk profile by comparison with equity investors. The fact that interest costs are paid out of corporate incomes before taxation, and take priority over payments to equity investors, reduces the risk to which debt providers are exposed. Interest costs are determined at the outset of the borrowing and are more likely to be paid than dividend payments. However, debt holders do not share in the potential upside of value of the firm, as the equity shareholders are the residual owners of the firm.

Debt and portfolio diversification

There is a further difference between debt and equity, at least in terms of how it is treated conventionally. As we saw in Chapter 1, rational equity investors invest in portfolios of equities, thereby eliminating their exposure to the specific risks associated with equity investments. Within a portfolio, for every investment that performs poorly due to specific risk factors another is likely to do well. Rational equity investors are therefore exposed only to risks that are systematic across all equity investments, and the cost of equity is a function only of systematic risk.

Debt investors also benefit from diversification. A rational lender should invest in a portfolio of bonds, or lend to a range of entities. This limits the degree to which the investor is exposed to the specific risk associated with one or a small number of borrowers.

The promised and expected yield on debt

However, diversification works in a slightly different way in the case of debt. Because interest payments and the principal repayment are contractually defined, and debt investors do not share in any upside, there is a ceiling on the payments received by debt investors. In the event that a business to which an investor has lent money is successful due to specific risk factors the debt investor simply receives the contracted interest payments and the repayment of the principal. This is referred to as the 'promised yield' on debt.[1] It is what the borrower promises to pay in the event that the business generates sufficient cash to honor the contracted obligations.

In the event that a business to which a debt investor has lent money is unsuccessful due to specific risk factors, the debt investor faces a downside – interest payments might be delayed or reduced, and the principal might not be repaid in full (or at all). This is referred to as the risk of default on a bond or loan. Prior to making any debt investment the rational lender should take a view on the likely probability of default. Combining the promised yield and the probability of default enables the debt investor to calculate the 'expected yield' on debt.

> From the point of view of the debt investor, it would be foolish to regard the promised yield as the relevant figure as default is a possibility. From the point of view of the borrower, the ability to default in adversity reduces the effective cost of borrowing.

The expected yield is the true cost of debt. Because businesses can (and do) default, the promised yield exaggerates the cost of debt. From the point of view of the debt investor, it would be foolish to regard the promised yield as the relevant figure as default is a possibility. From the point of view of the borrower, the ability to default in adversity reduces the effective cost of borrowing.

Similarly, for the rational portfolio debt investor, since the debt payments from successful investments cannot rise above the contracted level to offset those investments where there is a full or partial default, it follows that a debt investor with a portfolio of debt investments will anticipate an expected return on the whole portfolio which is below the contracted return.

For debt investors, diversification is still beneficial, as it eliminates variability in this expected return arising from specific risk factors. A debt investor with a diversified portfolio is only exposed to systematic risks that tend to affect the probability of default on all debt investments simultaneously. As we saw in Chapter 1, these are generally risks associated with the performance of the economy.

So far, so similar to equity. However, conventionally in business applications when practitioners refer to 'the cost of debt' they actually mean the *promised* yield on debt (i.e. the contractually agreed payments, not taking into account the possibility of default) and not the expected yield on debt (which, because it recognizes the possibility of default, is the true measure of the cost of debt).

This seemingly small and unimportant distinction has two main implications. First, if you see a cost of capital calculated using the promised yield on debt as a proxy for the cost of debt then, strictly speaking, this overstates the true cost of debt and the true cost of capital. However, as this is the conventional approach it would be normal to see this. In part this is because the cost of capital is often calculated and applied in situations where there is an underlying assumption that default will not occur – e.g. in business valuations which assume a company is a 'going concern,' or in the calculation of an allowed return on capital for a regulated business where the regulator has a duty to ensure that the company can finance its operations.

And in truth, for many companies for which the cost of capital is calculated the risk of default is small and hence the distinction between the promised and expected yield is a fine one. Because the contracted yield is easily observed and well understood it is more practical to stick with the promised figure, even if in principle it should be reduced.

The exception to this is for companies in or near financial distress. The promised yield on debt can be very high – well above the cost of equity – but the true, expected yield is much lower because of the high risk of default. Failing to adjust the promised yield to an expected yield can have odd consequences, as Example 5.1 shows.

Example 5.1 The promised and expected cost of debt

The authors once saw some analysis of the cost of capital for a business where the probability of default was high and hence the promised cost of debt was also high (to compensate debt investors for the high risk of default and thus provide a reasonable expected return).

The analyst erroneously applied the convention that the promised yield was the true cost of debt. On this basis the cost of debt was well above the cost of equity (which he had calculated conventionally, using the capital asset pricing model). The analyst noted that this could not be the case – the cost of debt must be lower than the cost of equity, as debt providers have a prior call on the company's cash flow.

He therefore concluded that a minimum value for the cost of capital must be his calculated cost of debt – since the cost of equity must be above the cost of debt, then the cost of capital, being a weighted average of the cost of equity and the cost of debt, must be at least as large as the cost of debt.

In fact he would have done better to apply the reverse logic – that the cost of debt must be lower than the cost of equity, so an upper bound for the cost of capital was provided by the cost of equity. This would have got him much closer to the correct answer.

That he didn't do so is probably down to the apparent 'science' of observing a contractually agreed rate of interest on debt compared with the 'conjecture' of building a theory, or model, to explain the cost of equity. But in relying on the promised cost of debt he ignored the risk of default and that, for the business in question, was significant.

The second main implication is that, if the conventional i.e. promised definition of the cost of debt is applied, then this cost of debt *does* include an uplift for specific risk.

Portfolio theory tells us that the expected cost of debt will not include any premium for exposure to specific risk, because such risk can be eliminated by holding a portfolio of loans. However, this is because a debt holder faces upside as well as downside risk on the expected return on any debt investment. There is no possible upside on the promised cost of debt – debt investors do not share in the higher returns if a company is successful, they simply receive the contracted debt repayments.

> Portfolio theory tells us that the expected cost of debt will not include any premium for exposure to specific risk, because such risk can be eliminated by holding a portfolio of loans. However, this is because a debt holder faces upside as well as downside risk on the expected return on any debt investment.

So the promised cost of debt necessarily includes an uplift for the risk of default, and this risk is affected by factors specific to a company or investment as well as systematic factors. Effectively what happens is this. For any debt investment the debt provider requires an expected return that takes into account only the systematic risk to which that investment exposes him. To set the promised cost of debt (the interest rate on the loan or the coupon on the bond) the debt provider calculates the contractual return necessary such that, taking into account the risk of default, the investment should yield the expected return.

Thus the promised cost of debt is calculated by uplifting the expected cost for default risk; and default risk comprises both company specific and systematic factors. This is another reason why specific risk matters despite the ability of investors to eliminate exposure to such risk through diversification – the conventionally used cost of debt will be higher the more specific risk associated with an investment.

For the remainder of this chapter, unless stated otherwise, when we refer to the cost of debt we mean the conventionally used cost of debt – the promised return on debt.

Different types of debt finance

Debt instruments have become much more complex in recent years, and carry a variety of different terms. This reflects the expansion of fixed income markets, the globalization of businesses, and also tax and currency issues for borrowers and lenders. A casual glance in the notes to the accounts of a large company will usually reveal a large array of debt instruments. Treasury departments will use money markets to raise short-term funds or cover currency positions, and may also use the bond markets to secure long-term financing and cover cash flows in many currencies. Some debt instruments are reasonably simple, but more complex debt instruments are now frequently used that include additional benefits, like options to convert or subscribe for equity.

Example 5.2 illustrates the many different sources of debt, using the example of a UK company, National Grid.

Example 5.2 A typical debt portfolio of a large company

Amounts falling due within one year:	£m
Bank loans and overdrafts	144.5
Commercial paper	52.5
6% mandatorily exchangeable bonds 2003	242.6
5.5% US dollar bonds 2001	197.6
US medium-term notes 2001	18.7
7.375% bonds 1999	–
Other loans	13.1
	669.0

Amounts falling due after more than one year:	£m
Bank borrowings 2002–04	1,000.0
Pollution control revenue bonds 2018–22	232.4
4.25% exchangeable bonds 2008	469.0
5.875% bonds 2024	443.3
US medium-term notes 2002–28	299.7
8% bonds 2006	238.9
European Investment Bank Swiss franc loan 2004	173.2
US private placement notes 2001–15	78.4
Zero coupon bonds 2002	26.2
US tax exempt bonds 2001–17	16.4
5.5% US dollar bonds 2001	–
Other loans	28.7
	3,006.2
Total borrowings	3,675.2

Source: National Grid, *Annual Accounts 2000*

Additionally, some companies may raise debt finance through affiliates or related parties; these forms of 'off-balance sheet' finance can be extremely complex and may have a significant effect on the company value that is available to equity investors. The costs and obligations in such cases may not be readily apparent from the financial accounts of a company. This was brought home to investors sharply by the collapse of Enron in December 2001.

The weighted average cost of debt

In principle, where a company such as National Grid uses a wide variety of debt instruments, to establish the overall cost of debt it is necessary to calculate the cost of debt for each individual instrument and then combine these into a weighted average cost of debt for the company as a whole taking into account the proportion of total debt accounted for by each instrument.

In practice it is often simpler to calculate an estimate of the generic long-term cost of debt for the firm, and then consider whether any complex financial arrangements actually in place give any reason to change this generic cost of debt.

So how is a generic cost of debt calculated? We shall first consider bonds as a simple, transparent source of debt pricing information, and then briefly consider other sources of debt finance.

Calculating the pre-tax cost of debt

The pre-tax cost of debt can be expressed as:

$$K_d = R_f + DM$$

where K_d = The pre-tax cost of debt
       R_f = The risk-free rate
       DM = Debt margin for default risk

As we saw in Chapter 1, when this pre-tax cost of debt is incorporated in the WACC calculation then the tax shield on debt interest must be deployed in the WACC formula.

The risk-free rate

The issues in deriving the risk-free rate (e.g. choice of government debt instrument, real versus nominal yield, choice of maturity, etc.) are exactly the same when calculating the cost of debt as they are when using the CAPM to calculate the cost of equity. Chapter 2 gives a blow-by-blow account of how to derive the risk-free rate for the CAPM, so all we need to say here is that the same applies for the cost of debt. Indeed, if you need to calculate a WACC, then it is important that the same risk-free rate be used in estimating both the cost of equity and the cost of debt.

Chapter 2 recommended the use of the redemption yield on an appropriately dated government security, issued by a highly creditworthy country, as a proxy for the risk-free rate.

Debt margin

As we saw in Chapter 2, government bonds are used as the basis for calculating the risk-free rate because it is assumed that lending money to a government exposes the lender to very little default risk. In much of the developed world it is extremely unlikely that any government will ever fail to pay government bond holders the agreed coupons and par redemption value, because of the wealth of the countries and the stability of government finances (backed by the ability to raise taxes if necessary).

In contrast, investors providing debt to companies expose themselves to greater risk. Companies, even those considered 'blue chip,' can and do default on their obligations to lenders, whether they be banks or bond holders. To compensate them for taking on this default risk lenders require a higher return for lending to a company rather than a government. This is known as the *debt margin*, the difference in the redemption yield on a corporate bond and the yield on a government bond (the risk-free rate).

> Investors providing debt to companies expose themselves to greater risk. To compensate them for taking on this default risk lenders require a higher return for lending to a company rather than a government. This is known as the *debt margin*, the difference in the redemption yield on a corporate bond and the yield on a government bond (the risk-free rate).

Figure 5.1 shows typical yield curves for government (sovereign) debt and corporate debt, illustrating the higher yield investors require for investing in corporate debt. The gap between the curves represents the debt margin (or spread), a measure of the higher yield that compensates for the default/credit risk of the corporate bond.

FIGURE 5.1
Required yield on corporate bonds over sovereign debt

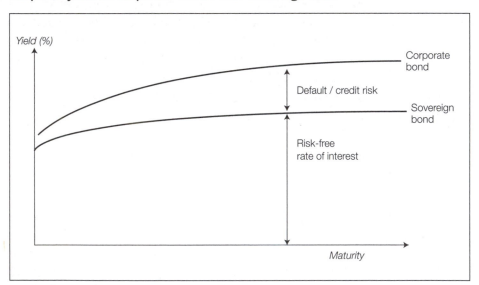

This spread represents the additional return with which bond investors are actually being rewarded in the market, for taking the default risk associated with the corporate bond. If the bonds used in the calculation are actively traded in the market then the spread provides a consensus market view on the return needed to compensate for the default risk associated with the corporate bond. This is because, were this not the case, then the process of arbitrage would lead the price of the bond to rise or fall until it were so.

As the risk of corporate default increases so the returns required by investors also rise. Higher risk companies will have to offer higher interest payments to reward investors for the possibility that investors may not receive their coupon interest or even the original principal.

Calculating the debt margin

It should therefore be clear that debt margins can be calculated using information on bonds traded in the market. Debt margins are simply the observed difference, or 'spread,' between the redemption yield on a government bond and the redemption yield on a traded corporate bond of comparable maturity.

For a particular company there are two *direct* ways in which debt margins can be estimated (we will consider *indirect* methods later):

1. Directly from the debt margins of traded corporate bonds issued by the enterprise itself, or based on first hand information from the enterprise about very recently determined borrowing margins on debt provided to it by third-party banks.

2. Based on the debt margins of other enterprises that are good close comparators to the enterprise in question and that have traded debt.

In either case, the technique involves measuring the spread between risk-free government and traded corporate bonds at various maturities. It is important to recognize that because risk-free and corporate yield curves vary with maturity (they are upward sloping in Figure 5.1), for consistency it is necessary to compare risk-free redemption yields and corporate redemption yields of the same maturity.

> Good comparators are companies in the same sector or with similar business interests. Equivalent size, financial health, and gearing are also important.

Table 5.1 provides an example of the results the practitioner can expect using this sort of technique. Margins are measured using traded bond information for a handful of comparator companies in the telecommunications sector. Good comparators are companies in the same sector or with similar business interests. Equivalent size, financial health, and gearing are also important.

TABLE 5.1
Corporate bond debt margins of global telecommunications firms, April 2004

Corporate debt issuer	Credit rating	Maturity of tradable debt	Yield to maturity	Maturity of risk-free benchmark	Risk-free yield to maturity	Debt margin
Telstra	AA-	15/11/2012	6.85%	15/05/2013	5.97%	0.88%
Alltel	A	01/11/2013	5.19%	15/02/2014	4.43%	0.76%
Verizon Communications	A	01/05/2013	5.33%	15/02/2014	4.43%	0.90%
Telefonica	A-	14/02/2013	4.63%	04/01/2013	4.07%	0.56%
BT Group	BBB+	26/03/2020	5.97%	07/06/2021	4.97%	1.00%
France Telecom	BBB	28/01/2013	4.80%	04/01/2012	3.92%	0.88%
Deutsche Telekom	BBB	26/09/2012	4.66%	04/01/2011	3.75%	0.91%
Cia de Telecomunicaciones de Chile	BBB	15/07/2006	3.01%	31/03/2006	2.09%	0.92%
Telekomunikacja Polska	BBB	10/12/2008	4.52%	15/04/2009	3.47%	1.05%
CenturyTel	BBB	15/08/2012	5.65%	15/02/2014	4.43%	1.22%
AT&T	BBB	01/03/2007	3.72%	15/02/2007	2.52%	1.20%
Telus	BBB-	01/06/2011	5.17%	15/04/2009	3.44%	1.73%
Sprint	BBB-	15/04/2022	6.91%	15/02/2014	4.43%	2.48%
Rogers Wireless	BB	01/03/2014	7.72%	15/02/2014	4.43%	3.29%

Where a debt margin is required for a maturity where no bond information is directly available, a technique of interpolation may be used as long as it is possible to establish debt margins at shorter and longer maturities than the one required.

Where debt margins cannot be directly measured from the market, as briefly noted above, indirect methods can be used. These estimate the cost of debt either by using credit ratings available in the market, or by understanding the cause of default risk and using financial analysis to estimate synthetic credit ratings.

The cause of default risk

The risk of default in corporate lending arises because there is a possibility that pre-interest cash flows and cash reserves will not be adequate to pay interest costs and principal repayments. The risk of default therefore rises when available cash is squeezed. Lower revenues, higher costs or an unsustainable capital expenditure program are all factors that increase the risk of default. Increasing debt service costs, which could arise as a consequence of increasing interest rates on floating debt, will also increase the risk of default.

Measuring or estimating default risk

Armed with this insight into the causes of default, it is possible to evaluate the relative risks of different companies defaulting on their debt by examining their financial situation. Credit rating agencies analyze the projected financial performance of companies in order to assess their risks of default, and provide a ranking from the safest to the least creditworthy. Such agencies include Moody's, Standard & Poor's, Fitch, and Institutional Investor. While these rating agencies provide information in slightly different forms, fundamentally their common aim is to inform investors as to the risk of default for companies.

Standard & Poor's ratings are based on a sliding scale with 20 categories, where AAA represents extremely low default risk at one end of the scale and D represents total default risk at the higher end of the scale (see Table 5.2).

How is a rating assessed?

Rating agencies examine complex quantitative and qualitative risk factors to assess their ratings for companies.

TABLE 5.2
Example of rating scale – Standard & Poor's

Description	Rating category	Comments
Investment grade	AAA	The highest debt rating assigned. The borrower's capacity to repay debt is extremely strong
	AA	Capacity to repay is strong and marginally differs from the highest quality
	A	Has strong capacity to repay; borrower is susceptible to adverse effects of changes in circumstances and economic conditions
	BBB	Has adequate capacity to repay, but adverse economic conditions or circumstances are more likely to lead to risk
Sub-investment grade	BB, B, CCC, CC, C	Regarded as predominantly speculative, BB being the least speculative and C the most
	D	In default or with payments in arrears

Source: Standard & Poor's

The rating agency will assess company strength against each risk factor, assessing which are the most important factors for the company's future financial position, and in particular its ability to make debt service payments. For example, the agency is likely to concentrate on technology risks as being critical to, say, a pioneering telecommunications company, but is less likely to see such risks as being important for, say, a tobacco manufacturer.

Judgment is used to evaluate 'soft' factors that impact on company performance, such as the perceived quality of the management team.

How realistic are ratings at predicting corporate default?

The rating agencies are often criticized for being reactive to events, rather than providing a forward-looking measure of default risk. There have been instances where strongly rated companies and governments have unexpectedly suffered financial problems leading to defaulting on their debt.[2]

In their defense the rating agencies provide historical data that show that, over a long period and with a large sample size, the actual rate of default for those companies that they have rated more highly has indeed been lower. This is illustrated in Table 5.3, based on information from Moody's.

TABLE 5.3
Cumulative probability of corporate default, 1983–99 (%)

	Years to default							
Rating	1	2	3	4	5	6	7	8
Aaa	0.0	0.0	0.0	0.1	0.2	0.3	0.4	0.5
Aa1	0.0	0.0	0.0	0.2	0.2	0.4	0.4	0.4
Aa2	0.0	0.0	0.1	0.2	0.5	0.6	0.7	0.8
Aa3	0.1	0.1	0.2	0.3	0.4	0.6	0.6	0.6
A1	0.0	0.0	0.3	0.5	0.7	0.8	0.9	1.0
A2	0.0	0.0	0.1	0.4	0.6	0.8	0.9	1.2
A3	0.0	0.1	0.3	0.3	0.4	0.5	0.8	0.9
Baa1	0.0	0.3	0.5	0.9	1.3	1.6	2.0	2.3
Baa2	0.1	0.3	0.6	1.2	1.8	2.5	2.8	2.9
Baa3	0.3	0.8	1.3	2.2	2.8	3.8	4.7	5.7
Ba1	0.6	2.1	3.9	6.3	8.5	10.7	12.2	13.7
Ba2	0.5	2.6	5.1	7.3	9.2	10.5	11.9	12.8
Ba3	2.5	7.0	11.9	16.5	21.0	25.1	28.7	32.6
B1	3.5	9.3	14.8	19.6	24.5	29.8	34.9	38.4
B2	6.9	14.0	20.3	24.8	28.5	31.2	32.6	34.4
B3	12.2	20.7	27.3	32.5	37.5	40.7	44.0	47.8
Caa1-C	19.1	28.4	34.2	40.1	43.4	47.7	47.7	51.3
Investment-grade	0.0	0.2	0.3	0.6	0.8	1.1	1.3	1.5
Speculative-grade	3.7	8.3	12.7	16.6	20.2	23.4	26.2	28.7
All corporates	1.2	2.7	4.0	5.2	6.3	7.2	7.9	8.6

Source: Moody's, 2001

Table 5.3 shows the instances of actual historic defaults for a given number of years after a company was ascribed a certain rating. During the period covered by Table 5.3 only 0.5% of companies rated Aaa by Moody's defaulted on their debt within eight years of that rating being assigned, compared with an equivalent figure of 32.6% for a Ba3 rating. While there are a few anomalies, it is indeed the case that the lower the rating assigned by Moody's, the greater the observed incidence of actual default.

Use of credit ratings to establish debt margins

To recap, we have seen that the debt margin is the additional return on a corporate bond, over and above that on a government bond, needed to entice an investor to accept the default risk associated with the corporate bond. For bonds traded in the market the debt margin can be observed as the spread between the yield on a corporate bond and a counterpart government bond.

Credit rating agencies analyze the underlying causes of corporate bond default, and assign ratings to companies to reflect their view of credit risk. While the agencies do not always get it right, there is a clear past correlation between credit ratings assigned and the actual record of default.

So where is this taking us in calculating the cost of debt? If the business whose cost of debt is to be evaluated has issued bonds that are actively traded in the market, then the redemption yields on these can be observed, giving a direct measure of the pre-tax cost of debt. There is no need to fuss about with government bonds, spreads, and debt margins.

> Credit rating agencies analyze the underlying causes of corporate bond default, and assign ratings to companies to reflect their view of credit risk. While the agencies do not always get it right, there is a clear past correlation between credit ratings assigned and the actual record of default.

However, in some cases it is not possible to observe relevant corporate bonds directly. For example, a business that has not yet been started will not have issued bonds. Even if the business being examined has issued bonds these may not have the appropriate maturity dates for the purposes required (e.g. it may not have issued any long-term debt).

In addition, it is sometimes more convenient to derive a broad benchmark of the cost of debt for a company, rather than going to all the trouble of calculating the yields and interest rates on each of a company's debt instruments separately and then combining them into a weighted average cost of debt. Readers will recall Example 5.2 that showed how complicated the composition of debt for a company can be. A shortcut can look tempting in these circumstances.

In these cases it is possible to use credit ratings as the basis for evaluating a company's debt margin without the need to observe the yields on its debt directly. Credit ratings are intended to reflect the probability of default, and spreads widen with a higher risk of default. There is thus a relationship between observed market spreads and credit ratings. This is shown in Table 5.4, which gives average spreads observed in the market, by rating, on bonds of varying maturity. These spreads are expressed in terms of 'basis points,' the convention being that each basis point is equal to 1/100th of a percentage point. As the time horizon to maturity increases, the spread between corporate debt and sovereign debt increases, reflecting the cumulative increased risk of corporate default.

So, if an industrial company's credit rating is known, Table 5.4 suggests what a reasonable estimate of its debt margin should be for different maturity periods. Table 5.4 is only relevant to industrial companies. Bond spreads also vary between industry sectors, for a given rating. This variation is not uniform across different ratings as Table 5.5 illustrates.

TABLE 5.4

Bond spreads by maturity and credit rating for industrial companies, 2001

Rating	1 Yr	2 Yr	3 Yr	5 Yr	7 Yr	10 Yr	30 Yr
Aaa/AAA	36	42	47	62	78	85	97
Aa1/AA+	41	47	57	73	88	95	107
Aa2/AA	46	57	62	78	94	107	118
Aa3/AA−	51	62	67	88	104	118	129
A1/A+	61	72	88	105	124	138	150
A2/A	71	82	103	120	144	164	173
A3/A−	81	97	113	130	160	178	198
Baa1/BBB+	101	117	133	150	175	199	208
Baa2/BBB	121	137	153	170	190	210	230
Baa3/BBB−	141	152	163	180	205	225	245
Ba1/BB+	275	300	325	350	385	425	500
Ba2/BB	300	325	350	375	425	475	600
Ba3/BB−	350	400	425	475	500	550	725
B1/B+	450	475	500	575	625	675	800
B2/B	525	575	625	700	750	800	950
B3/B−	575	625	725	825	950	1,050	1,175

Source: *www.bondsonline.com*

TABLE 5.5

Ten year bond spreads by sector and credit rating, 2001

Rating	Industrials	Utilities	Banks	Transportation	Financials
Aaa/AAA	85	128	137	121	134
Aa1/AA+	95	135	147	131	146
Aa2/AA	107	143	150	141	151
Aa3/AA−	118	148	156	156	154
A1/A+	138	168	168	171	237
A2/A	164	175	171	191	242
A3/A−	178	186	174	196	247
Baa1/BBB+	199	201	239	216	275
Baa2/BBB	210	215	244	236	285
Baa3/BBB−	225	235	249	259	295
Ba1/BB+	425	440	460	350	490
Ba2/BB	475	475	470	450	500
Ba3/BB−	550	530	480	500	510
B1/B+	675	740	810	600	830
B2/B	800	840	820	700	840
B3/B−	1,050	890	830	850	850

Source: *www.bondsonline.com*

Thus data such as that contained in Tables 5.4 and 5.5 can be used to give an estimate of a company's debt margin where there is no direct traded corporate debt information available but the company has a credit rating. The relevant debt margin is obtained by looking at the observed average market spread for the same credit rating, maturity period, and industry sector as the company whose cost of debt is being evaluated. It is important to take care to use current data and also to consider how closely the company in question fits sector average characteristics. Because of the observed differences between sectors it is preferable to use sector specific information.

Use of financial ratios to synthesize a rating

Where no credit rating is available for the business some financial analysis is needed. Rating agencies would typically require at least three weeks to complete their review, but analysis of the financial ratios and associated ratings can provide a short cut to a sensible rating. Table 5.6 illustrates some of the key financial variables used by credit rating agencies, and gives the median value of each for each credit grade for US industrial companies. It illustrates that as the financial performance measures deteriorate, so too do the assigned credit ratings.

TABLE 5.6
Financial ratios and rating bands for US industrial companies

US Industrial long-term debt Three-year (1996–98) medians	AAA	AA	A	BBB	BB	B
EBIT interest coverage (x)	12.9	9.2	7.2	4.1	2.5	1.2
EBITDA interest coverage (x)	18.7	14.0	10.0	6.3	3.9	2.3
Funds flow/total debt (%)	89.7	67.0	49.5	32.2	20.1	10.5
Free operating cash flow/total debt (%)	40.5	21.6	17.4	6.3	1.0	(4.0)
Return on capital (%)	30.6	25.1	19.6	15.4	12.6	9.2
Operating income/sales (%)	30.9	25.2	17.9	15.8	14.4	11.2
Long-term debt/capital (%)	21.4	29.3	33.3	40.8	55.3	68.8
Short- and long-term debt/capital (%)	31.8	37.0	39.2	46.4	58.5	71.4

Source: Standard & Poor's

Such financial ratios do vary by sector. For example, an interest cover ratio of 4 is consistent, on average, with a credit rating of AA for a US electric utility (source: Standard & Poor's). For a standard US industrial company, a similar level of interest cover is on average associated with only a BBB rating (see Table 5.6). This is because US electric utilities tend to have very stable cash flows compared with standard US industrial companies, and hence the relatively small margin by which earnings exceed interest payments is less indicative of a risk of default for electric utilities. So while the general information contained in Table 5.6 is useful, it is often preferential to look at financial ratios for specific sectors or comparable companies.

Nevertheless, armed with some knowledge of the key financial ratios for a company, and information such as that in Table 5.6, it is possible to infer a credit rating for the company, and hence derive an estimate of the debt margin.

Such information is available most extensively in the US, thanks to the depth of company and rating information. It is becoming more widely available across Europe and other OECD countries as bond markets develop and ratings become more commonplace.

Calculating the debt margin – conclusions

We have identified four ways of calculating the corporate debt margin using the data sources referred to above. In order of preference (taking into account effort and accuracy) these are:

- If the company has long-term traded debt, then the cost of debt can be directly observed from the redemption yield on this debt.
- If the company has no long-term traded debt, but there are companies that are good close comparators, and these have long-term traded debt, then the debt margin can be observed from the bonds issued by these comparators. The selection of comparators should consider suitability in terms of comparable industry, size, and financial condition.
- If the company has a credit rating, then spreads observed for comparable rated companies, from bonds of equivalent maturities, can tell us the debt margin.
- Lastly, if the company has no traded debt, no suitable comparators with traded debt, and no credit rating, it is possible to use financial ratios to synthesize a rating and use this to calculate the debt margin (using the third approach).

The tax shield

We now move on to the impact of debt on company taxation. In the bulk of tax jurisdictions, interest cost is a tax-deductible expense – i.e. the amount a company pays in interest (on debt) is deducted from its earnings before calculating the corporation tax it must pay. Its tax bill is therefore reduced, the greater the amount of interest (on debt) that is payable. In this sense, having debt rather than equity 'shields' a firm from part of its tax bill.

So, taking the UK as an example, with a corporate tax rate of 30%, for every £1 of interest payment a company's cash tax burden is reduced by 30 pence. This saving reduces the post-tax cost of borrowing and enhances corporate value, to the benefit of shareholders. This can be illustrated with the simple example below where Company A is funded entirely by equity while Company B is partially funded using debt.

Example 5.3 Effect of tax shield on equity

		Company A	Company B
Capital	Equity	1,000	600
	Debt		400
EBIT		200	200
Interest @ 5%		0	20
PBT		200	180
Tax @ 30%		60	54
PAT		140	126
Total payments to debt investors			20
Total payments available to equity investors		140	126
Total payments to all investors		140	146
Return on equity		14%	21%

Company B's utilization of debt finance reduces its tax bill and increases total payments to providers of finance. Returns on equity are higher. By using a share buyback, financed by debt, Company A could unlock the same value for its shareholders.

To reflect this 'tax shield' advantage of debt in the WACC formula, the pre-tax cost of debt is multiplied by the percentage corporate tax rate subtracted from 1, to give the lower effective post-tax cost of debt borne by companies.

Practical issues – what tax rate to use for the tax shield?

It may not be straightforward to evaluate the tax rate for the tax shield. For a profitable company operating in one country the tax shield rate will be the statutory rate of corporate tax, but there are many instances where the effective corporate tax rate may not equal the statutory corporate tax rate.

For example, in 1998 the effective tax rate of Hanson plc, a UK-headquartered aggregates group with operations around the world, was 14.7% as compared to the UK statutory rate at the time of 31%. At that time Hanson plc had a net positive cash position and disclosed non-taxable items and 'other' items as the major factor for the reduction in tax charge below the statutory rate. Analysts' reports attributed these differences to the location of surplus cash balances in favorable countries and utilization of tax losses brought forward.

In circumstances where the statutory tax rate and the effective corporate tax rate are different it is important to understand why this is the case before deciding on the appropriate tax rate to use in the WACC formula. If the difference is short-term, or a timing matter, then over the long term one would expect a company to pay close to the statutory rate. If on the other hand the difference reflects a permanent taxation difference[3] due to the circumstances of the company, then the effective taxation rate may be more appropriate in the long term.

In circumstances where companies are loss making then no tax will be payable and the losses can be carried forward to offset future taxable profits. If the cost of debt is to be calculated as an input into a discount rate for a company valuation then in most circumstances there is an assumption that the corporate will become profit making at some time in the future, at which point tax will be payable. It remains the case that debt finance will still reduce the tax payments of the company, albeit with a timing difference. In these circumstances the statutory tax rate is likely to be more accurate than not assuming a tax shield at all, although the timing differences may mean that it is preferable to model the tax shield in detail (see Chapter 8 where we describe how this can be done).

Taxes in a global perspective

Taxes are further complicated by the global reach of multinational companies. Although an international group may have its headquarters in a particular country, some of its operations will be in other countries, and may attract tax at substantially different rates due to the impact of financing structures and different levels of profitability across the group. The marginal tax rate for a particular project and for tax relief on the project's finance may be completely different from the group's effective tax rate.

The effect of corporate tax on value calculation is clear – the tax shield will be more valuable if tax relief arises sooner, or at a higher rate, or both. Corporate tax rates for a number of the world's more common business locations can be found at *www.costofcapital.net*.

Capital structure – the mix of debt and equity

The previous chapters and sections have shown how to calculate the cost of equity and the cost of debt. To complete the WACC calculation we need to know the weights for the cost of capital components – i.e. the proportions of equity and debt in the total capital of the business. This is referred to as the *capital structure* of a business.

Deciding what capital structure to use for the purposes of calculating WACC requires us to cover a number of issues in turn:

- We first consider the relationship between the actual capital structure of a company, the actual proportions of debt and equity used in financing an investment, and the relevant capital structure to use in calculating the WACC to be applied to an incremental investment. We conclude that in principle a *target* or *optimal* capital structure should be used.

- We next discuss why there is such a thing as an optimal capital structure for a business and investment, and what determines its level.

- Finally, we discuss methods for calculating the optimal capital structure, including industry benchmarking and financial modeling.

Actual current capital structure

In calculating the capital structure for input into WACC, one obvious possibility open to us is to calculate the current proportions of debt and equity in the business, based on the current market value of each. However, at any given point in time, the current weights of debt and equity are specific to the current financing structure of the firm and this may not be representative of the future financing structure. A target forward-looking structure may therefore be more appropriate.

Target or optimal gearing structure

The need to use a target financing structure is particularly acute in the case of a company making a new investment (e.g. an acquisition of another company, or the launch of a new venture or project). When financing such a new investment, a company may simply issue new debt to cover the cost, or finance it out of retained earnings (equity). In the first case the source of finance is entirely debt, in the latter case it is entirely equity.

However, this distinction only traces the actual source of the cash financing rather than the underlying true opportunity cost. A company borrows at a group level and therefore it needs to take into account the impact the new investment has upon the overall company debt capacity.

As we shall see, different types of venture differ in their ability to support a large proportion of debt because of their cash flow characteristics. Even if as a matter of practical financing an incremental investment is financed entirely by debt, it is most unlikely that as a stand-alone investment this would have been possible. It is only possible within the group structure because the debt providers are relying on the cash flows and assets of the group as a whole to underwrite their loans. Thus the new investment is not entirely debt-financed in underlying terms: it relies on the equity in the business as a whole, and funding it entirely through debt uses up the debt capacity of the group.

> In evaluating the cost of capital for any investment it is important not to be misled by the source of the cash financing. The cost of capital for each investment needs to be calculated with respect to the characteristics of the investment itself – the risks to which it exposes both debt and equity investors, and the appropriate capital structure this implies.

In evaluating the cost of capital for any investment, therefore, it is important not to be misled by the source of the cash financing. The cost of capital for each investment needs to be calculated with respect to the characteristics of the investment itself – the risks to which it exposes both debt and equity investors, and the appropriate capital structure this implies. Methodologies for calculating the optimal capital structure are therefore an important ingredient for calculating the cost of capital in practice.

An additional practical benefit of using a target (optimal) capital structure is that this removes the circularity between cost of capital expressions and valuations. Because the market value of equity determines the gearing ratio, which in turn determines the equity beta and the cost of equity, which in turn determines the market value of the equity (through discounted cash flow analysis, as we shall see in Chapter 8), in practice this creates a cumbersome circularity. This can be avoided by iterative programming, but the target gearing ratio neatly removes the problem.

Does the capital structure matter?

Before we embark on an explanation of how to calculate optimal/target gearing it is worth saying a few words about whether there is such a thing. It has not always been accepted that capital structure matters in the sense that it affects business value. So are we embarking on a wild goose chase in determining the optimal capital structure?

Going back into postwar history, the 'traditionalist' view of capital structure was that as debt was cheaper than equity it was optimal to maximize the proportion of a business funded by debt.

The Nobel prize-winning work of Franco Modigliani and Merton Miller in 1958 (henceforth referred to as MM) questioned whether the source of financing mattered. They challenged the received wisdom of the day by suggesting that the value of an investment depended only on its stream of expected future cash flows, and the cost of capital. This was entirely independent of how it was financed. The practical implication of this assertion was that managers need not worry about the debt–equity ratio: it did not affect the cost of capital or value and there was no inherent advantage in one structure of finance over another.

Capital structure in the Modigliani and Miller world

It is not immediately obvious how MM reconciled their view with the traditional thinking that, for any investment, debt is almost always cheaper than equity – i.e. equity shareholders demand a risk premium that is usually higher than the margin debt holders require. So why could MM have argued that a firm that increased its proportion of debt would not reduce its cost of capital, and hence increase its value?

The reason is that as a firm 'gears up' (i.e. increases its reliance on debt finance), both debt and equity become more risky, and hence the costs of both debt and equity rise. In Chapter 2 we saw how financial leverage increases the size of an equity beta and hence increases the cost of equity calculated using the CAPM. Modigliani and Miller proposed that the expected return on (or cost of) equity rises in line with the debt–equity ratio. Earlier in this chapter we saw how debt margins are related to credit ratings that in turn are calculated according to financial characteristics of an investment. This material shows that an increase in the amount of debt in a business will result in a deterioration in some of the key financial ratios, leading to a lower credit rating and hence a higher debt margin and cost of debt. What therefore happens as a firm gears up is that cheaper debt replaces more expensive equity (which by itself would reduce the cost of capital) but at the same time both the cost of equity and the cost of debt increase. In the purest version of the theory these two effects exactly offset each other, and the WACC is invariant to the debt–equity ratio. The theoretical effect is as illustrated in Figure 5.2.

FIGURE 5.2
The Modigliani and Miller view of WACC at different gearing levels

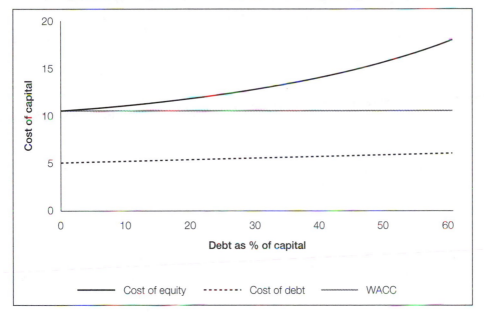

Capital structure in the real world

Unfortunately this elegant result depends on a set of assumptions that are not true in the real world. When tax is taken into account, the cost of capital falls steadily as the debt–equity ratio increases: the more a firm borrows, the more tax it saves. When tax is put into the MM framework, it delivers the awkward result that firms maximize their value by borrowing up to the hilt. This is clearly implausible, and it is not how managers behave – managers need a sensible amount of slack in the business, either to make the most of opportunities or to act as a buffer in financial downturns.

In reality, as debt increases, there is a risk of bankruptcy and this increases in a nonlinear way that is difficult to measure. The MM theory includes a formula (the formula relating the asset beta to the equity beta that we saw in

Chapter 2) explaining how the cost of equity increases with gearing, but does not provide a similar formula for the cost of debt. That it must rise is clear. But the way in which it does so is an empirical, not a theoretical, question.

Calculating the optimal capital structure

In practice, many believe there is an optimum level (or at least range) for the level of gearing of any firm. However, to determine this optimum borrowing level requires a complex calculation which both takes account of tax and also the pattern of changes in its borrowing costs as gearing increases. Clearly as the amount of debt increases, and a firm's interest cover becomes low, there is a serious risk that an unexpected cash flow shock will make it unable to meet its interest commitments and it may fall into bankruptcy or financial distress. Lenders add a substantial premium to reflect this risk. That is why bond yield spreads rise as debt ratios rise. Borrowing costs rise sharply as the interest cover approaches unity and financial distress and bankruptcy beckon.

Figure 5.3 provides a very simple illustration of the relationship between WACC and gearing (the ratio of debt to total business value), based on observations of actual movements in the cost of debt rather than the theoretical relationship used in Figure 5.2.

FIGURE 5.3
Illustrative example of relationship between WACC and gearing

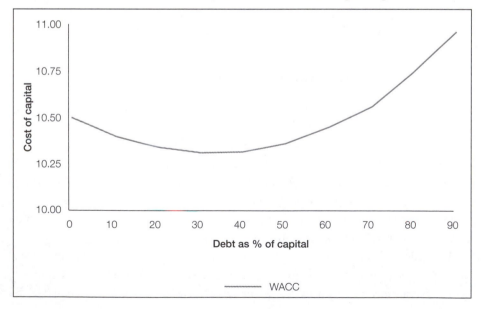

In Figure 5.3 the WACC falls (because of the lower post-tax cost of debt and despite increases in the costs of both debt and equity) as the debt-to-value ratio increases from zero to around 30%–40%. Beyond this point it starts to increase because the combined effects of additional gearing on the costs of debt and equity begin to dominate the advantages of having more debt.

What level of gearing will a firm choose?

If we assume that investors seek to maximize firm value, because this will enhance the value of their equity interest, and that management act in shareholders' interests in pursuing this goal, then it seems clear from the analysis embodied in Figure 5.3 that the key issues in choosing a level of gearing are the effects of gearing on the costs of debt and equity and the tax relief associated with debt.

In fact, it is somewhat more complicated than that in the real world for a number of reasons. The relationships between gearing and the costs of debt and equity are not clear and known; capital markets are not perfect; and managers and equity investors are human beings, not financial logic machines. As a result, in practice gearing levels are set on the basis of a range of factors, some of which are more to do with perception rather than actual hard numbers:

- If capital markets were efficient then a business that wished to invest in a value-enhancing new venture would be able to secure finance for it. Investors would see the rationale for the new investment and would provide debt and equity to fund it. In fact, because of capital market imperfections (e.g. constrained capital availability, imperfect knowledge of the investment's prospects on the part of investors, timing issues in raising capital for an urgent opportunity, etc.) finance might not be easily available. Firms might therefore wish to keep some 'slack' in the business (e.g. cash, or some untapped capacity to raise extra debt) to allow them to capitalize on emerging opportunities.

- As we have seen in Chapter 1, the assumption that managers always act rationally in the interests of shareholders is naïve. Managers may be reluctant to increase gearing to the optimal level for a number of reasons – for example, because it would increase the pressure on them to deliver strong financial results (remember, debt payments must be met, but dividend payments to equity investors do not need to be made, at least in the short term), or because it would increase the chances of company failure, taking the managers' careers with it.

- An alternative theory tries to reconcile observed gearing behavior with the assumption that managers do seek to maximize shareholder value. In a series of US market studies in the early 1990s, it was observed that, where companies raised large amounts of debt for the purposes of leveraged buyouts (LBOs), there was evidence of phenomena such as predatory pricing by competitors, suggesting that competitors were trying to drive the companies in question out of business by exploiting their lack of financial slack. So a manager may act in shareholders' interests by not gearing up if it would expose the company to such attack.

- On the other hand, if despite this risk management decides to take on the extra debt, then this might suggest to investors that managers are confident in the financial strength of the business. It may also suggest to potential investors that there will be more discipline on managers. This is the so-called 'signaling' theory.

Assessing the optimal capital mix in practice

Although things are complicated by the complex ways in which the interests of managers, shareholders, and the capital markets interact, the preceding sections suggest that there may be an optimal gearing level, or range. And as we have seen, it is this gearing level that is needed to complete our cost of capital calculation.

There are two main ways in which the optimal capital structure for a business can be assessed: *industry benchmarking* and *fundamental analysis*. Industry benchmarking seeks to evaluate the optimal gearing level for a particular investment with reference to the actual observed gearing levels of businesses in the same industry, whereas fundamental analysis investigates the debt capacity of a business based upon its projected future financial performance and what that implies for the ability to service debt.

We look at these in turn.

Industry benchmarking

Within an industry there is likely to be a range of gearing levels for different companies. However, while it is possible for firms to be temporarily significantly undergeared or overgeared, an efficient capital market should provide incentives for undergeared firms to increase their gearing (since they are failing to take advantage of opportunities to increase value, and should therefore face the threat of takeover), and if a firm becomes overgeared it will have incentives to restructure back to an optimal level. In aggregate, therefore, for an industry as a whole, the level of gearing should be reasonably close to the optimal level given the expected cash flow variability associated with the industry. It is possible therefore to use the relevant industry average gearing level as a benchmark for the optimal gearing level for a specific firm.

It is important to use the right industry benchmark, as gearing levels vary widely across different industries. This is illustrated in Figure 5.4. The differences between industries can be attributed to different degrees of revenue cyclicality, different growth potential, varying fixed costs of operation, and a host of other industry-specific factors.

Figure 5.4 also illustrates that firms in industries which expose equity investors to less underlying systematic risk (a low asset beta) are generally able to finance their businesses using a higher proportion of debt funding (gear up more) than those which are subject to higher systematic risk. This is because they can be more certain of making (fixed) interest and principal payments, even in the event of adverse cash flow movements caused by systematic shocks.

Industry benchmarking and optimal gearing

While the industry benchmark approach is appealing because of the relative ease in data collection, it has a drawback. It assumes that the actual industry gearing levels provide a good guide to the optimal levels.

While this would seem a reasonable assumption – after all, why should whole industries depart from the optimal level of gearing? – it is not necessarily accepted as being the case in every country. For example, gearing levels in the US have historically been much higher than those in Europe, where there has only relatively recently been a trend towards a higher dependency on corporate bond finance. If US companies are getting it right this might suggest that, at the time of writing, industries in Europe are undergeared relative to the optimal level. Alternatively, perhaps US companies are overgeared.

Fundamental analysis

So if, as some believe is the case in Europe, industries are all currently undergeared, and thus observed gearing does not give an accurate indication of optimal gearing, how can the right level of optimal gearing for a business be calculated? The alternative is to analyze the projected cash flows of the business to investigate its ability to support debt.

Financial models can be constructed which can simulate the performance of a business at different levels of gearing, calculating the resultant cost of equity,

FIGURE 5.4

Asset betas and gearing levels for UK industries, 2000

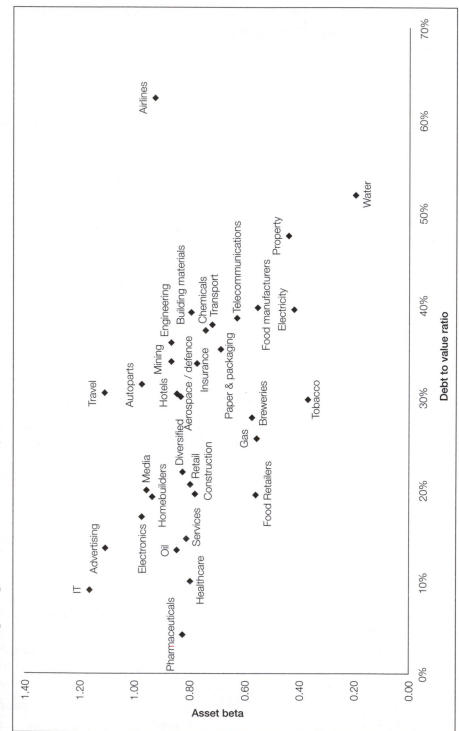

Source: Bloomberg L.P. (www.Bloomberg.com)

cost of debt, and firm value, to explore what level of debt in theory maximizes firm value. Such models use hard market information on debt margins, the probability of bankruptcy, etc., but may not fully reflect the effects of softer factors such as 'signaling' and management desire to charge a war chest for future activities.

A simple example of such an optimal gearing model, for a low risk regulated utility, is given below. First, Table 5.7 shows how the cost of equity at different gearing levels is typically simulated, using the gearing formula in Chapter 2, and assuming an asset beta of 0.13, a risk-free rate of 4.5%, and an EMRP of 5%.

TABLE 5.7

Simple optimal gearing model – simulations for the cost of equity

	Gearing (D/D+E)										
	20%	25%	30%	35%	40%	45%	50%	55%	60%	65%	70%
D/E	25.0%	33.3%	42.9%	53.8%	66.7%	81.8%	100.0%	122.2%	150.0%	185.7%	233.3%
Asset beta	0.13	0.13	0.13	0.13	0.13	0.13	0.13	0.13	0.13	0.13	0.13
Equity beta[1]	0.17	0.18	0.19	0.20	0.22	0.24	0.26	0.29	0.33	0.38	0.44
Cost of equity[2]	5.3%	5.4%	5.4%	5.5%	5.6%	5.7%	5.8%	6.0%	6.2%	6.4%	6.7%

Notes

[1] Equity beta has been calculated using the asset beta and applying the levering formula:

Equity beta = Asset beta [1 + D/E]

[2] Cost of equity calculated using CAPM formula:

$K_e = R_f + (Equity beta * EMRP)$

Typical simulations of the cost of debt are more complicated and may work as follows:

- As the level of gearing increases, so the amount of debt in the business increases, and this therefore means higher interest payments.

- As interest payments rise with gearing, so interest cover (the ratio of EBIT to interest) falls.

- Lower interest cover results in a lower credit rating being assigned to the business. As we have seen, this results in a higher debt margin being charged by lenders, and thus a higher cost of debt.

- The higher interest charges implied result in a further deterioration in the credit rating in a vicious circle.

The simulation of the cost of debt in Table 5.8 illustrates how, in our example, as debt and gearing levels increase, the interest cover falls from 7.5 to 1.9 and the simulated credit rating also falls from AA– to BBB. The resultant post-tax cost of debt rises from 3.98% to 4.49% and would be expected to rise even more dramatically as gearing increases beyond 70%.

TABLE 5.8
Simple optimal gearing model – simulations for the cost of debt

£m	Gearing (D/D+E)										
	20%	25%	30%	35%	40%	45%	50%	55%	60%	65%	70%
Debt	1,004	1,256	1,507	1,758	2,009	2,260	2,511	2,762	3,013	3,264	3,515
EBIT	428	428	428	428	428	428	428	428	428	428	428
Interest[1]	(57)	(71)	(86)	(101)	(116)	(132)	(146)	(169)	(189)	(205)	(225)
PBT	371	357	342	327	312	296	282	259	239	223	203
Tax	(111)	(107)	(103)	(98)	(94)	(89)	(85)	(78)	(72)	(67)	(61)
PAT	260	250	240	229	219	208	197	182	167	156	142
Interest cover[2]	7.50	6.00	5.00	4.23	3.70	3.25	2.93	2.54	2.26	2.09	1.90
Bond rating	AA–	AA–	AA–	A+	A+	A	A	A–	BBB+	BBB+	BBB
Pre-tax cost of debt	5.68%	5.68%	5.68%	5.75%	5.75%	5.82%	5.82%	6.10%	6.28%	6.28%	6.41%
Post-tax cost of debt	3.98%	3.98%	3.98%	4.03%	4.03%	4.07%	4.07%	4.27%	4.40%	4.40%	4.49%

Notes

[1] Interest charge = debt * pre-tax cost of debt.

[2] Interest cover is EBIT divided by interest payments.

Having separately simulated how the cost of debt and cost of equity change with gearing, these are combined into a WACC in Table 5.9 which is used to find the optimal capital structure. The firm is optimally geared at the point where the WACC is minimized and hence the value of the firm is maximized. In this example, the value of the firm has been calculated using a perpetuity formula, rather than a forward-looking DCF analysis.

Table 5.9 illustrates that as debt levels are increased at low levels of gearing the overall cost of capital falls. But beyond the optimal gearing point the higher costs of debt and riskier equity outweigh the advantages of debt. This also illustrates that the gains from increased gearing can quickly be lost if too much debt is issued. The graphical representation of this appears in Figure 5.5.

Our example has illustrated a very simple, 'static' financial model. More complex optimal capital structure analysis would analyze the optimal level of debt in the context of a dynamic model, which would take into account the different risk factors that could affect the firm's cash flows, and simulate the

TABLE 5.9
Simple optimal gearing model – simulations for WACC and value

	Gearing (D/D+E)										
	20%	25%	30%	35%	40%	45%	50%	55%	60%	65%	70%
Cost of equity – K_e	5.3%	5.4%	5.4%	5.5%	5.6%	5.7%	5.8%	6.0%	6.2%	6.4%	6.7%
Post-tax cost of debt – K_d	3.98%	3.98%	3.98%	4.03%	4.03%	4.07%	4.07%	4.27%	4.40%	4.40%	4.49%
Post-tax WACC	5.06%	5.03%	5.00%	4.99%	4.97%	4.97%	4.95%	5.03%	5.10%	5.09%	5.15%
FCFF (£m)	150	150	150	150	150	150	150	150	150	150	150
Growth rate – g	1.9%	1.9%	1.9%	1.9%	1.9%	1.9%	1.9%	1.9%	1.9%	1.9%	1.9%
New firm value (£m)[1]	4,885	4,926	4,967	4,983	5,021	5,025	5,061	4,919	4,817	4,825	4,740
Current firm value (£m)	5,022	5,022	5,022	5,022	5,022	5,022	5,022	5,022	5,022	5,022	5,022
Change in firm value (£m)	(137)	(96)	(55)	(39)	(1)	3	39	(103)	(205)	(197)	(282)

Current position:	
Firm value (£m)	5,022
Gearing	40.0%
Post-tax WACC	4.97%

Optimal position:	
Firm value (£m)	5,061
Gearing	50%
Post-tax WAAC	4.95%

Notes

[1] New firm value is obtained by discounting the FCFF at the WACC, assuming a stable growth rate. Hence:

$$FV = FCFF\ (1 + g) / (WACC - g)$$

FIGURE 5.5

Graphical representation of optimal gearing analysis

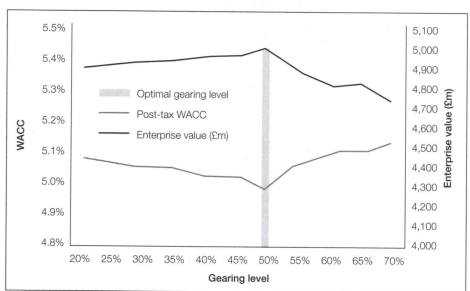

reaction of key financial ratios under uncertain and dynamic conditions. Such a model could take a more sophisticated approach to the interaction between different financial ratios and credit rating, and could, by giving more comprehensive output on financial performance, also allow qualitative account to be taken of factors such as 'signaling.'

For further illustrations of optimal capital structure models refer to the website: *www.costofcapital.net*.

Key points from the chapter

- In theory the cost of debt should be estimated as the promised yield (i.e. the yield implied by the agreed rate of interest on the loan or the coupons on the bond) reduced for the possibility of default to give the expected yield. In practice, for most purposes practitioners use the promised yield as a proxy for the true cost of debt.

- The cost of debt is made up of the risk-free rate and a debt margin. The debt margin is the difference in yield on a company bond and a risk-free instrument of equivalent maturity.

- The debt margin rises with increasing default risk. For bonds that are traded it is possible to calculate the debt margin directly by observing the actual differences (spreads) in yields between corporate bonds and government bonds issued by highly creditworthy countries.

- Credit rating agencies assess the default risk associated with companies. The credit ratings they assign can be used to assess the debt margin where no market information is available. Where a company does not have a credit rating it is possible to assign one through analysis of its financial ratios.

- Where a company or a project is expected to pay tax, the post-tax cost of debt is lower than the pre-tax figure. This is because of the tax shield on debt interest payments.

- Tax shields will be dependent upon the effective corporation tax rate. This may vary across companies, but in the longer term should be close to the statutory rate.

- Debt is a cheaper form of financing than equity and at low levels of gearing it is advantageous to increase the proportion of debt. However, as gearing rises, so too do the cost of equity and the cost of debt. Finding the right balance between debt and equity is a difficult balance between financial efficiency and investor perceptions.

- Optimal gearing can be analyzed by looking at industry benchmarks, but more rigorous approaches use static and dynamic financial simulation techniques.

Notes

1   It should be noted that for a bond, this 'promised yield' is unlikely to be the same as the coupon on the bond. It is the redemption yield on the bond, taking no account of default on the coupon and principal payments by the borrower. Readers should refer to the discussion of the risk-free rate in Chapter 2 for an explanation of the difference between the redemption yield (the 'promised yield' here) and the coupon.

2   For example, US company Enron's debt was mostly rated at BBB/Baa or higher only months before it fell into default in December 2001.

3   Examples of permanent taxation differences include income that is not taxed, such as dividends which have already been taxed, or expenses that are not tax deductible, such as amortization on certain assets acquired, entertaining, and fines.

6

INTERNATIONAL WACC AND COUNTRY RISK

This chapter in the field guide section of our book demonstrates how the cost of capital (or WACC) can be calculated in international markets. While estimation of the cost of debt is relatively straightforward (even in international markets) estimation of the cost of equity is not. We therefore spend most of this chapter focusing on the models that calculate the international cost of equity, and how they can be applied in practice.

Models that estimate the international cost of equity are mainly adaptations of the CAPM.[1] Consideration is also given to non-CAPM alternatives we have seen in practice, so that readers are free to make up their own minds regarding the choices they may need to make.

We examine five different models of the international cost of equity – what we describe as the 'global' CAPM, the 'home' CAPM, the 'foreign' CAPM, and the 'relative volatility' and 'empirical analysis' models. Very different results are obtained from the different models. The highest numbers are likely to be obtained from the relative volatility approach, and the lowest from the global CAPM. The choice of which model to use is likely to depend on views of how international capital markets work and the particular circumstances associated with the investment in question.

The chapter concludes by considering how these international cost of equity models can be used in conjunction with a model of the international cost of debt to estimate international WACCs. An example is provided using a hypothetical telecommunications business in Vietnam.

Introduction

International considerations make estimation of the cost of capital more complicated. The purpose of this chapter is to examine models that can deal with this complexity, and to provide an objective critique of their advantages and disadvantages.

While the overall cost of capital (or WACC) is constituted from both the cost of equity and the cost of debt, determining an international cost of capital (international WACC) is largely driven by the choice of methodology for, and calculation of, the international cost of equity. That is why this chapter focuses largely on the international cost of equity.

Treatment of country risk

Before we embark on the substance of this chapter, which is a description of the most important of the various models available to calculate the international cost of equity, we need to set out clearly our treatment of a very important practical issue – country risk. By country (sovereign) risk we mean downward risks[2] to cash flows associated with those risk factors which have the potential to affect all investments in a particular country simultaneously. These include political, economic, financial, and institutional risks associated with a country. A good example would be the civil war in Mozambique in 1975–92, which had a detrimental effect on investments in that country. Such risks can be significant, particularly in emerging markets.

As we saw in Chapter 1, standard financial textbooks assume that all cash flow risks, including country risk, are dealt with by adjustment to forecast cash flows, thus deriving true expected cash flows to which a CAPM-based cost of capital can be appropriately applied. In practice, it is rarely the case that cash flows are adjusted for country risk, for the simple reason that it is difficult for a manager of a particular business or investment to make an objective assessment of the probability or impact of such risks.

For this reason, in the real world many practitioners adopt the pragmatic approach of adding a country risk premium (CRP) to a CAPM-based cost of capital in lieu of cash flow adjustment. The CRP for a country can be derived in a number of ways. Some practitioners simply add a premium (perhaps two or three percentage points) based on subjective judgment. More sophisticated approaches infer the relevant CRPs for different countries by examining the yield spreads on sovereign bonds – these are considered helpful as they provide estimates of differences in the returns actually required by market investors when investing in different countries. A fuller explanation of such an approach can be found at our website, *www.costofcapital.net*.

> In the real world many practitioners adopt the pragmatic approach of adding a country risk premium (CRP) to a CAPM-based cost of capital in lieu of cash flow adjustment.

In this chapter we have assumed that cash flows are *not* adjusted for country risk factors, and hence it is appropriate to include an uplift for country risk in the WACC calculations for an international investment. We have taken this approach because we believe this will be of most practical use in the actual situations readers will encounter. However, should this not be the preferred approach, we have presented the models in such a way that it should be easy to adapt them to exclude the CRP, or set the value to zero.

Country risk issues

The sovereign spread approach to determining a CRP is sometimes adopted by investors as an international cost of capital model in its own right. In fact, as we shall see, two out of our five models – the global and home CAPM approaches –

both rely on the addition of country risk premia (likely to be based on sovereign bond spreads) to calculate the cost of equity capital. In these circumstances, they may also be termed 'sovereign spread approaches' although we choose to call them the 'global' and 'home' CAPM to distinguish the way in which other variables in the calculation – e.g. beta and the EMRP – are calculated.

There is also another point we must make in relation to country risk and the sovereign spread technique. The CRP estimated from the sovereign spread approach is a debt spread (because the base information is measured from sovereign bond spreads). For more information on this see *www.costofcapital.net*.

But the same CRP is frequently used in calculations of the cost of equity. Some practitioners make an upwards adjustment to the sovereign debt spread to take account of this. For example, Aswath Damodaran suggests an upwards multiplication based on the ratio of equity market volatility to bond market volatility (for individual countries). Other practitioners consider this arbitrary or even an inappropriate adjustment (for reasons we will see later), and prefer to add the debt country risk spread to the risk-free rate. This has the advantage of adding a debt spread to a debt variable in the CAPM (the risk-free rate) and is the approach we adopt with our global and home CAPM approaches (as we shall see later, the foreign CAPM approach already implicitly imbeds a debt country risk premium in the foreign risk-free rate). This approach is therefore consistent for all our adapted CAPM approaches and also allows the practitioner to make separate adjustments for any additional equity country risk premium (to the EMRP) should this be thought desirable and appropriate.

Famous five?

As we have already highlighted, this chapter considers five approaches that can be adopted when calculating the cost of equity in international markets. These can be classified as:

1. the '**global**' CAPM model
2. the '**home**' CAPM model
3. the '**foreign**' CAPM model
4. the '**relative volatility**' model
5. '**empirical analysis**' based on country credit ratings.

In practice, these five approaches can give very different answers when applied in the same situation. This can clearly be seen from a worked example for a particular business set out in Table 6.1. Full details of the basis for this example are set out in Example 6.1 towards the end of this chapter. For now, readers should simply focus on the differences in the estimates of the cost of equity derived from the five approaches.

TABLE 6.1
Illustration of differences in international cost of equity estimates

Model	Nominal risk-free rate (%)	Country risk premium (%)	Beta factor	EMRP (%)	Relative volatility adjustment	Cost of equity (%)
Global CAPM	5.1	2.5	1.0	5.0	–	12.6
Home CAPM	5.0	2.5	1.1	5.0	–	13.0
Foreign CAPM	7.5	–	1.2	7.0	–	15.9
Relative volatility	5.0	2.5	1.1	5.0	2.58	21.7
Empirical analysis	–	–	–	–	–	25.0

Table 6.1 illustrates that using the different models can imply both different estimates of the input components (e.g. the risk-free rate, beta, EMRP) and significant variation in the calculated cost of equity (in this hypothetical example the highest estimate is almost double the lowest). The choice of model can therefore have a significant impact on valuations and investment decisions. For example, if it were believed that the business would generate a return of 15% per annum, then the business would be regarded as a good investment using two of the approaches, and a poor investment using the other three. We therefore make no apology for fully exploring the details behind these models and how they affect such calculations. Each of the five approaches is considered in turn.

The global CAPM approach

The basis of the global CAPM is that increased globalization broadens the appropriate definition of the market for all investors.

Unlike the conventional CAPM in Chapter 2 – which calculated the cost of equity based on an orthodox 'home' risk-free rate, an orthodox 'home' equity market risk premium (EMRP), and a beta measuring covariance with respect to the 'home' equity market (where by 'home' we mean the country of the investor and the investment) – the global CAPM essentially measures all of the variables assuming there is a global supply and global demand for all forms of capital.

The model is therefore based on a global risk-free rate, a single global EMRP and a global beta. It assumes that investors hold fully diversified international portfolios made up of stocks from around the world.

The global CAPM (including a CRP term – see discussion above) is usually written as:

$$K_e = (R_{f\,global} \&^3 CRP_{target\,country}) + \beta_{global} * EMRP_{global}$$

where:

K_e	=	(International) cost of equity	
$R_{f\,global}$	=	Global risk-free rate	
$CRP_{target\,country}$	=	Country risk premium of target country (if applicable)	
β_{global}	=	Equity beta of investment with respect to global portfolio	
$EMRP_{global}$	=	Global equity market risk premium	

It is common to implement the model in a particular currency. So, for example, the US implementation of the global CAPM would involve using the US risk-free rate and simply substituting a world equity index measured in dollars when beta is estimated. The following paragraphs explain how it is implemented in its pure form.

Global beta

Looking at the calculation of the global CAPM, and considering beta first, a useful source for the global market portfolio are the Morgan Stanley World Capital Indices (MSWCI). Estimates of global betas can be sourced from data-providers such as Bloomberg, by using one of the MSWCI indices as the relevant benchmark index in the beta calculation process.[4]

Since most individual stock markets are not perfectly correlated with the world market, betas measured with respect to the MSWCI indices can often be lower than betas calculated with respect to their home markets. Table 6.2 illustrates this, using a sample of mainstream UK companies.

TABLE 6.2
Home versus global betas for five UK listed companies, 2002

	British Energy	Cadbury Schweppes	Safeway	Lloyds TSB	Rentokil Initial
Home beta	0.99	0.48	0.62	1.29	0.72
Global beta	0.64	0.40	0.46	0.91	0.53

Source: Bloomberg L.P. (*www.Bloomberg.com*)

The most likely explanation for the lower global betas in Table 6.2 is that UK listed companies with significant parts of their business in the UK, such as Safeway and Lloyds TSB, are much more likely to be influenced by factors that affect the UK stock market than factors that drive the global index. The fortunes of these UK companies are therefore more UK-dependent – as opposed to globally influenced – and so changes in their share prices are much more sensitive to changes in the UK stock market than changes in the global index. Because betas are measured by correlating changes in companies' shares prices against changes in stock market indices, all other things being equal, this would lead to higher measured home betas than global ones.

Of course, it is always possible to find a company where this result is reversed. An example of this is provided in Table 6.3. The company in question is Petrobras (a Brazilian oil company).

In this case, returns on Petrobras shares appear to have greater sensitivity to the global market than the domestic Brazilian one. While this runs counter to the evidence from the UK companies in Table 6.2, it is not surprising given that oil companies, whatever their country of registration or operation, receive the majority of their income in US dollars through exporting a global commodity (oil) which is sold in global markets. However, for the majority of businesses, the relationship is the other way around.

TABLE 6.3
Home versus global beta for Petrobras, 2002

	Petrobras
Home beta	1.3
Global beta	1.7

Source: Bloomberg L.P. (*www.Bloomberg.com*)

It should also be noted that the phenomenon of global betas that are lower than home betas is consistent with the principle of incremental benefit from international investment, as empirically validated by Bruno Solnick. His work demonstrated that adding international investments to a domestic portfolio usually reduces the standard deviation of portfolio returns through greater diversification. This work is characterized in Figure 6.1. It is based on the same principle represented in Figure 1.3 in Chapter 1, where incremental (domestic) stocks were added to a portfolio and the standard deviation of the returns from that portfolio measured. In this case, the incremental stocks that Solnick added were listed in different markets.

FIGURE 6.1
International diversification and risk

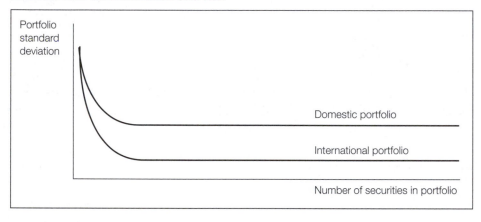

The importance of this work and analysis is that in situations where a company's shareholder register is largely dominated by investors holding fully diversified global portfolios, there are strong arguments for using the global CAPM approach.

In Figure 6.2 Solnick's work has been reproduced using the approach and methodology set out in Chapter 1, in order to confirm that the principle of international diversification still works. As with Solnick's analysis, the incremental stocks that are added to the portfolio are listed in different territories, thereby creating an international portfolio.

Figure 6.2 is consistent with Solnick's research and shows that the principle of incremental diversification through international investment would appear to hold.

FIGURE 6.2

The benefits of diversifying risk on an international basis

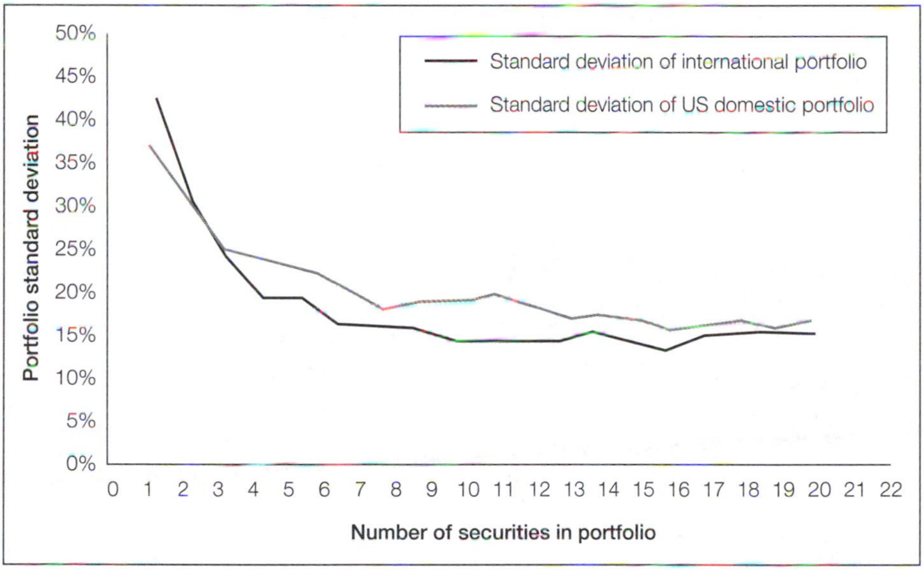

Source: Bloomberg L.P. (*www.Bloomberg.com*)

Global EMRP

Moving on from beta, estimation of the global EMRP is in principle straightforward. If it were appropriate to apply a global model, then there would be a single global EMRP, which could be observed or calculated in any country.

In practice, however, even if capital markets are integrated the EMRP may vary, because of the composition of stocks in certain markets. For example, a particular country might have a composition of stocks that is more skewed towards low risk sectors such as utilities, and it is reasonable to expect that these will generate returns that are below those of average beta stocks. In these circumstances, the EMRP may vary from country to country because of differential stock composition. Countries with lots of high systematic risk stocks will have relatively high EMRPs, and countries with lots of low systematic risk stocks will have lower EMRPs.

This tendency is particularly pronounced in emerging markets where the local market index may be dominated by a handful of large companies. Figure 6.3 – which is reproduced from Mark Mobius' book on emerging markets[5] – shows the extent of the problem. For a number of markets, it measures the share of overall market value accounted for by the top 10 stocks.

FIGURE 6.3
Percentage market capitalization of top 10 stocks in 21 countries, 1995

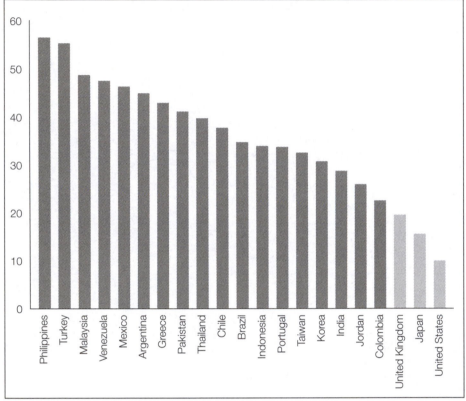

Source: Mobius (September 1995) *Mobius on Emerging Markets*; IFC

Taking the Philippines as an example, more than 50% of its total stock market capitalization was accounted for by only 10 companies. If these companies were, say, high systematic risk stocks then, all other things being equal, it would be expected that the observed EMRP for the Philippines would be relatively high.

Figure 6.3 shows that this phenomenon is generally more prevalent in emerging markets. It is not, however, just confined to emerging markets – it may also be an issue in certain OECD countries. A good example of this is provided by Finland, where Nokia (the mobile phone manufacturer) has, in the past, accounted for over 50% of the overall capitalization of the Helsinki exchange.

So the question arises as to how the global EMRP can be calculated when individual country EMRPs vary due to stock composition. A sensible approach – recommended by Ibbotson Associates – involves multiplying an EMRP that has been measured for a particular market (see Chapter 3) by the correlation of that market to the world index. In arithmetic terms, this amounts to calculating a 'beta' for individual world markets calculated with reference to the global index. So, for example, if the US EMRP is thought to be 5%, and the correlation (β) of the US market against a proxy for the world index obtained from the MSWCI is 0.87, then the world EMRP can be derived as:

$$\beta_{us}\ EMRP_{w} = EMRP_{us}$$

$$EMRP_{w} = \frac{EMRP_{us}}{\beta_{us}}$$

$$EMRP_{w} = \frac{5.0\%}{0.87} = \underline{\underline{5.75\%}}$$

Global risk-free rate

The final variable that needs to be considered in the context of the global CAPM approach is the appropriate risk-free rate (adjusted for country risk if applicable – see the introduction to this chapter). In principle, if it is considered appropriate to apply the global CAPM approach, then by definition this implies that there is a single market for capital, and hence a single global real risk-free interest rate. The only complexity arises where expected differential inflation and currency movements mean that nominal risk-free interest rates will differ between countries.

The most straightforward way to derive a global risk-free rate is to calculate the real rate of return on government bonds issued by any country that is considered to be of top-rated credit quality. As we saw in Chapter 2, this implies using bonds issued by OECD countries, preferably index-linked bonds (where available). This real figure can be converted into nominal terms – in whatever currency required – using the international Fisher arithmetic set out below.

> The most straightforward way to derive a global risk-free rate is to calculate the real rate of return on government bonds issued by any country that is considered to be of top-rated credit quality.

By way of illustration, suppose the world real interest rate is 3% (e.g. sourced from US index-linked Treasuries), and we want to calculate a global risk-free rate applicable to an investment with cash flows denominated in, say, Hungarian forints. If Hungarian inflation is forecast to be 5% into perpetuity, the calculation would be as follows:

$$(1 + \text{real } R_{f\,global}) * (1 + \text{Hungarian inflation}) - 1$$

$$= (1 + 0.03) * (1 + 0.05) - 1$$

$$= \underline{\underline{8.15\%}}$$

The home CAPM approach

Unlike the global CAPM, the home CAPM approach assumes that equity markets are segmented and calculates CAPM variables with respect to home benchmarks (by 'home' we mean the country where the investor is located). So, if the investor is American, the relevant CAPM variables would be the US risk-free rate (adjusted, if applicable, for the additional country risk associated with the country in which the investment being considered is located), beta calculated as the covariance with respect to the US market, and the EMRP based on US estimates.

The formula for the home CAPM is set out below:

$$K_e = (R_{f\,home} \&^3 CRP_{target\,country}) + \beta_{e\,home} * EMRP_{home}$$

where	K_e	= Cost of equity
	$R_{f\,home}$	= Home risk-free rate
	$CRP_{target\,country}$	= Country risk premium of target country (if applicable)
	$\beta_{e\,home}$	= Equity beta of investment with respect to home portfolio
	$EMRP_{home}$	= Home equity market risk premium

The key feature of the home CAPM approach is that it involves consideration of all the variables in the context of the home market portfolio. This is the relevant portfolio, because if investors held globally diversified portfolios – without home bias – the situation would be best approximated by the global CAPM approach.

Home beta

In the context of the home CAPM, the correct measure of systematic risk is given by a beta measured against the home portfolio. So, for example, if a US company were investing in a UK electricity utility, then the correct beta from the perspective of the home CAPM is the beta of UK electric companies calculated by performing a regression against the US market, *not* the beta of US electric companies against the US market. The latter, of course, would be used if the US investor were applying the CAPM in the context of a US investment. This point is often overlooked in applying the home CAPM approach.

Home EMRP

Moving on from beta, calculation of the EMRP for the home CAPM approach is in principle relatively straightforward – it is estimated just as in the standard CAPM context. However, for investments in some countries, particular emerging markets, practitioners sometimes add a premium to the EMRP calculated on a home basis. This is consistent with the Damodaran approach to country risk (which we mentioned earlier), where an upwards adjustment relating to the ratio of equity to debt market volatility is applied to a sovereign debt spread. In other words, Damodaran not only adds a debt CRP but also (through the equity/bond adjustment) implicitly adds an equity market CRP on top of this. A higher EMRP assumption can be considered to be the equivalent of this (although there is no reason why these two should be the same in numerical reality).

Careful thought needs to be given to the appropriateness of adopting higher EMRPs than would otherwise be adopted in conventional home markets. The home CAPM approach is often adopted where there is a need to consider an international investment in the context of an investor whose other investments are either concentrated in the home market or only partially diversified internationally. As we have seen, the evidence suggests that, far from adding to the overall risk to which an equity investor is exposed, adding stocks from international countries to a home portfolio can actually *reduce* overall portfolio volatility. This undermines the case for increasing the EMRP.

> The evidence suggests that, far from adding to the overall risk to which an equity investor is exposed, adding stocks from international countries to a home portfolio can actually *reduce* overall portfolio volatility. This undermines the case for increasing the EMRP.

Even for an investor with a fully diversified international portfolio it is not clear that a higher EMRP should be applied in the case of an investment in an emerging market. Remember that the key issue in deciding the cost of equity for any investment is the extent of systematic risk to which the investor is exposed as a result of this investment.

Home risk-free rate

The risk-free rate is relatively straightforward to calculate in the home CAPM context although, as we have already seen in this chapter, care needs to be exercised in order to ensure that if a nominal rate is used this is appropriate to the currency denomination of the cash flows, and that a CRP is applied if the cash flows have not already been adjusted for country risk.

The foreign CAPM approach

It is also possible to estimate CAPM variables using foreign market information (by 'foreign' we mean the country where the investment is located). By way of illustration, if the investment is located in India one would include the Indian risk-free rate, an Indian company beta derived by regressing the company's stock with respect to the Indian market, and the EMRP based on Indian estimates.

The formula for the foreign CAPM is set out below:

$$K_e = R_{f\,foreign} + \beta_{foreign} * EMRP_{foreign}$$

where K_e = Cost of equity

$R_{f\,foreign}$ = Foreign risk-free rate

$\beta_{foreign}$ = Equity beta of investment with respect to foreign portfolio

$EMRP_{foreign}$ = Foreign equity market risk premium

There are several difficulties in applying the foreign approach. Most notably:

- It is often very difficult to find sufficient or reliable financial information in developing markets.

- Even where such information exists, it may not be of sufficient duration to meet statistical needs (for example, as we saw in Chapter 2, measurement of beta typically requires five years of stock market information).

- Estimates of the EMRP are unlikely to be available (either historic or forward looking).

Because of this it may not often be possible to use this approach. For example, in Zambia, the Lusaka stock exchange has only been operational since 1994 and only a handful of stocks are traded in significant volumes (see *www.luse.co.zm*). This makes the validity of the results from the foreign CAPM approach in Zambia questionable.

Where it is possible to implement the foreign CAPM approach with confidence, we might expect it to yield slightly higher figures than the home approach. This is because foreign EMRPs may be higher than home EMRPs (particularly if the 'foreign' country is an emerging market and the 'home' country is an OECD country). As we have already highlighted, this is theoretically contentious. Specifically, it is interesting to note that a higher observed foreign EMRP may be considered consistent with the Damodaran country risk adjustment but, on the other hand, it is arguably inconsistent with the additional diversification achieved by international investment.

It should also be emphasized that the cost of equity derived using the foreign CAPM approach is applicable to cash flows denominated in the foreign currency in nominal terms, which have not been adjusted for country risk. This is because the yield on foreign government bonds used to determine a foreign risk-free rate will implicitly include a premium for country risk, and so the foreign CAPM automatically includes a country risk adjustment.

Lastly, as with the other approaches, it is possible to adjust a cost of equity figure derived from the foreign CAPM to make it applicable to cash flows calculated on a different basis (e.g. in home country currency, quoted in real terms, and/or probability-weighted for country risk). However, in the foreign CAPM case the adjustments are necessarily in the opposite direction.

The relative volatility approach

The relative volatility approach is predominantly associated with Bank of America and, to a lesser extent, Goldman Sachs, but has also been adopted from time to time by other investment banks.

The distinguishing characteristics of the relative volatility model are that two adjustments are made to the familiar CAPM model. These are:

- A familiar adjustment of the risk-free rate for country risk. Implicitly, therefore, this model assumes that the cash flows are not adjusted for country risk.

- A less familiar additional adjustment for the relative market volatility of the country in question.

The formula for the model is set out below:

$$K_e = (R_{f\,home} \&^3 CRP_{target\,country}) + \beta_{home} * EMRP_{home} * (\sigma_{target\,country} / \sigma_{home})$$

where K_e = Cost of equity
       $R_{f\,home}$ = Home risk-free rate
       $CRP_{target\,country}$ = Country risk premium of target country (if applicable)
       β_{home} = Equity beta of investment with respect to home
                                     portfolio
       $EMRP_{home}$ = Home equity market risk premium
       $\sigma_{target\,country}$ = Volatility of target country market
       σ_{home} = Volatility of home market

Relative volatility factor

The adjustment for relative volatility is based on the ratio of the volatility of the foreign stock market (i.e. that of the target country) to the volatility of the home country stock market. So, for example, if the volatility of the Zambian market were three times greater than the US market, then the adjustment coefficient that a prospective US investor would apply to a Zambian company would be three. The home market EMRP – in this example, the US EMRP – would be multiplied by this adjustment coefficient.

Because emerging markets are typically more volatile than more developed markets, the adjustment coefficient is usually greater than one when the model is applied to emerging markets. This means that the model typically produces relatively high discount rates in emerging markets.

Table 6.4 provides some illustrative adjustment coefficients calculated in 1999, and the implications for the adjusted EMRP, assuming the home EMRP is 5%.

The relative volatility model and diversification

A criticism leveled at the relative volatility model is that it ignores the benefits of international portfolio diversification.[6] In the context of the home CAPM approach, we have already discussed the pros and cons of increasing the EMRP when calculating the cost of equity for an investment in a relatively volatile market, such as an emerging market. That debate is also highly pertinent in the context of the relative volatility model since, as Table 6.4 shows, it suggests that the EMRP should be increased substantially for investments in some emerging markets. Readers should refer back to the subsection on the Home EMRP for the debate.

TABLE 6.4
Relative volatility adjustments in 1999

Country	Home EMRP	Relative volatility adjustment coefficient	Resultant risk premium
UK	5.0%	1.00	5.0%
Germany	5.0%	1.00	5.0%
Holland	5.0%	1.00	5.0%
Austria	5.0%	1.00	5.0%
Greece	5.0%	1.38	6.9%
Finland	5.0%	1.00	5.0%
Norway	5.0%	1.00	5.0%
Switzerland	5.0%	1.00	5.0%
Czech Republic	5.0%	1.47	7.4%
Poland	5.0%	1.49	7.5%
Hungary	5.0%	1.47	7.4%
Romania	5.0%	2.65	13.3%
US	5.0%	1.00	5.0%
Canada	5.0%	1.00	5.0%
Australia	5.0%	1.03	5.2%
New Zealand	5.0%	1.09	5.4%
Japan	5.0%	1.00	5.0%
Malaysia	5.0%	1.59	8.0%
Indonesia	5.0%	2.62	13.1%
Philippines	5.0%	1.86	9.3%
Thailand	5.0%	1.79	8.9%
Vietnam	5.0%	2.58	12.9%
China	5.0%	1.55	7.7%
Hong Kong	5.0%	1.43	7.1%
Singapore	5.0%	1.00	5.0%
South Korea	5.0%	1.48	7.4%
Taiwan	5.0%	1.07	5.4%
India	5.0%	1.91	9.5%
South Africa	5.0%	1.91	9.6%
Zambia	5.0%	3.00	15.0%
Oman	5.0%	1.72	8.6%
Saudi Arabia	5.0%	1.59	7.9%
Brazil	5.0%	2.16	10.8%
Argentina	5.0%	1.99	9.9%
Chile	5.0%	1.38	6.9%
Peru	5.0%	2.15	10.8%
Mexico	5.0%	1.75	8.8%
Colombia	5.0%	2.00	10.0%
Venezuela	5.0%	2.31	11.6%
Dominican Republic	5.0%	2.45	12.2%

Where emerging market stock exchanges are dominated by a relatively small number of stocks then the measure of overall volatility will disproportionately reflect the risk characteristics of these stocks.

There are also practical measurement issues that relate to points already touched upon in this chapter. For the ratio of relative volatility to be the appropriate factor by which to adjust the EMRP it is important that there be sufficient reliable data to calculate it accurately. As we have seen the information available from emerging markets is not always reliable. Furthermore, where emerging market stock exchanges are dominated by a relatively small number of stocks then the measure of overall volatility will disproportionately reflect the risk characteristics of these stocks. They may not be appropriate comparators for the particular investment being considered.

Pragmatic justifications for the relativity volatility model

So are there any other reasons why the practitioner should consider applying the relative volatility model? We identify two justifications below, which suggest it may be applied as a pragmatic response to practical issues that arise in international investment appraisal. In neither of these cases is there any theoretical justification for the approach.

First, some have argued that management concerns about the total risk associated with international investments may provide a justification. A paper published in the *Bank of America Journal of Applied Corporate Finance*[7] argues that:

> Management at some level [are] likely to be concerned with the total risk of cross-border projects, rather than simply the marginal risk that remains after the recognition of potential diversification benefits.

This quotation appears to suggest that the driving force behind using the model is management's concerns. We saw in Chapter 1 that managers' interests and shareholders' interests are not necessarily aligned when it comes to questions of diversification – the so-called *'agency problem.'*

The relevance of this issue in the context of the relative volatility model is that the specific risk associated with an emerging market investment can be highly significant. Of course, we know that shareholders can eliminate their exposure to specific risks by investing in a diversified portfolio of equity investments. Managers, however, cannot. They may be concerned about exposing their company to significant specific risk, and hence exposing themselves to uncertain career and remuneration prospects. The adoption of the relative volatility approach in these circumstances may protect managers' interests even if it leads to decisions that are contrary to the interests of shareholders and shareholder value.

The second reason why the relative volatility approach may be adopted in practice concerns the quality, or perceived quality, of cash flow information available to investors and managers contemplating investments in international markets (particularly emerging markets).[8]

In many emerging market situations, the quality of cash flow information can be particularly poor. In these circumstances, it may be the case that there are significant (downside) specific risks (other than country risk) of relevance to the performance of the business that have not been properly captured (or which managers suspect may not have been captured) in the cash flows used for appraisal. In this case, it is possible to see the adoption of the relative volatility approach (with its higher discount rates) as a pragmatic response to poor, upwardly biased, cash flow projections.

Of course, purists would quite rightly assert that there is no sound basis for adjusting discount rates upwards to compensate for overly ambitious cash flow projections, and that cash flows should instead be reduced (for an illustration of the difficulties in adjusting discount rates see Chapter 7).

Empirical analysis based on credit scores

The fifth approach of which readers should be aware is empirical analysis procedures based on country credit scores. Typically, these procedures involve regressing observed equity returns against sovereign credit scores provided by rating agencies and other sources such as Institutional Investor or the Economist Intelligence Unit (EIU).

An illustrative extract from a seminal article[9] is reproduced in Figure 6.4. It shows the observed relationship between 13-year historic equity returns and country credit scores provided by Institutional Investor.

The idea behind this approach is that there is a direct relationship between returns and credit score, and that this can be quantified using historic data. Having derived this relationship, if it is possible to obtain a credit score for a particular country expressed in numerical terms, then it is possible to estimate a country specific cost of equity for that country. For example, if a country has an Institutional Investor credit score of 60, Figure 6.4 suggests that the average cost of equity in this country is between 20% and 30% (as the returns used in Figure 6.4 are quoted on a US dollar basis, the cost of equity is applicable to cash flows denominated in US dollars).

FIGURE 6.4

Relationship between historic equity returns and country credit scores

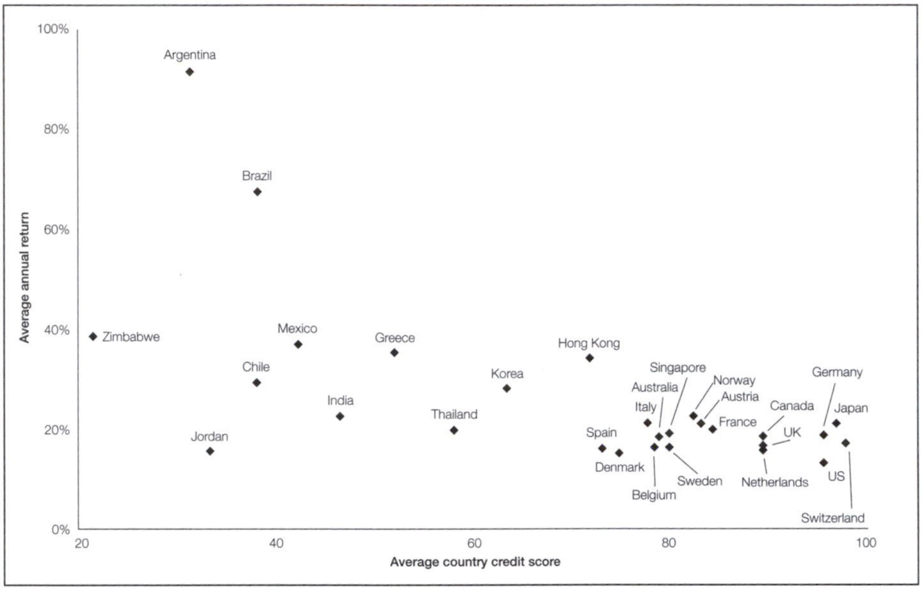

Source: Erb, Harvey and Viskanta (1995), *Journal of Portfolio Management*, Institutional Investor

The model has a number of drawbacks as well as some attractions. Dealing with the attractions first:

■ The approach can be easily applied across a number of countries.

■ The model is derived using objective capital market information.

■ It is convenient, as it allows the cost of equity to be calculated directly on the basis of credit score.

On the other hand, the approach:

■ Is unable to distinguish between different costs of equity for different sectors and companies within a country (the technique simply estimates the cost of equity for the market portfolio in each country).

■ Is constrained by data availability – not many emerging markets have a sufficient track record of historic returns making it difficult to calculate the relationship.

■ Has suffered from the critique that even 13-year periods of actual observations may not be sufficient to measure proper expected returns. This is because of data bias and statistical noise. For example, to quote the late Fischer Black (of Black-Scholes option pricing fame), 'We need decades of data for accurate estimates of average expected return.'[10]

It will be interesting to see whether the model becomes more useful as the amount and quality of the available data increases for less developed markets.

Summary of various models

A high level summary of the various models is set out in Table 6.5. It provides the reader with a handy guide as to how the various models work, and the input assumptions that are typically required.

TABLE 6.5
Summary of international cost of equity models

Model	Risk-free rate	Country risk premium	Beta	EMRP	Relative volatility adjustment
Global	Any low-risk country interest rate	Can be added if needed	Measured against global index	Global measure (Ibbotson technique)	✗
Home	Home interest rate	Can be added if needed	Measured against home index	Home (possibly adjusted for emerging markets)	✗
Foreign	Foreign interest rate	Can be deducted if not needed	Measured against foreign index	Foreign	✗
Relative volatility	Home interest rate	Can be added if needed	Measured against home index	Home	✓
Empirical analysis based on credit ratings	Not applicable	Not applicable	Not applicable	Not applicable	Not applicable

A flavor of the general results obtained from each approach is summarized in Table 6.6. This is based on Example 6.1 – a hypothetical Vietnamese telecommunications company.

Example 6.1 Cost of equity for a telecommunications company in Vietnam

Suppose that an investor wants to calculate a 10-year nominal US dollar cost of equity (to be applied to cash flows unadjusted for country risk) for a telecommunications business ('Telco') in Vietnam using each of the cost of equity approaches identified in this chapter. The assumptions used by the investor are as follows:

- World real risk-free rate = 3.0%
- Projected 10-year US inflation = 2.0%
- Yield on 10-year US government Treasury bond (nominal US dollars) = 5.0%
- Yield on 10-year Vietnamese government bond (Fisher-adjusted to nominal US dollars) = 7.5%
- Vietnam arithmetic country risk (from a country risk model) = 2.5%
- Equity beta for Telco (estimated with respect to a global index) = 1.0
- Equity beta for Telco (estimated with respect to US index) = 1.1
- Equity beta for Telco (estimated with respect to Vietnamese index) = 1.2
- US EMRP = 5%
- Vietnamese EMRP = 7%
- Global EMRP = 5.75% (using Ibbotson methodology)
- Debt margin = 150 basis points (1.5%)
- Relative volatility coefficient of Vietnamese market to US market = 2.58
- Institutional Investor country credit score for Vietnam = 60

In these circumstances, the costs of equity from the five approaches can be calculated as:

(i)   Global CAPM
      $[(1.030 * 1.020) - 1] * 100 + 2.5 + 1.0 * 5 = 12.6\%$

(ii) Home CAPM
      $(5 + 2.5) + 1.1 * 5 = 13.0\%$

(iii) Foreign CAPM
      $7.5 + 1.2 * 7 = 15.9\%$

(iv) Relative volatility approach
      $(5 + 2.5) + 1.1 * 5 * 2.58 = 21.7\%$

(v)   Empirical analysis based on credit ratings

      By inspection from Figure 6.4 using credit rating of 60: 25%

Note that the input figures are illustrative only, providing an indication of the likely magnitude of the variables in question. It has also been assumed for simplicity that the CRP is simply added on to the risk-free rate whereas in practice it is sometimes applied multiplicatively using Fisher arithmetic. The summary results at Table 6.6 do, however, give a flavor of the responsiveness of the different approaches.

TABLE 6.6
Illustrative output from international cost of equity models

Model	Nominal risk-free rate (%)	Country risk premium (%)	Beta factor	EMRP (%)	Relative volatility	Cost of equity (%)
Global CAPM	5.1	2.5	1.0	5.0	–	12.6
Home CAPM	5.0	2.5	1.1	5.0	–	13.0
Foreign CAPM	7.5	–	1.2	7.0	–	15.9
Relative volatility	5.0	2.5	1.1	5.0	2.58	21.7
Empirical analysis	–	–	–	–	–	25.0

It should be clear from Table 6.6 that there is a tendency for the empirical analysis and the relative volatility approaches to produce higher numbers than the other models. Often the global CAPM produces the lowest figure.

Choice of approach

Which of the models is considered most appropriate will depend, in part, on the view the practitioner takes in relation to several key issues. These include:

- the degree of integration of world capital markets;
- the concept of the marginal investor and the markets in which capital is raised;
- the robustness of the cash flow information in hand;
- the availability of data.

Integration of world capital markets

The degree of integration of world capital markets is clearly an important issue influencing the choice between using the global CAPM approach, or the models that implicitly assume segmented conditions (e.g. the home and foreign CAPM approaches). The main conclusion of academic analysis is that money and bond markets are more integrated than equity markets, and that OECD-type markets are more integrated than emerging ones.

It is interesting to note that if the home CAPM approach is adopted, on the basis that world equity markets are not fully integrated, then two investors – armed with identical cash flow information and expectations – could estimate different costs of equity and arrive at differing valuations of a business. This is to be expected if capital markets are not fully integrated.

> The degree of integration of world capital markets is clearly an important issue influencing the choice between using the global CAPM approach, or the models that implicitly assume segmented conditions (e.g. the home and foreign CAPM approaches).

For example, consider an American and an Indian investor each applying the 'home' approach in the context of a possible investment in a UK utility company. The Indian could arrive at a different cost of equity compared with the US investor (each applying the home approach) because of differences in the UK utility company's beta when estimated with reference to the Indian stock market as opposed to the US stock market, and potentially differences in the Indian and US EMRPs applied.

So regardless of other differences the two potential investors might perceive (e.g. in terms of different tax rates, etc.), they could value the investment differently purely due to differences in their estimates of the cost of equity. This would not be the case if world capital markets were fully integrated, as assumed by the global CAPM.

The concept of the marginal investor

The concept of the marginal investor also potentially has an important role to play in the choice of an appropriate model. Because firms in principle should target returns on opportunities that just sufficiently remunerate the marginal suppliers of equity capital, it is the marginal investor who determines the cost of equity.

The difficulty, of course, lies in identifying the marginal investor in the business. A sensible proxy may be to identify the main market in which the capital that will fund the investment is raised. While this does not necessarily capture the position of the marginal investor, it at least captures the position of the majority of the investors and avoids explicit speculation regarding the location and attitudes of the marginal investor. It is also likely to have intuitive appeal to those making the investment decision.

For a public company this would imply looking at the shareholder register to identify the location of the majority of shareholders (which may differ from the location of the company itself).

Robustness of the cash flow information

As we saw in the discussion of the relative volatility approach, some practitioners seem to justify this model on the basis that the higher EMRP it implies for emerging markets is a pragmatic reaction to a perceived upward bias in cash flows.

If it is perceived that the cash flow forecasts sourced from emerging markets are of an unreliable nature then conceptually the proper response, whatever the investor's views regarding the strengths and weaknesses of the different international cost of equity models, is to adjust the cash flows downwards to true expected values.

If this is not, or cannot be, done for whatever reason, then some addition to the cost of equity is necessary to avoid excessive value being assigned to the investment. This does not necessarily mean that the relative volatility approach should be chosen. It is possible to add a premium to the cost of equity derived from any of the five models. However, there is no accepted methodology for calculating this addition, as we shall see in Chapter 7. Whichever model is used, if a CRP is being applied, it is important not to raise the cost of equity for the cash flow risks associated with country risk factors, as the CRP should already be adding on the appropriate amount for these.

Availability of data

A final factor driving the selection of approach is that data must be available to make the model work. For example, as explained earlier in the chapter, it is not always possible to gather sufficient information to implement the foreign CAPM approach.

International cost of debt and WACC

So far, we have focused solely on models that can be used to calculate the international cost of equity. To estimate an international WACC, it is necessary to consider how the international cost of debt can be calculated so that the cost of debt and cost of equity can be brought together to estimate an international WACC.

Because the standard WACC formula is still relevant, the international WACC formula should look familiar:

$$\text{International WACC} = \text{International K}_e * \frac{E}{V} + \text{International K}_d * (1 - T) * \frac{D}{V}$$

where K_e =   International cost of equity
          K_d =   International cost of debt
          E   =   Market value of equity
          D   =   Market value of debt
          T   =   Corporate tax rate
          V   =   Market value of equity plus market value of debt

International cost of debt

We have already dealt with estimation of the international cost of equity. Estimation of the international cost of debt is more straightforward. This is because the cost of debt in an international context is simply a function of three underlying variables. These are:

■ The risk-free rate of interest. This should be calculated on the same basis as that used in the calculation of the cost of equity.

■ A premium for any country risk associated with the country of the investment. This must always be included, as debt investors, unlike equity investors, are unable to eliminate country risk through portfolio diversification (assuming the convention that the promised cost of debt is used). Remember, however, that if the foreign CAPM has been used for calculating the cost of equity then the estimate of the risk-free rate will include a premium for country risk already and it is not necessary to add a CRP.

■ A relevant corporate debt premium (corporate margin or spread).

In simple arithmetic terms, the international cost of debt can therefore be calculated as:

$$\text{International K}_d = R_f \,\&^3\, \text{CRP} + \text{DM}$$

where K_d =   International cost of debt
          R_f =   Risk-free rate (calculated as for cost of equity)
          CRP =   Country risk premium
          DM =   Debt margin

So, for example, if the risk-free rate has been calculated as 5% for the purpose of calculating the cost of equity, the relevant debt margin is 1.5% (150 basis points) and the country risk premium of the country in question is 2.5%, the international cost of debt calculated on a simple arithmetic basis is:

$$5\% + 2.5\% + 1.5\% = \underline{\underline{9\%}}$$

Alternatively, the cost of debt is sometimes estimated geometrically, in which case the formula is adapted slightly and becomes:

$$\text{International } K_d = (1 + R_f) * (1 + CRP) * (1 + DM) - 1$$

Using the same input figures as above[11]:

$$K_d = (1.05 * 1.025 * 1.015) - 1$$
$$= \underline{\underline{9.2\%}}$$

The choice of arithmetic versus geometric calculation techniques can make relatively little numerical difference (as the examples above demonstrate). It is, however, important to be clear about the calculation methodology and avoid problems with inconsistency: variables that have been calculated arithmetically should not be applied geometrically and vice versa.

Estimation of international WACC

Now we have seen how to estimate the international cost of debt, the final piece of the jigsaw is in place. We can calculate an international WACC.

Let us consider the hypothetical situation set out in Example 6.2.

Example 6.2 International WACC for a telecommunications company in Vietnam

Consider the earlier Vietnamese telecommunications (Telco) example used to calculate various costs of equity. Suppose that the task is now to calculate an international WACC using the home version of the CAPM. The assumptions given are:

▶

■ Yield on 10-year US government Treasury bond (nominal US dollars) = 5.0%

■ Arithmetic Vietnam country risk (from a country risk model) = 2.5%

■ Equity beta for Telco (estimated with respect to the US index) = 1.1

■ US EMRP = 5%

■ Arithmetic debt margin[1] = 150bp (1.50%)

■ Tax rate = 30%

■ Target capital structure = 50/50

■ Projected 10-year US inflation = 2.0%

■ Projected 10-year Vietnamese inflation = 8%

Notes
[1] Based on cost of debt for comparator companies of 6.5% and a government bond yield of 5.0%.

Using the arithmetic basis for country risk and debt margin the international WACC for Telco can be calculated:

■ in the home currency of the investor (i.e. US dollars);

■ in the currency of the target company (i.e. Vietnamese dong).

Example 6.3 Illustrative international WACC calculations

'US' cost of equity = (5 + 2.5) + 1.1 * 5 = 13.0%
'US' cost of debt = (5 + 2.5) + 1.5 = 9.0%
'US' WACC = 13 * 0.5 + 9 * (1 – 0.3) * 0.5 = $\underline{9.65\%}$

This discount rate would be used to discount expected cash flows from Telco, expressed in US dollars.

'Vietnamese' WACC = [(1.0965 * (1 + 0.08) / (1 + 0.02)] – 1
= $\underline{16.10\%}$

This discount rate would be used to discount expected cash flows from Telco, expressed in Vietnamese dong.

Key points from the chapter

This chapter has dealt with models that can be used to estimate the cost of capital in an international context. The key points are as follows:

International cost of equity

- A number of models can be used to estimate the cost of equity in overseas markets, including:
  1. the '**global**' CAPM
  2. the '**home**' CAPM
  3. the '**foreign**' CAPM
  4. the '**relative volatility**' approach
  5. '**empirical analysis**' based on country credit ratings.
- Each of the models can be used to calculate the cost of equity with or without an uplift for country risk. It is appropriate to apply a higher cost of equity reflecting country risk only if the cash flows for the investment whose cost of equity is being analyzed have not been adjusted for country risk.
- It is possible to use the five models to estimate the cost of equity capital in most markets, although some of the models require data that can be difficult to obtain, particularly in emerging markets.
- The choice of the most appropriate model will depend on the circumstances in question, the judgment of the practitioner and issues such as the identity of the marginal investor.
- The highest cost of equity figures are typically generated by the relative volatility approach – which increases the EMRP to reflect observed volatility of share prices in international markets – or the empirical analysis approach, which is based on historic analysis of the relationship between equity returns and country credit scores.
- The lowest figures are typically generated by the global CAPM – which assumes that capital markets are fully integrated and that investors hold portfolios of equity investments that are diversified internationally.

International cost of debt

■ Calculation of the international cost of debt is more straightforward. The cost of debt will be a function of the risk-free rate of interest, an appropriate debt margin for the target business and an adjustment for country risk.

International WACC

■ International WACCs can be calculated in either home currency terms or in the foreign currency of the target business. Arithmetic or geometric calculation processes can be used. The chapter provides an illustrative calculation based on a US investor considering an investment in a Vietnamese telecommunications business.

Notes

1 We call these models adaptations of the CAPM because that is exactly what they are (practical real world adaptations). However, financial purists would not necessarily recognize these models as 'official' CAPM approaches because they have not been theoretically derived.

2 This differs from the standard concept of risk in financial analysis introduced in Chapter 1 which means potential for variation (up or down) around a central estimate.

3 The CRP can in principle be applied either as a simple arithmetic addition or as a geometric addition (using the Fisher arithmetic). We adopt the notation '&' to denote that either application occurs in practice.

4 For many MSWCI indices currency fluctuations are dealt with by expressing all global equity market movements in US dollar terms.

5 See *Mobius on Emerging Markets* (1996) 2nd edn, FT Pitman.

6 Some commentators have also expressed concern that by including terms covering total volatility in the formula the model infringes the basic tenet underpinning the CAPM that the cost of equity is affected only by volatility due to systematic risk factors. We do not share this concern, as the volatility terms in question are for markets as a whole. They therefore reflect properly the volatility to which equity investors, *fully diversified in those markets*, would be exposed.

7 *Bank of America Journal of Applied Corporate Finance*, Fall 1996, p. 89, 'A Practical Approach to Calculating Costs of Equity for Investments in Emerging Markets', by Stephen Godfrey and Ramon Espinosa of Bank of America.

8 For more information on shareholders' perceptions of the standards of financial reporting in different markets, visit: *www.opacity-index.com*.

9 *Journal of Portfolio Management*, Winter 1995, 'Country Risk and Global Equity Selection', by Claude B. Erb, Campbell R. Harvey, and Tadas E. Viskanta.

10 Black, F. (1993) 'Estimating expected return', *Financial Analysts Journal*, Sept–Oct, pp. 36–8.

11 In practice, one would not use the same input figures. If the inputs themselves (debt margin, CRP, and so on) have been estimated arithmetically they should only be applied in arithmetic calculations. If a geometric technique is preferred, the input variables need to be estimated geometrically in order to be consistent. This is shown in more detail in Examples 6.3 and 6.4.

7

CASH FLOWS, THE DOT.COM BUBBLE, AND ALL THAT

This is the first chapter in the section of our book that deals with the application of the cost of capital.

The cost of capital plays a key role in investment appraisal and company valuation, through its application as the discount rate in discounted cash flow analysis. However, the existence of stock market bubbles, such as the one seen in the dot.com sector in the recent past, casts doubt on the continued applicability of the discounted cash flow approach to valuations. Some dot.coms were highly valued in the market despite generating negative cash flows and having very uncertain future prospects. Moreover, dot.com share prices sometimes fluctuated significantly during periods when underlying business prospects apparently changed little.

While the same fundamental principles apply in the new economy as the old – value is based on future expected cash flows discounted at an appropriate cost of capital – there are difficulties in applying the standard techniques. In particular, investments in dot.coms at the time of the bubble could probably be best regarded as being investments in options. Hence, option valuation techniques would have been necessary to attempt to explain dot.com stock market values.

Furthermore, market sentiment and speculation may also have played an important role in influencing the stock market values of dot.coms. Because current information on fundamentals such as cash flow and risk is of limited use in judging future performance, stock prices can fluctuate significantly due to the cumulative impact of the decisions taken by individual investors as they each try to pick companies that will be popular with other investors.

Introduction

The previous section of this book explains the theoretical underpinning for the calculation of the cost of capital, and many implementation issues for successfully applying it. In this chapter we explore how the cost of capital is used as a key element – the discount rate – in discounted cash flow analysis, the most commonly used technique for investment appraisal and business valuation.

Through its use in discounted cash flow analysis, the cost of capital plays a key role in making real-life business and government investment decisions, and this is where its importance lies – in its application. What, for example, can cost of capital theory say about the valuation of Internet businesses? The values ascribed to dot.coms in the recent past seemed to defy conventional logic. For example, between 1998 and 1999 the market capitalization of Amazon.com increased by over 50% at the same time as its losses mounted, contravening normal assumptions about the link between value and current cash generation.

There have also been some bewildering fluctuations in dot.com share prices. Figure 7.1 shows the huge fluctuations in the returns of Scoot.com relative to the UK market between January 1998/December 2001.

FIGURE 7.1

Fluctuations in Scoot.com returns relative to the FTSE All Share Index, 1998–2001

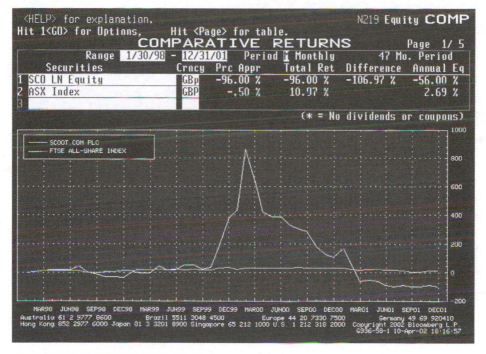

Source: Reprinted with permission from Bloomberg L.P.

This chapter will hopefully shed some light on these perplexing observations. But to do so, it is necessary to take a step back and explain how in the standard analysis the risk-adjusted discount rates discussed in the previous section are applied to cash flows in order to inform investment decisions and perform valuations. This analysis yields further insights into the interpretation of cost of capital theory, for example with regard to the relevance of specific as opposed to systematic risks.

Once we have done this, we can extend the analysis to draw some conclusions about the dot.com bubble. The structure of this chapter is therefore as follows:

- It begins with an explanation of the net present value (NPV) approach to taking investment decisions.

- It then emphasizes the importance of using *expected* cash flows in performing NPV calculations.

- It goes on to consider alternatives to NPV for taking investment decisions – internal rate of return, payback, book rate of return, and economic profit.

- Finally, it considers techniques for valuing companies, with specific reference to real option valuations and its relevance to the dot.com bubble.

Risk, return, and investment decisions

We examined in the previous section the theory and practice of a cost of capital based on the risk associated with investments. We now explain how the cost of capital can be incorporated into judgments regarding company and project value, and the appraisal of investments.

The concept of present value

As we have seen, the cost of capital is the annual return required by investors on funds committed to a business, given the risks to which that business exposes the investors. If the cost of capital is 10%, and $10 is invested in year 1, then the business will need to be worth $11 ($10 * (1.1)) to investors in year 2 in order to meet the required return.

Put another way, from the investors' perspective, a cash flow of $11 in year 2 is equivalent to cash of $10 in year 1 given the cost of capital of 10%. Hence, the *present value* in year 1 of $11 in year 2 is $10, and this is calculated by dividing the year 2 cash figure by (1 + the cost of capital).

Similarly, the required value in year 3 would be $12.1 (calculated as $10 * (1.1) * (1.1)). And hence the present value of $12.1 in year 3 is $10, calculated as $12.1 divided by ((1 + the cost of capital) squared).

More generally the formula for the present value (PV) of a stream of cash flows can be calculated as follows:

$$\text{Present value} = \Sigma \ \frac{CF_t}{(1 + r)^t}$$

where CF_t = Cash flow in period t

r = discount rate, or cost of capital

The present value states in a single figure the value of a stream of cash flows from a business or venture, taking into account the required return to investors, given the timing of those cash flows and the risk characteristics of the business. Performing the calculation of present value is often referred to as 'discounted cash flow' (DCF) analysis, and the rate of return used in the calculation is referred to as the 'discount rate.' Cost of capital theory tells us how to calculate the appropriate discount rate.

The net present value rule

Net present value (NPV) is the term given to the discounted (present) value of future cash flows less the value of the initial investment. Any investment which offers a positive expected NPV adds to wealth and shareholder value, because the risk and time-adjusted expected future financial rewards associated with the investment outweigh the initial investment cost. The optimal investment strategy is to put money into companies and projects which maximize NPV.

This simple investment decision is optimal regardless of individual investors' preferences for the balance between consumption now and in the future. One investor might want to consume as much as possible today, while another might want to forego consumption now in order to consume more in the future. But if they both follow an investment strategy of maximizing NPV in their investments they will maximize the size of the consumption 'cake' to which they have access. The first investor can then borrow to boost his consumption today, while the second investor can lend to enjoy higher consumption tomorrow, assuming there are well-functioning capital markets. (A formal exposition of this is available at our website, *www.costofcapital.net*.)

Separation of ownership and management

The finding that there is a simple rule regarding investment – namely, that firms should always seek to increase NPV, and that this holds true regardless of the preferences which individual investors have for different patterns of consumption – is extremely important for the operation of a capitalist economy. It enables companies to be owned by many individuals with different preferences, and for those investors to delegate the business of managing the companies to other individuals (managers). For their part, these managers have a relatively simple rule to follow – they should run the business in such a way as to maximize the expected NPV of future cash flows. This is the underpinning of the NPV approach to investment appraisal and to value-based management.

Two important points

This has two implications which can sometimes cause confusion. First, if two investments have the same NPV (correctly calculated) and involve the same initial outlay, they are equally attractive, regardless of the amount of systematic or specific risk to which they expose the investor. Intuitively, it might be expected that the project with the less variable cash flows would be favored on the grounds that individuals are, as discussed in Chapter 1, 'risk averse.' However, for an equity investor, the only risks that count are systematic risks, and these are reflected in the cost of equity part of the discount rate used to calculate the NPV. In a portfolio, variability in returns arising from specific factors is irrelevant. Indeed, when adding an investment to a portfolio it could be the case that a more variable return is actually helpful in mitigating risk by offsetting variations in existing investments. Secondly, it is important to note that the relevant risk to take into account in calculating the NPV is that of the investment itself, and not the company making the investment. An investment in a venture which has a high degree of systematic risk is always risky, irrespective of the company or individual which makes the investment. It would be inappropriate, and illogical, for the identity of the investor to affect the appraisal of the investment[1] other than in cases where this affected some fundamental aspect of the cash flow of the investment (e.g. if one company were able to achieve cost savings or revenue enhancements through synergies which were not available to others). In such a case the higher value of the investment to the company able to realize the synergies would properly be reflected in more bullish cash flow forecasts, and not a lower discount rate.

> For an equity investor, the only risks that count are systematic risks, and these are reflected in the cost of equity part of the discount rate used to calculate the NPV.

> It is important to note that the relevant risk to take into account in calculating the NPV is that of the investment itself, and not the company making the investment.

This means that the discount rate at which a company assesses an investment opportunity should be calculated separately for that opportunity, and will not necessarily be the same as the overall cost of capital for the company. A company which is subject to relatively little risk, such as a utility, should not use its overall cost of capital when assessing much more risky projects in other areas. This remains the case even if it can apparently obtain debt finance at relatively low interest rates to fund a small additional project (once again, interested readers can surf to *www.costofcapital.net* for a technical exposition of this).

Ultimately, the application of cheap finance to risky ventures would change the risk profile of a company, resulting in a rise in its overall cost of capital affecting the whole business, not just the marginal venture.

This point also relates to the observation regarding diversification made in Chapter 1. Managers sometimes believe that a lower discount rate should be applied in appraising a project or acquisition which diversifies the activities of their company (e.g. into a new business or geographic area). The cost of capital should not be reduced for this reason. Investors are better able to diversify their investments than companies and can do so more cheaply. Any genuine cash flow benefit (e.g. the achievement of synergies, the reduced incidence of the costs of financial distress, or the ability to attract higher calibre managers) should be reflected in value through better cash flow forecasts.

The general rule therefore is that a good project is a good project, and a bad project is a bad project, and they both need to be assessed on their own merits in relation to their own risks. Beauty is not in the eye of the beholder.

The importance of expected cash flows

The discussion of the NPV rule above simply refers to the cost of capital being applied to 'the cash flows' of the investment under consideration. This is generally the approach taken in the theoretical texts.

What this fails to make clear is the importance of using the appropriate estimates of cash flows. In particular, as we saw in Chapter 1, implicit in the theory of a portfolio approach to calculating the cost of capital is an assumption that the resulting figure is to be applied to a probability-weighted assessment of cash flows. This is most easily explained in Example 7.1.

Example 7.1 Cash flows in an uncertain world

The table below gives the cash flows associated with a very simple 10-year project, involving an investment of $5,000 in year 1.

	1	2	3	4	5	6	7	8	9	10
Investment	–$5,000									
Success		$3,000	$3,000	$3,000	$3,000	$3,000	$3,000	$3,000	$3,000	$3,000
Failure		$1,000	$1,000	$1,000	$1,000	$1,000	$1,000	$1,000	$1,000	$1,000
Expected	–$5,000	$1,600	$1,600	$1,600	$1,600	$1,600	$1,600	$1,600	$1,600	$1,600

▶

In the event that the project is successful, the investment is assumed to return positive cash flows of $3,000 per annum in years 2 to 10. If it is unsuccessful, it returns only $1,000 per annum. It is also assumed that in the event of failure the venture continues and that the investment has no residual value at the end of the 10-year period.

Assuming that the probability of success is 30% and the probability of failure 70% the probability-weighted cash flow in each of years 2 to 10 is $1,600 (0.3* $3,000 + 0.7* $1,000).

Example 7.1 gives a very simple example of a project that can either be successful or unsuccessful. The true expected outcome is a probability-weighted average of the two actual possible outcomes. It is this cash flow to which the portfolio cost of capital should be applied. On a probability-weighted basis the risk that the cash flows will be lower than expected is symmetrically offset by the possibility that they will be higher than expected. If the only risks to which the project is exposed are specific then it would be appropriate to appraise this investment by discounting the expected cash flows at a risk-free cost of capital.

The problem with this analysis is that this logic is not always made explicitly clear in the financial textbooks, and that in any case it is not intuitively appealing to commercial people. In the real world, it is difficult to assign probabilities to success and failure. The number of possible outcomes is infinite, and the cash flows associated with each are highly uncertain. Calculating an expected value is therefore difficult.

Furthermore, even if it were possible with certainty to characterize a project in the way that is done in Example 7.1 – for example, if there were two possible outcomes, one where a particular contract was won, the other where it was lost – in a real world situation there would be a reluctance to consider the expected cash flow in the way set out. To manage such a project, budgets and targets need to be set. The natural tendency is to set these against the cash flows of the successful outcome – there would be little purpose in monitoring progress against a purely fictitious, 'expected' cash flow that in reality will never arise (i.e. it is impossible to win 30% of a contract).

Hurdle discount rates

For this reason, many businesses investing in projects with high specific risks will evaluate them on the basis of high investment *hurdle* rates rather than on the basis of the much lower discount rates suggested by the portfolio approach to the cost of capital. Implicitly what they are doing is evaluating on the basis of an assumed successful outcome, and judging that against a higher discount rate which is implicitly adjusted upwards for the probability of failure. Example 7.2 elaborates on the example in Example 7.1 to illustrate this.

Example 7.2 Hurdle rates versus NPV in the context of uncertainty

Assume that the appropriate discount rate (cost of capital) for the project described in Example 7.1 is 10%. It can be shown that at this discount rate the NPV[2] of the probability-weighted cash flows is $3,831 (go to our website, *www.costofcapital.net*, to see this). The same result can be obtained by discounting the cash flows associated with the successful outcome at a discount rate of approximately 27%. Thus, if 27% were used as a hurdle discount rate and applied to the cash flows associated with the favorable outcome this would give exactly the same NPV result as applying the true risk-adjusted cost of capital to probability-weighted cash flows.

There are many real-life situations where there is a big difference between the discount rate appropriate to true expected cash flows and that appropriate for the cash flows associated with a favorable outcome. For example, it has been estimated that the probability of making a commercial oil or gas discovery in the UK sector of the North Sea is just one in 11. In 10 out of 11 cases costs are incurred in exploration but no oil or gas produced. Overall investment in North Sea wells gives returns of less than 10%, in line with the market cost of capital for the industry. This implies that the target rate of return for the one in 11 successful wells must be substantially in excess of this in order to compensate for the negative returns on those wells which fail.

The problem with this pragmatic approach is that there is no theoretical basis for setting the hurdle rate – this is a matter of custom and judgment. Portfolio theory, on the other hand, suggests a rigorous basis for identifying the cost of capital, and sets out the approach that needs to be adopted to cash flows to make this valid. While it can be argued that in practical commercial situations the calculation of probability-weighted cash

> An advantage of the portfolio approach is that it disciplines businesses to think carefully about the actual risks they face, and the way they would impact on cash flows.

flows is difficult, arguably it is no more difficult to achieve than to adjust the discount rate by the appropriate amount (in fact, implicitly the calculations involved are very similar). An advantage of the portfolio approach is that it disciplines businesses to think carefully about the actual risks they face, and the way they would impact on cash flows.

Alternatives to the NPV investment rule

There are a number of alternative investment appraisal methodologies which are applied by companies in place of the NPV. This section briefly considers the most important of these, explaining how they work and setting out the reasons why they are inferior to the NPV approach.

The internal rate of return

Probably the most credible of the alternative methodologies is the use of the internal rate of return (IRR), sometimes referred to as the discounted cash flow rate of return. This is closely related to the NPV, so that in many cases the two methodologies are interchangeable. However, as we shall see, if applied properly the IRR requires equal or more effort than the NPV, and there are situations in which the IRR is not directly applicable or gives misleading or ambiguous results. In practice, the NPV is therefore the superior methodology.

Defining the IRR

The IRR is defined as *the discount rate that results in the NPV of cash flows being zero*. It expresses in a single figure what the returns on a given set of cash flows actually are.

To illustrate the calculation of the IRR, consider the simple four year project cash flows set out in Table 7.1.

TABLE 7.1
Cash flows for IRR example

Year	1	2	3	4
Cash flow	−$4,000	$1,500	$2,000	$1,500

To calculate the IRR of the cash flows in Table 7.1 it is necessary to identify the discount rate that results in the NPV of the cash flows being zero. Let us first try using a discount rate of 5%. The NPV is calculated as:

$$NPV = \frac{-4{,}000}{1.05} + \frac{1{,}500}{(1.05)^2} + \frac{2{,}000}{(1.05)^3} + \frac{1{,}500}{(1.05)^4} \quad \text{(see note}^2\text{)}$$

This gives an NPV at 5% of $512.75. Using a discount rate of 20% the NPV turns out to be –$410.88. It is clear therefore that the IRR – the discount rate which sets the NPV to zero – lies somewhere between 5% and 20%. Figure 7.2 shows the relationship between the NPV and the assumed discount rate for the cash flows in Table 7.1 (go to *www.costofcapital.net* to see the derivation of Figure 7.2).

FIGURE 7.2
Relationship between discount rate and NPV for example in Table 7.1

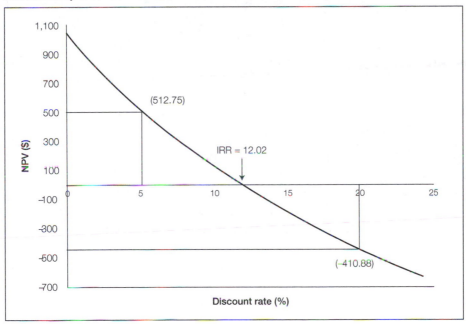

It can be seen from the diagram that the NPV becomes zero at a discount rate of almost exactly 12%. Hence, the IRR of these cash flows is 12%. Most spreadsheets have functions that will carry out the iterative calculation to derive this number but the value must be treated with caution as under some conditions more than one possible result can arise (see below).

Using the IRR rule

Having calculated the IRR, how can we use it as a tool for taking investment decisions? The answer is, we compare this IRR with a target rate of return, and accept the investment if and only if the IRR exceeds this target rate of return.

Those who use the IRR approach in preference to the NPV approach sometimes argue that it is easier to apply since it avoids the need to calculate the appropriate cost of capital discount rate for an investment. This task is, of course, inherent to the calculation of the NPV. Thus, these people argue that the advantage of the IRR is that it eliminates the need to understand books like this one.

There is a flaw in this logic. Where does the target rate of return to which the IRR is compared come from? It is clearly crucial that this is set at the appropriate rate if the right investment decisions are to be taken. In fact, the only acceptable way of setting this target rate of return is to calculate the cost of capital for the investment under consideration. If this is done, then the IRR technique involves just as much work as the NPV but, as we shall see, does not perform as well. If the required rate of return is not calculated in this way (for example, if a simple hurdle rate of the type described above is set) then the IRR rule can lead to incorrect decision taking.

> Application of a blanket IRR rule to a range of investments with different characteristics will tend to lead to the selection of more risky investments.

Furthermore, application of a blanket IRR rule to a range of investments with different characteristics will tend to lead to the selection of more risky investments. Suppose a company has set a hurdle discount rate of 10%. It will undertake all investments which have an IRR of 10% or above, and reject those with IRRs of less than this. Recall from Chapter 1 that in competitive markets with arbitrage opportunities expected equity returns on investments are driven down to a level commensurate with the systematic risks to which the investment exposes the investor. This implies that only relatively risky projects are likely to pass the firm's decision rule. Furthermore, some of these projects, while returning more than 10%, may destroy shareholder value – given their risk profile, the IRR they are expected to achieve, while being above 10%, may be below the appropriate risk-adjusted cost of capital.

Three problems with the IRR decision rule

Even if the IRR rule is applied correctly (i.e. the IRR is compared with an appropriate risk-adjusted target rate of return on an investment-by-investment basis) it still suffers three drawbacks which make it inferior to the NPV decision rule.

First, it cannot handle variable discount rates. As we touched on in the discussion on the risk-free rate in Chapter 2, there is generally a *term structure* to interest rates. The interest rates on long-term government bonds are generally higher than they are for short-term Treasury bills. Within the NPV framework this is easy to incorporate – the discount rates for individual periods can be tailored to reflect the changing interest rates. It is not so clear what can be done when using the IRR. The methodology relies on calculating a single IRR and comparing it with a single target rate of return.

Second, the IRR gives ambiguous results when the cash flows 'change signs.' In the example set out in Table 7.1, the convention was adopted of having an investment period up front where cash flows are negative, followed by a payback period where cash flows are positive. Now consider the second example in Table 7.2.

TABLE 7.2
Cash flows for second IRR example

Year	1	2	3
Cash flow	–$1,000	+$2,500	–$1,530

Table 7.2 shows the cash flows for a very simple three-period investment. It begins with an investment in year 1 of $1,000, followed by a positive cash flow in year 2 of $2,500, finishing with a further negative cash flow in year 3 of $1,530. While such a cash flow profile might be considered unusual, such situations do occur – for example in the nuclear and mining sectors, where there are clean-up and closure costs once the productive life of the investment has come to an end.

In Figure 7.3 we have plotted the NPV for this investment at various discount rates (again, the calculations can be found at *www.costofcapital.net*).

The figure shows that there are two IRRs for this project – one at around 7% and another at around 43%. Suppose the company has used rigorous cost of capital analysis to calculate the appropriate rate of return for this project on a risk-adjusted basis, and that this rate is 15%. The IRR rule now gives ambiguous results. If the IRR is regarded as 43% the investment should be undertaken. If it is regarded as 7% it falls below the target rate of return. By contrast, the NPV rule gives an unambiguous result. Using a discount rate of 15%, the NPV is $14.79. The investment thus generates positive value and should be undertaken.

Third, the IRR can give misleading results when it is applied to mutually exclusive projects. Consider Table 7.3. The first row gives the cash flows for the simple investment considered in Table 7.1. The second row sets out the cash flows for an alternative, mutually exclusive investment (for example, these might be two ways of using the same piece of land, and therefore there is a choice of doing one or the other but not both).

FIGURE 7.3
Relationship between discount rate and NPV for example in Table 7.2

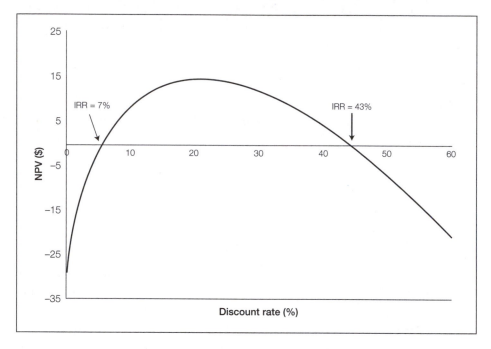

TABLE 7.3
NPV versus IRR

Year	1	2	3	4	NPV @ 10%	IRR
Cash flows A	−$4,000	$1,500	$2,000	$1,500	**$130**	12%
Cash flows B	−$2,000	$750	$1,000	$800	$99	**13%**
Cash flows (A–B)	−$2,000	$750	$1,000	$700	$31	**11%**

Suppose the appropriate cost of capital at which to discount each of these projects is 10%. Using the NPV rule, the NPV of investment A is just over $130, while the NPV of investment B is around $99. If the two investments are mutually exclusive, therefore, most value will be added by undertaking investment A.

Using the IRR rule gives the opposite result. As we saw earlier the IRR for investment A is approximately 12%. The IRR for investment B, on the other hand, is approximately 13% (see *www.costofcapital.net* for the figures). Thus the IRR can give the wrong conclusion when mutually exclusive projects are considered.

In fact, it is possible to modify the IRR rule so that it continues to give the appropriate results. Rather than separately calculating the IRRs for the two investments, it is better to look at the IRR for the incremental cash flows associated with the larger of the two investments. In this case, investment A represents a bigger outlay than investment B. The incremental cash flows associated with the larger investment are set out in the third row of Table 7.3 where the cash flows of the second investment are subtracted from the first. The IRR of these incremental cash flows is approximately 11%, above the target discount rate of 10%. Hence, when the IRR rule is applied in this way, it correctly identifies that the additional investment in investment A is justified because it yields a rate of return in excess of the cost of capital.

However, this does not altogether resolve the difficulties. Such incremental calculations become horribly complex where there are multiple mutually exclusive projects. Furthermore, when incremental cash flows are being considered there is a distinct likelihood of multiple 'sign changes' resulting in the IRR giving the ambiguous results discussed above. Finally, if projects are mutually exclusive due to a capital constraint the IRR is less helpful in prioritizing investment than the NPV. The latter allows us to compare investments in terms of the amount of NPV added for each dollar of investment (how much 'bang for our buck').

IRRs and exits

In addition to these three ways in which the IRR approach can give results which are at best misleading, and at worst plain wrong, there is another area where the IRR must be used with caution – when considering exits from early-year ventures.

It is frequently the case that venture capitalists and equity funds invest in a portfolio of start-up ventures where the probability of success for each individual venture is relatively low. In the event that a particular investment proves successful, the venture capitalist or equity fund will often seek to exit by selling its equity stake, either in a trade sale or through an initial public offering (IPO). This crystallizes the value of the successful venture, and provides cash that can be used to fund further investments.

However, care needs to be exercised in determining the value of such a strategy. The authors are aware of equity funds which promise a high IRR for their investors, and as we shall now see, this gives them an artificial incentive to achieve an early exit for a successful investment, even if by doing so they actually destroy shareholder value.

To see how this happens let us once again consider the investment introduced in Examples 7.1 and 7.2. To recap, this involves an outlay of $5,000 in year 1, followed by positive cash flows in years 2 to 10. In the event that the investment is successful, these are $3,000 per annum; if unsuccessful they are $1,000 per annum. With a 30% chance of success and a 70% chance of failure, the NPV of the expected cash flows of the investment is $3,831 (assuming a discount rate of 10% is appropriate).

It is often the case with new ventures that after a relatively short time there is far greater certainty over the likely outcome. For some investments, involving new products or services, the critical uncertainty is likely to surround the first few years' sales figures – will the level of demand be towards the top end or bottom end of predictions? In others, much of the risk may be associated with the construction phase – will the necessary capital investment be completed on time and on budget?

Let us assume that for our investment that the critical uncertainties are whether the investment can be completed in a single year within the budget of $5,000, and whether the level of demand will be as high as $3,000 per annum or as low as $1,000. We will assume that if the investment has been successfully completed, and two years' track record of demand at the $3,000 level has been observed, then it will be accepted by all investors, existing and potential, that the investment will continue to be successful to year 10. In other words, the uncertainties associated with the project at inception will have been resolved by the end of year 3, since the investment will have been completed and the level of demand will have been established.

Assume, then, that in years 1 to 3 the cash flows are those of the successful scenario set out in Example 7.1, and that this leads all interested parties to conclude that the future cash flows will also be those associated with the successful scenario. In this event a typical venture capital company or equity fund might seek to sell its stake in the venture, perhaps through a trade sale. Table 7.4 sets out the implications of this for the NPV and the IRR of the venture.

TABLE 7.4
NPV, IRR, and exits

	Investment	Years 2–3	Sale Year 3	Years 4–10	NPV	IRR
Expected	−$5,000	$1,600 pa	Na	$1,600 pa	$3,831	29%
Actual	−$5,000	$3,000 pa	Na	Na	Na	Na
Hold	−$5,000	$3,000 pa	Na	$3,000 pa	$11,161	59%
Sale (1)	−$5,000	$3,000 pa	$14,605	Na	$11,161	120%
Sale (2)	−$5,000	$3,000 pa	$5,000	Na	$3,944	60%

The first row of Table 7.4 shows the expected value of the venture of $3,831 immediately prior to investment, taking into account only a 30% chance of success. The IRR at financial close is 29%.

The second row shows the actual observed cash flows in the first three years of the venture's life, which indicate to investors that the venture will prove successful. The probability of success has now risen from 30% to 100%. If the original investor were to retain its investment in the venture and hold it until the life of the venture was completed at the end of year 10, then the cash flows it would receive are given in the third row. The NPV has risen to $11,161 and the IRR to 59%.

Suppose instead the original investor were to sell its interest in the venture (i.e. its entitlement to receive cash flows of $3,000 per annum in years 4 to 10) in year 3. This is illustrated in the fourth row of Table 7.4. It would receive a payment of $14,605 for this, $14,605 being the value of $3,000 per annum for years 4 to 10 discounted back to year 3 at the appropriate discount rate of 10% (this is what a third-party investor would be prepared to pay for the remaining cash flows). The NPV of the entire investment from the point of view of the original investor is once again $11,161. This is not surprising. The original investor should be indifferent between selling its stake at a fair price, and holding on to its investment.

However, the IRR associated with the sale option is 120%, slightly more than double the 59% achieved if the investment is retained. Thus, where a venture capital company or equity fund sets itself an IRR target it will tend to prefer to exit early from successful projects in order to maximize its rate of return.

This could lead to inappropriate decision taking. Suppose the original investor was offered less than $14,605 at exit – say, $5,000. This would still give an IRR of 60%, slightly better than the 59% achievable without an exit. But the NPV associated with this sale option would be below $4,000, not much more than a third of the $11,161 achievable by holding on to the investment. All these figures can be seen at *www.costofcapital.net*.

So following an IRR objective might give an inappropriate incentive to exit a successful investment. What is happening here? Well, we have assumed that the key cash flow risks are concentrated in the first three years of the project's life. Once this period has been successfully completed, the future cash flows are known with certainty. By exiting at this point, and selling at a fair value, the original investor essentially concentrates the entire IRR for what is a 10-year project into just three years, artificially boosting the reported IRR. The NPV calculation, in contrast, accurately reflects that no additional value is created if the investor's interest in the project is sold at a fair value.

Of course, it may well be the case that the original investor's best option is indeed to exit at the earliest opportunity. Equity funds and venture capital companies often do so, because their expertise in managing investments is greater in overseeing start-ups rather than more mature ventures, and exiting also provides a source of cash to enable them to pursue new opportunities. The latter rationale is related to the concept of real options which we discuss later in this chapter.

The payback rule

There are alternatives to NPV and IRR. Some companies apply the payback rule, whereby they require all investments to repay the original capital outlay within a certain specified time period. For example, they might reject any project that failed to repay the initial investment within a certain number of years. There appear to be several potential underlying reasons for adopting such a rule:

- In a fast moving world such as electronics, there might be a view that if a new venture did not pay back within two or three years, it would be unlikely ever to make a positive return.

- A cash-strapped company might wish to target early payback of investments, simply in order to ensure that positive cash flow returns will be available quickly to fund the next investment opportunities.

- The use of a payback period might reflect skepticism regarding investments which rely on forecasts of positive cash flows some years into the future. For example, company directors or shareholders might reason that a line or project manager might wish to promote a project for his or her own short-term interest, and might be prepared to make extravagant promises regarding some future period when he or she might have changed job. This reasoning would suggest that it is easier to test the reliability of returns in the near future, and it is more likely that managers can be held accountable for failure to perform.

Problems with the payback rule

Whatever the underlying logic, it is easy to show that the payback rule is inferior to NPV. Consider Table 7.5. Investment A is the same investment that we have seen previously. Investment C requires the same initial capital outlay as investment A, but it generates a larger positive cash flow in year 3, offset by a smaller positive cash flow in year 4.

TABLE 7.5
The payback principle

Year	1	2	3	4
Investment A	−$4,000	$1,500	$2,000	$1,500
Investment C	−$4,000	$1,500	$2,500	$500

If we compare investment A and investment C on the basis of the payback rule, it is clear that investment C is superior. It pays back the initial investment in year 3, while investment A does not return the initial outlay until part of the way through year 4. Indeed, if the company payback rule was that all investments must pay back in year 3, the company would accept investment C but reject investment A.

If we apply the NPV rule, however, investment A is superior to investment C. Recall that if the appropriate cost of capital discount rate to assess the investment is 10%, investment A returns a positive NPV of around $130. By contrast, the NPV of investment C discounted at 10% is *negative* to the tune of around $177. Hence, if 10% is the appropriate cost of capital, investment A adds to shareholder value while investment C destroys shareholder value. In fact, the IRR of investment A is about 12% (as we have seen), while the IRR of investment C is only about 7%. Thus, if the appropriate discount rate lies between 7% and 12% investment A should be accepted while investment C should be rejected, contrary to the payback rule (once again you can find these figures at *www.costofcapital.net*).

The reason why the payback rule gives the wrong result is that it applies implicit discount rates which are wholly inappropriate. If the rule is applied as a cut off (e.g. reject all projects which fail to pay back by the end of year 3) it implicitly applies a discount rate of zero to the cash flows in years 1 to 3 (it simply adds these up, giving no differential weighting according to the year in which the cash flow arises), while applying an infinite discount rate to all cash flows beyond year 3 (implicitly they are discounted out of the calculation altogether).

The NPV rule attaches less importance to a cash flow the further in the future it arises, but does this on a smooth basis, properly taking into account opportunity cost and risk. It does not employ any arbitrary cutoff date.

Discounted payback

Before moving on it is worth briefly mentioning the hybrid, *discounted payback* methodology. Arguably, this has a superior pedigree to the straight payback approach, particularly if used for information rather than decision purposes. In some situations it may be helpful to know when an investment is expected to achieve payback on a discounted cash flow basis. It gives the investor a sense of when, on an appropriate basis taking into account the risk-adjusted time value of money, the original sum invested is returned.

> In some situations it may be helpful to know when an investment is expected to achieve payback on a discounted cash flow basis. It gives the investor a sense of when, on an appropriate basis taking into account the risk-adjusted time value of money, the original sum invested is returned.

All other things being equal, there is an advantage in funds being released more quickly because it potentially opens up new investment opportunities, or options. The treatment of *real options* is considered later in this chapter.

Book rate of return

The three investment rules considered above (NPV, IRR, and payback) all rely on knowing the cash flows associated with an investment. Rather than using cash flow information, some companies take investment decisions on the basis of accounting figures. One method used is to calculate the average return on the book value of an investment, and compare this with some target rate of return.

This methodology is most easily explained by using again the cash flows of our old friend investment A. You will recall that this involved an investment of $4,000 in year 1, resulting in the generation of positive cash flows in years 2 to 4. To derive accounting figures for this investment, all we need to do is split out revenue and direct costs within the assumed cash flows, and make assumptions regarding depreciation. The easiest assumption for the latter is that the original investment is depreciated on a straight line basis across years 2 to 4.

Table 7.6 sets out a stylized income statement for investment A.

TABLE 7.6
Income statement for investment A

Year	2	3	4
Revenue	$3,000	$4,000	$3,000
Direct costs	$1,500	$2,000	$1,500
Cash flow	$1,500	$2,000	$1,500
Depreciation	$1,333	$1,333	$1,333
Net income	$167	$667	$167

For simplicity Table 7.6 assumes that there are no taxes. The cash flow row is identical to the figures included in the earlier tables for investment A, but here an assumption has been made about the breakdown between revenue and direct costs in order to make this look like a standard income statement. The $4,000 investment is depreciated on a straight line basis over three years, resulting in a depreciation charge of just over $1,333 per annum. Reported accounting net income is therefore $167 in years 2 and 4, and $667 in year 3. Average net income is $333 per annum.

We can also derive an accounting balance sheet for our investment – see Table 7.7.

TABLE 7.7
Balance sheet for investment A

Year	1	2	3	4
Gross book value	$4,000	$4,000	$4,000	$4,000
Cumulative depreciation		$1,333	$2,667	$4,000
Net book value	$4,000	$2,667	$1,333	$0

Table 7.7 shows that the gross book value of our asset remains at $4,000 throughout the life of the investment, but the net book value falls in line with the cumulative accounting depreciation. On average, the net book value across the four years of the project is $2,000. The average return on book value is then calculated by dividing the average net income per annum ($333) by the average net book value of the asset ($2,000). This gives an average return on book value for investment A of 16.67%. This would need to be compared with some target average book rate of return, for example with some industry norm or that achieved by the company as a whole.

Once again, it is relatively easy to demonstrate that this accounting approach to investment decisions can give incorrect results. Tables 7.8 and 7.9 give the income statement and balance sheet for an alternative investment, investment D.

TABLE 7.8
Income statement for investment D

Year	2	3	4
Revenue	$2,000	$3,500	$4,500
Direct costs	$1,500	$2,000	$1,500
Cash flows	$500	$1,500	$3,000
Depreciation	$1,333	$1,333	$1,333
Net income	–$833	$167	$1667

TABLE 7.9
Balance sheet for Investment D

Year	1	2	3	4
Gross book value	$4,000	$4,000	$4,000	$4,000
Cumulative depreciation		$1,333	$2,667	$4,000
Net book value	$4,000	$2,667	$1,333	$0

Investment D involves the same initial outlay as investment A, and in cash terms exactly the same positive future cash flows. However, in investment D the cash flows are significantly more backend loaded.

The average book rate of return measure for investment D is identical to that of investment A. Both have average net income of $333 per annum, against an average net book value of $2,000, giving an average book rate of return of 16.67%. Hence, on the basis of the average book rate of return, there is nothing to choose between the two investments. However, because investment D's cash flows are relatively backend loaded, in NPV terms it is an inferior investment to investment A. In particular, if the appropriate cost of capital discount rate is 10%, as we have seen investment A returns a positive NPV of around $130, while the NPV of investment D is *negative* to the tune of $47 (see the figures at our website, *www.costofcapital.net*).

The use of average book rate of return is therefore flawed. It ignores the cash flows, does not consider a proper risk-related opportunity cost of capital, and does not provide any proper basis for benchmarking what the returns on an investment should be.

Economic profit

An increasingly common way of linking investment decisions to the accounting numbers is through the use of *economic profit* calculations. Economic profit (sometimes under the trademarked name of Economic Value Added, EVA) is the old concept of residual income resurrected.

Economic profit is calculated by taking profit before interest and after tax (PBIAT) and deducting a capital charge. The capital charge is calculated as the cost of capital multiplied by the capital invested in the business. For example, a business with $1,000 of capital and a cost of capital of 10% has to earn a PBIAT of more than $100 to generate economic profit. Economic profit simply says that a business must earn its cost of capital on the capital it employs in order to create value.

Economic profit is used by many leading companies as a performance measure. It is used in internal monthly management reporting and in reporting to shareholders. It is also often linked to management incentives. Thus, if it is possible to evaluate investment decisions with the same measure, this establishes a straightforward way of linking investment decisions to business performance.

Fortunately there is an important mathematical relationship that enables us to do this. The net present value of future economic profits plus opening capital *equals* the net present value of future cash flows (all discounted at the cost of capital).

Typically economic profit analysis is used to support traditional discounted cash flow analysis so that the impact on future business performance can be tracked. The benefit is that one measure can be used to link the investment decision with subsequent performance.

Economic profit is not without its critics. Some commentators criticize economic profit for discouraging investment and say that it is a tool best suited to mature, capital intensive industries. There are also measurement challenges in applying it to new economy businesses – for example, how does one measure the capital base? Nevertheless, it is a useful addition to management's toolkit.

A conclusion on alternatives to NPV

If you want to be sure that you are appraising investment opportunities properly there is no short-cut – you must use the NPV approach. Only this approach will properly consider the time value and opportunity cost of investments, set against the risk of the particular investment in hand.

If applied properly, the IRR approach is sound, but it does not save any effort and can potentially yield ambiguous results. Payback and average book rate of return are conceptually flawed and are not recommended. The only justification for using them might be in a well-established business making very similar investments on a repetitive basis, where a simple rule of thumb can suffice because basic project parameters are well known and do not vary. Such circumstances are unlikely to interest readers of this book, however, as such decisions can be taken on the basis of gut feel and there is no need to understand the derivation of the cost of capital.

> If applied properly, the IRR approach is sound, but it does not save any effort and can potentially yield ambiguous results.

Real option valuations

A drawback of the NPV approach is that it is not well-suited to handling situations where a follow-on investment is linked to an initial investment. Such situations are extremely common in business life. Examples include any expenditure on R&D, on marketing or product positioning, or on investment in the first element of an investment program which is capable of later expansion.

It is easiest to demonstrate how the NPV approach can be misleading in such situations by using a numerical example. Table 7.10 gives the expected cash flows for two linked investments. Investment A is the same project with the same cash flows as we have seen in earlier examples. Investment E involves an outlay of $2,500 in year 4 followed by positive cash flows in years 5 to 7.

TABLE 7.10
How NPV can give misleading results when real options exist

Year	1	2	3	4	5	6	7
Investment A	–$4,000	$1,500	$2,000	$1,500			
Investment E				–$2,500	$1,000	$850	$850
Combined	–$4,000	$1,500	$2,000	–$1,000	$1,000	$850	$850

Table 7.10 also gives the year-by-year cash flows for the two projects taken together. Assuming that the appropriate risk-adjusted discount rate for an investment of this nature is 10%, the NPV of the combined investment is –$40. In other words, if the two investments are assumed to be undertaken together, and are appraised prior to the first investment being made, the conclusion will be that no investment should be made as this would destroy shareholder value.

If, however, making the initial investment in investment A does not *commit* the investor subsequently to fund investment E, then it is clear that this conclusion is incorrect. Recall that in Table 7.3 it was established that investment A has a positive NPV of $130 at a discount rate of 10%. If the investor, having funded investment A, has the choice whether or not to fund investment E, then an NPV of $130 is the *worst* outcome possible. At the point at which the second investment needs to be made, if the projected NPV of investment E is negative then the correct decision is simply not to make the investment. Whatever happens, the investor will receive the NPV of $130 from investment A, and any subsequent investment will only be made if it adds to this NPV.

Furthermore, if it is assumed that the ability to make investment E is conditional on having already made investment A (e.g. investment A represents an initial entry into a new market, and investment E is a subsequent expansion opportunity), then by making investment A an investor has secured an *option* to make investment E. He or she will exercise this option only if it is valuable to do so.

Implicitly, by discounting the overall cash flows in Table 7.10, we assumed that investment E would follow automatically after investment A. On the basis of a discount rate of 10%, the NPV of investment E is –$170, more than offsetting the positive NPV of $130 associated with investment A. (You can find these calculations at *www.costofcapital.net*. Note that for ease of explanation, we ignore the complexity that it may be more appropriate to use a different discount rate for investment E during the period of delay).

Where cash flows are contingent on decisions that will only be made once various uncertainties affecting the asset value are resolved, standard deterministic discounted cash flow is less appropriate. Real option valuation (broadly defined) provides a basis for explicit valuation of the opportunities (options) deriving from the ability to make or revise decisions in response to changing circumstances. The term *real option* reflects the analogy between financial options and management flexibility to respond to events in an uncertain world.

Real option valuation is useful in looking at the value of start-up businesses with high but uncertain growth potential and intangible assets such as trademarks, patents, or R&D portfolios, as well as businesses whose revenues are affected by volatile commodity prices. It is particularly relevant when considering the value of high technology businesses including e-businesses. Some typical examples of real options are given in Table 7.11.

TABLE 7.11
Some examples of real options

Option	Example
Growth options	Brand extensions where new markets become attractive
Deferral options	Natural resources where development may be deferred pending the acquisition of geological data on reserves and favorable commodity prices
Flexibility options	Dual-firing power plant to enable fuel substitution
Exit/abandonment options	To stop R&D where technical results are poor/market prospects become unfavorable
Staged investment options	Design for expansion but defer additional capacity pending better understanding of potential market size
Operating strategy options	Own production versus contracting out depending on demand

There are two principal approaches to valuing real options:

- decision analysis based approaches.
- financial options modeling based approaches.

Decision analysis

The decision analysis approach involves applying a *decision tree* approach to the calculation of NPV. Figure 7.4 sets out the decision tree for the investments in Table 7.10.

In Figure 7.4 the investor must choose whether or not to make investment A. If no investment is made then the outcome is simply an NPV of zero. If investment A is undertaken, then the investor faces a further decision concerning investment E. Whether or not that investment should be made will depend on prospects for investment E in year 4 when the decision must be made.

For this purpose it has been assumed that prospects for the success of investment E will depend on the level of demand observed in year 4, and that there are two possible states of the world – a high-demand scenario, with a 40% probability, where the NPV of cash flows for years 5 to 7 will be $2,500, and a low-demand world, with a probability of 60%, where the cash flows for the same period will be $900.

The combination of two states of the world with two possible investment decisions leads to four possible outcomes. If the decision is made to invest in investment E, then this will yield an additional NPV of $793 ($2,500 – $1,707, the latter figure being the present value of the $2,500 investment needed in year 4) if demand is high, and an NPV of – $807 ($900 – $1,707) if demand is low. In both these cases, the NPV of investment E should be added to the NPV of investment A of $130. If investment E is not made, then the outcome is simply $130, the NPV of investment A.

The benefit of the decision tree is that it enables earlier decisions to be made on the basis of understanding future options and decisions. This is achieved by working backwards through the decision tree, establishing at each point from right to left what the best option is. In this simple case, we start with the investment E decision in year 4. It is clear that if demand is high the optimal decision is to make the additional investment in investment E, with an overall NPV (including the NPV of investment A) of $923 ($130 – $1,707 + $2,500).

If, on the other hand, demand is low, the optimal decision is not to invest in investment E in which case the overall NPV is simply the value of investment A, $130.

FIGURE 7.4
Decision tree analysis

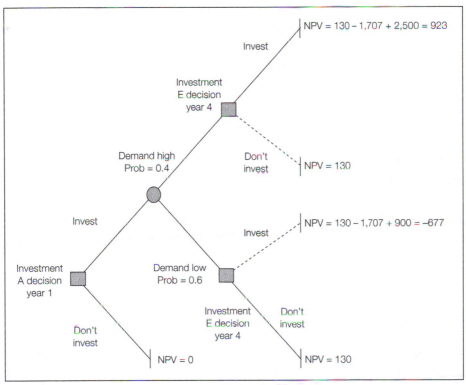

While it is impossible to know at the beginning of year 1 (when the initial investment decision in investment A must be taken) what demand actually will be in year 4, it is clear that if the initial investment in investment A is made, then in the event that demand is high an overall NPV for the combined project of $923 is achievable, while in the event that demand is low the overall NPV is $130. Weighting these two outcomes by their respective probabilities (40% probability of high demand, 60% probability of low demand) gives an overall weighted NPV of $446 if the initial investment is made (compared with $0 if it is not made). It is clear, therefore, that it is appropriate to invest in investment A. Contrary to the original analysis, the linkage of investment E with investment A adds value of some $316 ($446 – $130), rather than destroying value to the tune of $170.

The reason that the initial analysis got things so badly wrong was that it implicitly assumed that investment E would *inevitably* go ahead once the decision had been taken to make investment A. Thus the initial decision would immediately expose the investor to the downside risk that demand would be low in future years but it would still be necessary to expand capacity with a large negative NPV implication. Essentially the decision tree analysis enables the investor to identify future actions which he or she will be able to take to minimize or eliminate downside risk. In our simple example, only one of the four possible outcomes yields a negative NPV, and it is clear that the investor can avoid this simply by deciding not to make the subsequent investment in investment E in the event that demand turns out to be low. The swing in NPV of the combined value of the two investments from –$40 to $446 illustrates how important it is to recognize options and the value these can confer. The overall NPV of $446 effectively comprises $130 for investment A, together with an option value of $316 for investment E.

A problem with the decision tree approach is that the diagrams can become horrendously complicated. This example is simple in that it only involves two decisions, with two discrete states of the world and two possible decisions. In reality, there are likely to be many more possible states of the world to consider. Furthermore, uncertainties do not necessarily fall neatly into dual states of the world and therefore *probability distribution functions* are required rather than a simple either/or situation.

Nevertheless, the approach can be powerful. Software packages are available to aid the calculations, and the process of identifying the range of uncertainties and options available is often, of itself, an extremely useful process in helping managers increase the value of investments.

> A problem with the decision tree approach is that the diagrams can become horrendously complicated.

Financial options

The second principal approach to undertaking real option valuations is to use approaches employed in evaluating financial options. These have a theoretical elegance but are in practice only applicable in very specific situations. To use financial options models correctly, deep technical and mathematical skills must be available, as many potential pitfalls may not be apparent to nonexperts. Moreover, financial options methods are not particularly transparent when compared to decision trees. This can limit the extent to which assumptions can be discussed with, and adopted by, management.

It is nevertheless useful to consider the analogy of financial options with real options as this provides a ready insight into the value generated by optionality. For example, in the world of financial options, a 'call option' for a stock gives the owner of the option the right (but not the obligation) to buy that stock at a specified price (the 'exercise' price) at some future date. Where the option may be exercised only on a specified date, the call option is known as a 'European' call; where it can be exercised before or on the specified date it is known as an 'American' call.

There is a clear parallel between a European call option and the option to make investment E in the example above. By investing in investment A our investors secured the rights to make investment E in year 4 at an exercise price equal to the necessary investment.

If we put aside for now some of the technical problems and accept that such 'real options' are analogous to financial options, it is possible to use the tools developed for valuing financial options – such as the well known Black-Scholes formula – to inform real investment decisions.

In order to value a call option for a stock the Black-Scholes formula uses information on the exercise price, the current stock price, the time to expiration of the option, and the standard deviation of the returns on the stock. In terms of a real option, the parallels for these variables are the capital expenditure required to undertake the optional investment, the current view of the present value of operating cash flows the investment will secure, the time between now and the date at which the investment will need to be made, and the standard deviation of the returns associated with the investment. These are set out in Table 7.12 .

TABLE 7.12

Inputs for Black-Scholes option pricing formula

Financial option parameter	Notation	Analogous real option parameter	Impact on the value of the real option of an increase in the size of the parameter
Exercise price	X	Expenditure (investment) to commence exploitation of asset	Reduces value
Stock price	S	Present value of operating the asset	Increases value
Time to expiry	t	Length of time decision to exercise option may be deferred	Increases value: there is more opportunity for S to increase and the holder earns r for longer
Volatility	σ	Riskiness of project assets (variability of S)	Increases value: there is a higher potential upside
Risk-free rate the return	r	Time value of money (usually the risk free rate, but here we use the project discount rate)	Increases value: r represents the return during the time to expiry

Returning once again to the simple example set out in Table 7.10, the present value of the capital expenditure associated with investment E is $1,707 (equivalent to the exercise price in a financial option), the present value of the operating cash flows is $1,537 (equivalent to the current stock price), and the deferral time is four years. The most difficult parameter to assess is the volatility, as we have no current market proxy for the volatility associated with the follow on investment. Nevertheless, let us assume that the standard deviation of returns is 30%.

The Black-Scholes formula uses this information on exercise price, stock price, deferral time, and volatility to calculate the call option value as a percentage of operational cash flows.[3] For our example, the Black-Scholes model calculates a call option value of $303. Hence, the total value of making investment A according to this approach is $433, comprising $130 of NPV from investment A itself, and $303 option value associated with investment E.

Using real option valuation

It should be noted that real option valuation techniques are evolving, and while the main principles are well established there are still areas of debate. Probably the most significant issue is the extent to which the market's valuation of risks can be captured through the probabilities applied to market risks in the cash flows, allowing the use of the risk-free rate. This is a complex area where specialist advice is required.

Real option valuation obviously adds to the complexity of the valuation process and requires more information than standard discounted cash flow analysis. Ideally management information is required which, depending on the nature and purpose of the valuation, may be difficult to obtain. The depth of analysis will depend on the information available as well as the likely sensitivity of the valuation to the existence of option value. The valuer will need to exercise judgment in deciding whether to carry out real option valuation.

The valuation of dot.coms

We are now finally in a position to return to the thorny subject of valuing dot.coms. The high market capitalizations that have at times been ascribed to some Internet-based companies, and the wild fluctuations in share prices observed, have been sources of bewilderment to many equity analysts and valuation experts.

In part this bewilderment has stemmed from the fact that many of the standard stock market valuation techniques cannot be employed in the e-business world, and so the traditionalists have been unable to relate the market capitalization figures they have seen to observable measures with which they are familiar. The standard techniques are based on price-earnings multiples, revenue multiples, book value of assets, and reliable estimates of future growth. But Internet-based companies have virtually no tangible assets, they often have negative earnings, and future growth prospects are highly uncertain.

This can be illustrated with reference to two of the best known dot.coms – Amazon.com and Yahoo!. Table 7.13 shows that the market capitalization of these companies has been large at times of negative earnings, and that some big increases in market capitalization have been achieved at the same time as earnings performance apparently deteriorated (see, for example, Amazon.com in 1999). In contrast, the market capitalization of Yahoo! fell significantly in 2000 despite a significant improvement in pre-tax profit.

TABLE 7.13
Market capitalization of two dot.coms ($ million)

	1995	1996	1997	1998	1999	2000	2001
Amazon.com							
Market cap	Na	Na	1,438	16,950	25,942	5,543	4,022
Pre-tax profit	(0.3)	(6.2)	(27.6)	(124.5)	(643.2)	(1,106.7)	(526.4)
Yahoo!							
Market cap	Na	451	2,985	23,384	113,901	16,514	10,105
Pre-tax profit	(0.8)	(2.9)	(23.6)	43.3	104.4	264.1	(85.5)

Source: Thomson DataStream

Valuation metrics

With the traditional methods breaking down, some equity market analysts sought to replace them with other rule of thumb measures, such as market capitalization per user, revenue per subscriber, and market cap per monthly page view. However, there was little or no science behind these measures, and because e-business companies differed in the services they were providing and the ways in which value was to be created, there was no hard and fast rule to suggest what these metrics should be.

Applicability of discounted cash flow analysis

Calculating present value through discounted cash flow analysis is regarded by some as providing a potentially useful framework within which to value dot.coms. The argument goes that, ultimately, for such companies to have value they must return a positive cash flow to investors in the future, and this can be valued in a discounted cash flow model.

Some analysts have employed discounted cash flow techniques to explain the high market capitalization at particular points in time of some of the more well-known Internet-based companies. For Amazon.com, for example, analysts have in the past claimed to have been able to explain the share price by using plausible assumptions about the future size of the US book and music markets, the proportion of these markets which will be accounted for by sales on the Internet, Amazon.com's projected share of the Internet sales, and the margins that Amazon.com will be able to make on the sales.

Such analysis is interesting because it emphasizes that even e-businesses must conform to the laws of economics and cash flow. Arguably, the big reductions observed in dot.com capitalization from its peak may have resulted from investor realization that traditional valuation techniques such as price/earnings multiples and discounted cash flow analysis would assign little or no value to such companies. Nevertheless, the discounted cash flow framework is not terribly helpful in valuing these businesses. For one thing, to forecast cash flows requires the adoption of numerous heroic assumptions regarding market shares which are simply impossible to make with any degree of certainty.

Use of real option techniques

More importantly investments in e-business are effectively investments in options. The soaring capitalization at times of certain e-businesses has indicated that the market believes the Internet could be the next 'big thing' – perhaps akin to the development of electricity, the telephone, or the computer on its impact on our way of life.

The market would therefore expect important companies to emerge from this sector, and at times has attached a lot of value to companies which have been early movers and have invested aggressively, presumably because it believed they would achieve some first-mover advantage on which they would capitalize later. Essentially investors buying shares in such businesses have effectively purchased an option that they will be well-placed to capitalize on the e-business opportunities that might emerge in the future.

Whether the likes of Amazon.com ever attain the profits figures implicit in some of the market capitalization figures seen to date will depend on factors such as growth in the use of the Internet, customer loyalty, and the ease with which competitors can replicate their products or offer strong alternatives. A deep knowledge of the Internet, and insights into public reaction to it, can help inform opinions about these variables. Nevertheless, any view that a particular company will ultimately be successful is highly speculative given the extent of uncertainty.

Dot.com valuations and market sentiment

Finally, it must be recognized that the high capitalization of many Internet-based companies which contributed to the dot.com bubble is now ascribed by many to the 'irrational exuberance'[4] of equity investors. This view argues that, for many investors, in picking e-business stocks, valuation techniques take a back seat to gut feel and the love of a gamble.

There is much truth in this. Given that at the time of the bubble many dot.coms were years away from delivering positive cash flows to investors, the large fluctuations in market capitalization did not represent movements in actual results, but rather market sentiment regarding likely future results, and indeed market sentiment about share price movements. In these circumstances one might take the advice of someone who was himself a highly successful stock market investor:

> Professional investment may be likened to those newspaper competitions in which the competitors have to pick out the six prettiest faces from a hundred photographs, the prize being awarded to the competitor whose choice most nearly corresponds to the average preferences of the competitors as a whole; so that each competitor has to pick, not those faces that he himself finds prettiest, but those which he thinks likeliest to catch the fancy of the other competitors, all of whom are looking at the problem from the same point of view. It is not a case of choosing those which, to the best of one's judgement, are really the prettiest, nor even those which average opinion genuinely thinks the prettiest. We have reached the third degree where we devote our intelligences to anticipating what average opinion expects the average opinion to be. And there are some, I believe, who practise the fourth, fifth and higher degrees.

This apposite advice comes courtesy of John Maynard Keynes no less, writing in *The General Theory of Employment, Interest and Money* in 1936. Plus ça change . . .

Key points from the chapter

- Net present value (NPV) is the term given to the discounted value of future cash flows less the value of the initial investment. Any investment which offers a positive NPV adds to wealth and shareholder value, because the risk and time adjusted financial rewards associated with the investment outweigh the initial cost. The optimal investment strategy is to maximize NPV.

- Cost of capital analysis is relevant to discounted cash flow analysis because it provides the basis for calculating the discount rate. The appropriate cost of capital calculation should be based on the risk profile for the investment being analyzed, not the cost of capital of the potential investor (which may be different if the investment is not in the investor's core business area).

- When calculating the NPV of an investment it is vital to use probability-weighted cash flows that fully reflect the upside and downside risks associated with the investment.

- The internal rate of return (IRR) of a project is the discount rate which gives an NPV of zero. The IRR can be compared with some required rate of return in order to decide whether or not to proceed with the investment. However, the IRR is inferior to NPV as an investment decision tool. To be applied properly it requires the same degree of analysis as the NPV, but it is not as flexible (it cannot deal with variable discount rates), can give ambiguous results, and can give misleading results when applied to mutually exclusive projects.

- Some companies use a simple payback rule – requiring investments to repay the original outlay within a certain specified time period. This can lead to incorrect decision taking as such a rule does not properly take into account opportunity cost and risk.

- Similarly, it is inappropriate to take investment decisions on the basis of the book (accounting) rate of return. This approach ignores cash flows, does not consider a risk related opportunity cost of capital, and does not provide any proper basis for benchmarking what the returns on an investment should be.

- Real option valuations (ROV) are being increasingly used. ROV techniques enable account to be taken of the value in an investment associated with future opportunities that may arise (e.g. the option to expand the initial investment if conditions prove favorable). ROV can be applied using a decision tree approach or, in certain circumstances, using financial options modeling techniques such as the Black-Scholes formula.

■ Wild fluctuations in the market capitalization of dot.coms have led some commentators to conclude that the 'new economy' cannot be analyzed using traditional investment analysis tools. ROV gives some insights, as essentially investors are buying options: they hope that by investing in an Internet start-up they will be able to capitalize on growth in e-commerce in the future. Picking winners is a highly speculative exercise however, and enormous fluctuations in individual share prices have been observed.

Notes

1   Although readers will recall from Chapter 6 that the nationality of the investor could affect the cost of equity applied if capital markets are segmented and investors are not internationally diversified.

2   This calculation of the NPV assumes that the first year cash flow is discounted by the full amount of the discount rate, i.e. it implicitly assumes that the first year investment is incurred one year from the reference date for the NPV calculation. It is important when calculating NPVs that the reference date is clearly understood and the appropriate discount rate used for each period. For example, if the reference date was the start of year 1, and it was assumed that the $4,000 investment was spread evenly throughout year 1, then the appropriate discount rate to apply to the $4,000 investment would be $1.0247 = (1.05)^{1/2}$. This is sometimes referred to as mid-year discounting or the mid-year convention.

3   Specifically, the Black-Scholes formula is: Call option value = [N(d1) * S] – [N(d2) * PV(X)]; where d1 = [ln(S/X)] / (σ*$\sqrt{t}$) + [(σ*$\sqrt{t}$) / 2], d2 = d1 – (σ*$\sqrt{t}$), and the function N(d) is the probability that a normally distributed random variable will be less than or equal to d. S, X, σ and t are as defined in the text. PV(X) is the present value of X, calculated by discounting at the risk-free rate, r.

4   The phrase coined by Federal Reserve Board Chairman, Alan Greenspan, in December 1996.

USING THE COST OF CAPITAL IN BUSINESS VALUATIONS

Most people who use the cost of capital in the real world are interested in valuing a business or shares in a business. This is often in the context of listed companies or private companies, but can also be in the context of more unusual situations such as valuing financial interests in an organization owned by its members, valuing businesses in the public sector, or valuing equity in a special purpose vehicle or joint venture.

We have already touched on various methodologies that exist for assessing value in Chapter 7. By far the most robust and frequently used technique is discounted cash flow ('DCF'). This approach is capable of incorporating a far richer and greater amount of information than the majority of other techniques and has an intuitive appeal that has led to widespread adoption within the financial community.

Different DCF techniques exist. These include the well-known Weighted Average Cost of Capital ('WACC') approach – which discounts the operational cash flows of a business at the weighted average cost of capital (the blended return required to remunerate all providers of finance) – and the less common Flows to Equity ('FTE') approach – which discounts the cash flows distributable to equity providers at the cost of equity. Finally, there is the Adjusted Present Value ('APV') approach. This is seldom used in practice, but is technically perhaps the most reliable of all the techniques. It separates and distinguishes between the value generated from the operations of a business and any value generated by the financial structure that is put in place. It adds the two values together to generate an overall value for the enterprise.

We examine how these various DCF techniques may be employed and in what circumstances they may best be used. Each approach is considered in turn and the linkages back to cost of capital theory and practice explored.

Introduction

In the real world, value is extremely important. This is because having a sound understanding of value will allow practitioners to:

- *make better acquisitions and disposals* – identifying acquisitions that are purchased at values less than the value they provide to the purchaser (same applies in reverse for disposals), or spotting equities that are currently undervalued and will subsequently increase in price as their true performance becomes apparent to others;

- *determine the best corporate strategies* – through the evaluation of which strategies are most likely to add the most value; and thereby
- *maximize shareholder value* – the prime function of management.

In short, value matters like nothing else. An understanding of value is central to good commercial decisions, yet many commercial practitioners are content to express their views of value without a proper understanding of the techniques that can be used to crosscheck and underpin their judgments.

Practical valuation – the starting point

Assuming that we are interested in undertaking a business valuation, the most common starting point is to use DCF techniques to calculate an Enterprise Value ('EV') for the business. So what is this EV and what does it mean? And how do practitioners calculate it?

Enterprise Value ('EV')

Enterprise value is the value of a business before any debt liabilities are deducted. It represents the overall value generated for all investors in a business (both equity and debt) from the operations in their entirety.

As an example, if the equity value of a business is 500 and debt is 300, then the overall enterprise value is 800. This is because if debt liabilities are 300 and if the value of the business to shareholders is 500, the enterprise must be generating 800 of value prior to any financial claims (remember that debt has a prior claim on enterprise cash before equity; so if the market values the equity at 500, then this must imply that there is also sufficient cash to meet the prior claims of 300 debt).

There are two ways to estimate EV. Either:

- estimate the value of the overall operations of the business prior to any financial claims; or
- estimate the value of the equity investors' part of the business and add to this the value associated with stakes held by the providers of all other forms of (debt) finance.

For a listed company, it is easiest to adopt the second method because a market exists in the company's shares allowing the practitioner to infer the value of the equity investors' share of the operational cake. In practice, what this means is that the total number of shares in issue can be multiplied by current market price and added to the value of interest-bearing obligations. This is also called 'market value of invested capital' ('MVIC') and the approach assumes that shares in the company are fairly priced when compared with their value.[1]

Valuing businesses using DCF analysis

This section of our chapter examines three widely used DCF valuation methodologies to identify present value – be it an enterprise value or an equity value. The techniques are:

- **The standard WACC approach** – which discounts expected post-tax operating cash flows at a rate that reflects the blended returns required by all investors – the weighted average cost of capital ('WACC').

- **The flows to equity ('FTE') method** – which discounts cash flows attributable to shareholders at the (levered) cost of equity.

- **The adjusted present value ('APV') approach** – where post-tax operating cash flows are discounted assuming the asset has no leverage, with the value of the tax shield (tax relief on debt) being separately identified and added to the unlevered value to calculate the full present value of the asset.

The standard WACC and APV techniques both produce enterprise values of the firm, whereas the flows to equity approach will produce an equity value. Because it is a relatively simple process to calculate equity values from enterprise values (and vice versa), the key issue for practitioners is to select one approach or another regardless of whether an enterprise or equity value is required. But do the different approaches provide financially consistent results? The answer is yes – and we show this to be the case.

Although all three approaches adopt a different discount rate, each discount rate is appropriate given the measure of cash flow being valued. As a result, the values calculated under the three approaches can be reconciled to one another given certain assumptions. This is set out more fully in the section below.

We also consider different ways in which the WACC can be calculated (different, that is, from what we have termed the standard WACC approach). These different WACC approaches are associated with different WACC and beta unlevering formulae (different from what we have seen so far in this book). They are important because they account for the risks surrounding the tax effects of financing in different but plausible ways. They therefore employ different cost of capital expressions compared with our standard WACC approach. These techniques are as follows:

> it may not be clear to the reader at this stage, but our standard WACC approach – using the conventional unlevering formula – effectively involves an implicit assumption that interest tax shields are discounted at the unlevered cost of equity.

■ **The Modigliani-Miller (MM) WACC approach** – which discounts expected post-tax operating cash flows using a WACC that implicitly discounts interest tax shields at the cost of debt (rather than the unlevered cost of equity).

■ **The Miles-Ezzell (ME) WACC approach** – which discounts the interest tax shield for the first period using the cost of debt and then for all subsequent periods using the unlevered cost of equity.

It may not be clear to the reader at this stage, but our standard WACC approach – using the conventional unlevering formula that we first saw in Chapter 2 – effectively involves an implicit assumption that interest tax shields are discounted at the unlevered cost of equity.

Below, we identify which approach is the most appropriate methodology for valuation in different circumstances.

Standard WACC approach

The method most commonly used in the world of corporate finance for valuing a company or project that is in part debt-financed, is the standard WACC method.[2] In Chapters 1 and 2, we introduced our standard approach to calculate the WACC. The valuation of a company using this approach is summarized in Figure 8.1.

The first step of the WACC approach is to estimate the operating cash flows that would be available to the providers of capital to the business after corporate taxes are paid, but without taking into account any reductions accruing from the presence of tax shields from interest payments. We refer to this amount of tax payable as 'unlevered tax' because the tax is estimated on the same basis as if the business was unlevered, in which case corporate tax would not be reduced by any tax relief on interest payments.

FIGURE 8.1

Calculation of equity value for a company using the standard WACC approach

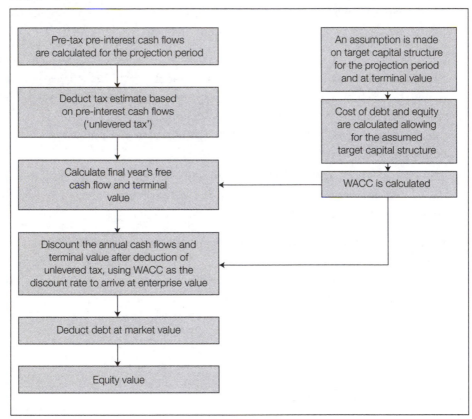

It is necessary to assess the cash flows on this unlevered tax basis because our standard WACC formula already includes an adjustment to the cost of debt component (the (1 – T) term in our standard formula first introduced in Chapter 1) that takes into account the impact of the tax deductibility of interest payments. To model this impact twice (in the cash flows as well as the discount rate) would therefore constitute double counting. The unlevered tax is then deducted from the pre-interest cash flows to calculate post-tax, pre-interest cash flows.

But this approach does not ignore the implications of debt financing. All of the debt implications to the equity holders of the business are reflected in:

■ The gearing adjustment to equity betas, capturing the increased risk that equity providers face from the presence of debt (which has a priority call on cash generated by the enterprise).

- The reflection of the tax benefit of debt financing – the 'interest tax shield' – through the tax adjustment to the cost of debt in the WACC formula.
- The impact of debt on the overall discount rate, where the cost of debt is weighted with the cost of equity through the WACC formula.
- The deduction of debt (at its market value) from enterprise value to derive equity value.

The approach assumes that the business adopts a single target capital structure for the projection period and for the calculation of terminal value. This assumption on current and longer-term capital structure is made normally with reference to actual data on both the company and/or a peer group or industry norms and factors such as interest cover, as described in more detail in Chapter 5.

The approach therefore implies that the management of the business will constantly strive to achieve a constant target gearing over time. It works on the assumption that debt is rebalanced each year to maintain a given gearing ratio. This means that if the value of debt is $500 and the value of equity is $1,000, if the market value of equity subsequently rises to $2,000, the management of the business will increase the amount of debt issued to $1,000 so that the debt equity ratio remains constant at 50%. Consequently, this approach is strictly applicable only in a situation where there is a single constant capital structure for the enterprise.

The WACC is calculated using the methodology first described in Chapter 1. It employs the formula first seen in Chapter 1:

$$\text{WACC} = K_e * \frac{E}{V} + K_d * (1-T) * \frac{D}{V}$$

$$
\begin{array}{lll}
\text{where} & K_e & = & \text{Cost of equity} \\
& K_d & = & \text{Cost of debt} \\
& E & = & \text{Market value of equity} \\
& D & = & \text{Market value of debt} \\
& T & = & \text{Corporate tax rate} \\
& V & = & \text{Market value of equity plus market value of debt}
\end{array}
$$

The approach typically employs the CAPM (the Capital Asset Pricing Model) for the cost of equity calculation. As we have seen this provides that investors require a premium above the risk-free rate of interest that reflects the systematic (or market) risks associated with the investment. The cost of equity is calculated accordingly, employing what is termed a 'levered' equity beta that reflects the riskiness of shareholder returns that arise as a result of fixed debt service commitments and the underlying riskiness of the firm's assets (as described in Chapter 2). Our conventional formula we have adopted for levering the asset beta (β_a), to create a levered equity beta (β_e), is sometimes referred to as the 'Harris-Pringle' formula. This is set out below:

$$\beta_e = \beta_a \left[1 + \frac{D}{E}\right]$$

The final term introduced in Figure 8.1 that needs introduction is the terminal value – the cash expectation left at the end of the period for which cash flows have been projected. In practice, a terminal value is most often calculated as a perpetuity, this being derived as the annual cash flow at the end of the projection period, plus one year's growth, divided by the estimated long-term WACC less a growth factor relevant to the business. This long-term growth rate is that for the sector in which the company or division operates. It would not normally be expected to be different from that of the economy to which the company is exposed.

The estimated post-tax WACC is used to discount the post-tax, pre-interest free cash flows, and also to discount the terminal value to produce an estimate of the present value of the business.

Example 8.1 provides a simple illustration of how present value can be calculated using the WACC approach.

Example 8.1 Present value of a business – our standard WACC approach

Assume that for a business the following inputs are appropriate:

Corporation tax rate	30%	Asset beta	1.15
Risk-free rate	5%	Debt to value	50%
Equity market risk premium	5%	Debt premium*	0%

* Assumed to be zero for simplicity.

Using the methods we have described in this book, the inputs produce the following results:

Debt to equity	100%	Equity beta	2.3
Cost of debt	5%	Cost of equity (levered)	16.5%
Post-tax WACC	10%	Cost of equity (unlevered)	10.75%

We assume that the business produces pre-interest, pre-corporation tax, operating cash flows of $100m per annum in perpetuity. Post-tax cash flows (where tax is calculated as 'unlevered tax' and we ignore the effect of interest payments) are therefore $70m per annum (given 30% corporation tax), because the 'unlevered' amount of tax payable is $30m.

In year 5, the terminal value of all future cash flows is equal to the next cash flow, divided by a discount rate equal to the long-term WACC minus the long-term cash flow growth rate. As there is assumed to be no change to the capital structure of the business, the long-term WACC is equal to our current WACC (10%). The growth rate of cash flows is assumed to be zero. Consequently, the pre-tax terminal value in year 5 is equal to the next cash flow ($100m), divided by the WACC (10%), which equals $1,000m. To reach an estimate in terms of its current value (in year 0 in our example), we need to deduct tax based on pre-interest cash flows and discount it using the same discount rate as used for the year 5 cash flow.

From these assumptions we can calculate present value, as the sum of the discounted cash flows. The results, looking at the first five years and the subsequent terminal value are as shown in the table below.

$m	0	1	2	3	4	5	Terminal value
Cash flows: pre-int, pre-tax	0	100	100	100	100	100	1000
Cash flows: pre-int, post-tax	0	70	70	70	70	70	700
*Discount factor (WACC)**	*1.00*	*1.10*	*1.21*	*1.33*	*1.46*	*1.61*	*1.61*
Present value	0	63.64	57.85	52.59	47.81	43.46	434.64
Enterprise value (PV)	**700**						
PV of debt	**350**						
PV of equity	**350**						

* The convention we use for discount rates is to present them in tables as a denominator that will reduce future values into present value terms.

The present value of the post-tax cash flows discounted with a post-tax WACC provides an estimate of the enterprise value. As the debt to value ratio is assumed to be 50%, the equity of this business is valued at 50% of the enterprise value, or $350m.

Flows to equity ('FTE') approach

A second possible DCF approach to the valuation of a business is the FTE approach. The FTE approach produces an estimate of the present value of equity based on the post-interest, post-corporation tax cash flows of the business. This time tax needs to be modeled as *actual* tax paid after the impact of any tax shields (rather than the notional 'unlevered' tax charge), because there is no debt component in the discount rate and therefore the impact of the tax shield cannot be modeled this time in any other way than in the cash flows. These cash flows are discounted using the *levered* cost of equity – the same cost of equity used to calculate a standard WACC – where the beta is adjusted for the financial risk of the company arising from the amount of debt financing adopted.

The valuation of a company using the FTE approach is summarized in Figure 8.2.

FIGURE 8.2

Calculation of enterprise value for a company using the FTE approach

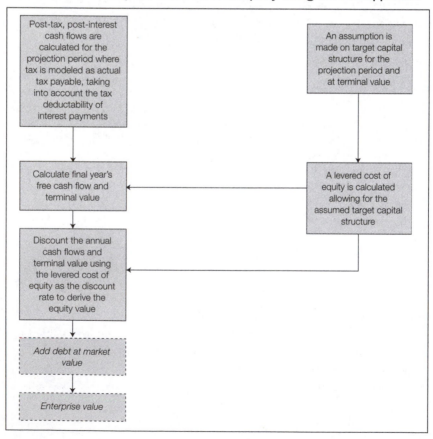

Unlike the WACC approach (and the APV approach discussed below), the FTE approach does not require the practitioner to deduct the market value of debt from the estimated enterprise value to reach an estimate of the present value of equity.

The methodology is particularly useful, in practice, for valuing financial services firms where companies' funding structure are such that they make money on the spread between borrowing and lending; therefore debt financing is not a financial engineering decision but becomes part of the normal day-to-day business operations. It may also be appropriate for special purpose vehicles with complex debt arrangements that are best modeled in financial spreadsheets.

> Unlike the WACC approach and the APV approach, the FTE approach does not require the practitioner to deduct the market value of debt from the estimated enterprise value to reach an estimate of the present value of equity.

To highlight the relationships between the WACC approach and the FTE approach, in Example 8.2 we use the same assumptions as in Example 8.1 to calculate the PV of equity using the FTE approach.

Example 8.2 Present value of a business – the FTE approach

We use the levered cost of equity of 16.5% derived in Example 8.1 to discount the post-tax post-interest cash flows, and use the estimate of the market value of debt ($350m) provided by Example 8.1 to calculate interest payments. Using the same assumptions, we find the following results.

$m	0	1	2	3	4	5	Terminal value
Cash flows: pre-int, pre-tax	0	100	100	100	100	100	606.06
Interest payments (5%)	0	17.5	17.5	17.5	17.5	17.5	106.06
Cash flows post-int, pre-tax	0	82.5	82.5	82.5	82.5	82.5	500
Cash flows post-int, post-tax	0	57.75	57.75	57.75	57.75	57.75	350
Discount factor (levered cost of equity)	1.00	1.17	1.36	1.58	1.84	2.15	2.15
Present value of equity	0	49.57	42.55	36.52	31.35	26.91	163.09
PV of equity	350						
PV of debt	350						
Enterprise value (PV)	700						

In this simple example, the FTE approach produces the same estimate for the PV of equity ($350m) as the WACC approach, and therefore after adding back debt of $350 the enterprise value is also the same, at $700m.

Adjusted present value ('APV') approach

A third approach to DCF valuation of a business is known as the APV approach. This was first promulgated in 1974 but, at present, appears to be much less used than the WACC framework, although this may change as the advantages of APV become more widely known. The basic philosophy behind the approach is that the value of an asset is dependent on two factors:

- the fundamental value from the operation of the asset;

- any value associated with financial structure (primarily interest tax shields).

In practice, the approach treats the business as being debt free – in order to calculate a fundamental value of the business – and isolates the effect of debt financing in a separate calculation. The valuation of a company using this approach is summarized in Figure 8.3.

The APV approach to business valuation separates the valuation of operations from financing. For the valuation of operations, post-unlevered tax cash flows are discounted using an 'unlevered' cost of equity, reflecting the assumption that there is no debt financing. An unlevered cost of equity is calculated using an estimate of the unlevered, asset, beta of the business, as described in Chapter 2.

> The effects of different tax rates, different interest rates and different timings of deduction can be explicitly modeled when using the APV approach.

The tax effect on business value of debt financing – the interest tax shield – is a valuation of the tax deductions that arise from a decision to finance using debt. The effects of different tax rates, different interest rates, and different timings of deduction can be explicitly modeled when using the APV approach. As a consequence, the discount rate that should be used to calculate the present value of the interest tax shield should reflect the risk associated with obtaining the tax deductions, which in turn will reflect:

- The risk of variation in the corporate tax rate.

- The risk of variation in the company's tax rate because of changes in cash flow profiles – if the company posts a loss (and so is unable fully to meet interest payments) in a particular year, then the tax deduction will be deferred until the company is back in profit; this has an impact on timing and therefore present value.

- Lack of freedom in controlling the capital structure of the business – if the business needs to maintain a constant gearing ratio, then the interest tax shield will vary in line with enterprise value, as the level of debt must be kept at a constant ratio to enterprise value.

FIGURE 8.3
Calculation of equity value for a company using the APV approach

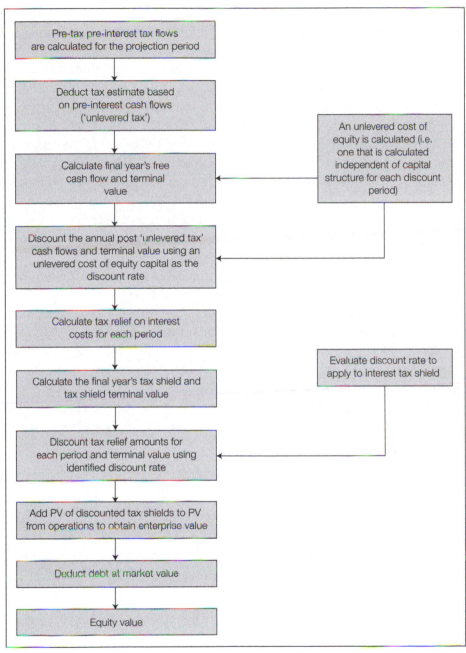

If a company is able to maintain a fixed level of debt financing, which will *never* need to vary in response to changes in the market value of equity (and hence the enterprise value), then the risk to the interest tax shield arises from the risk to the corporation tax rate and the risk to the company's existence. These risk factors are probably best reflected in the cost of debt, as they are similar to the risks that bond investors face. This suggests that the interest tax shield of such a business should therefore be valued using the cost of debt as the discount rate.

Alternatively, if a company has to maintain a constant gearing ratio, perhaps in order to maintain a constant credit rating, then the level of debt financing (and therefore the interest tax shield) will vary according to variations in enterprise value. The unlevered cost of equity estimates the discount rate that investors use to derive enterprise value, as it represents the rate of return that investors expect when the firm is entirely financed by equity. As the interest tax shield will vary in line with enterprise value if there is a constant gearing ratio, this suggests that the unlevered cost of equity is the appropriate discount rate to use to value the interest tax deductions of such a business.

In practice, the freedom of the company to control its capital structure may lie somewhere between these two extremes: for example, if the company faces pressure to maintain the gearing ratio broadly in line with a target gearing ratio, but does not need to change the level of debt instantly in response to change in enterprise value. In this case, the appropriate discount rate would lie somewhere between the cost of debt and the unlevered cost of equity, and an element of judgment would be required by the cost of capital practitioner.

To highlight the relationships between the three approaches to DCF valuation, in Example 8.3 we use the same assumptions as Examples 8.1 and 8.2 in applying the APV approach to valuation.

Example 8.3 Present value of a business – the APV approach

We use the same interest payments as in Example 8.2. We discount the interest tax shield using the unlevered cost of equity, as this implicitly assumes that the gearing ratio is kept at a constant level, consistent with the assumptions of our standard WACC approach.[3]

Using the asset beta of 1.15 we calculate that:

Cost of equity (unlevered) = 5% + (1.15 * 5%) = 10.75%

The following table summarizes the results from the APV approach.

$m	0	1	2	3	4	5	Terminal value
Cash flows: pre-int, pre-tax	0	100	100	100	100	100	930.23
Cash flows: pre-int, post-tax	0	70	70	70	70	70	651.16
Discount factor (unlevered cost of equity)	*1.00*	*1.11*	*1.23*	*1.36*	*1.50*	*1.67*	*1.67*
Present value	0	63.21	57.07	51.53	46.53	42.01	390.81
PV of unlevered business	**651.16**						
Interest payments	0	17.5	17.5	17.5	17.5	17.5	162.79
Interest tax shield	0	5.25	5.25	5.25	5.25	5.25	48.84
Discount factor (unlevered cost of equity)	*1.00*	*1.11*	*1.23*	*1.36*	*1.50*	*1.67*	*1.67*
Present value of tax shield	0	4.74	4.28	3.86	3.49	3.15	29.31
PV of tax shield	**48.84**						
Enterprise value (PV)	**700**						
PV of debt	**350**						
PV of equity	**350**						

Relaxing the assumptions

In the simple example used in Examples 8.1–8.3, the three valuation methodologies (Standard WACC, FTE, and APV) deliver the same figure for the present value of equity. Both the APV methodology and the flows to equity approach require computation of the value of debt, which requires the calculation of the enterprise value from the WACC approach, so in this simple example the WACC methodology is the easiest to use in practice.

We have, however, only been able to reconcile the three different approaches as we have maintained the same simplistic assumptions, which result in the three approaches being mathematically identical. The assumptions are that:

- The gearing ratio is kept constant in perpetuity.
- The corporation tax rate is constant in perpetuity.
- The interest rate on debt is constant in perpetuity.

These are assumptions that underlie our standard WACC approach described above, and if we do not employ these assumptions the WACC approach is no longer as useful to us.[4,5] Numerous cost of capital academics and practitioners have criticized the use of the WACC approach for the unrealistic assumptions that it requires. The APV approach, on the other hand, can be employed when these assumptions do not hold, as the value of debt financing is calculated separately. The APV approach is therefore a more dynamic tool that allows specific treasury and tax strategies to be modeled.

To highlight the potential importance of the assumptions employed by our standard WACC approach, in Example 8.4 we use the three DCF approaches described above – WACC, FTE, and APV – to estimate the present value of a business identical to that in the previous three examples, except that now the business is free to maintain its *level* of debt at a constant $350m, even if the enterprise value were to fluctuate. Thus we are relaxing the assumption that the debt to value ratio *must* be kept constant.

Example 8.4 Constant level of debt

As the cash flows in our simple example remain constant at $100m in perpetuity and the level of debt is held at $350m, the gearing ratio does not *actually* change over the lifespan of the company. But the point we are making is that it could and this means that the present value of the future interest tax shield is now higher to the company. This is because the ability to maintain a constant level of debt makes the tax shield more certain than if the company must vary the level of debt in line with uncertain enterprise value. The main risk to the level of debt, and therefore the interest tax shield, arises from the risk of corporate default, which is captured by the cost of debt. The company would therefore discount future interest tax shields using the cost of debt, not the unlevered cost of equity.

The only difference with the assumptions made in Examples 8.1, 8.2, and 8.3 is that the company would wish to discount future tax shields at a lower discount rate, a factor which is not captured by our standard WACC or FTE approach using the Harris-Pringle unlevering formula, because both implicitly discount future tax shields by the unlevered cost of equity. Consequently, both standard WACC approach and our FTE approach would continue to value the company at $700m.

The results produced by the APV approach do change, however, as the APV model does take account of the tax shield being relatively safe in this example, and can apply a discount rate equal to the cost of debt. The results for the APV approach are summarized in the following table.

$m	0	1	2	3	4	5	Terminal value
Cash flows: pre-int, pre-tax	0	100	100	100	100	100	930.23
Cash flows: post-tax	0	70	70	70	70	70	651.16
Discount factor	*1.00*	*1.11*	*1.23*	*1.36*	*1.50*	*1.67*	*1.67*
(unlevered cost of equity)							
Present value	0	63.21	57.07	51.53	46.53	42.01	390.81
PV of unlevered business	**651.16**						
Interest payments	0	17.5	17.5	17.5	17.5	17.5	350
Interest tax shield	0	5.25	5.25	5.25	5.25	5.25	105
Discount factor	*1.00*	*1.05*	*1.10*	*1.16*	*1.22*	*1.28*	*1.28*
(cost of debt)							
Present value of tax shield	0	5.00	4.76	4.54	4.32	4.11	82.27
PV of tax shield	**105**						
Enterprise value (PV)	**756.16**						
PV of debt	**350**						
PV of equity	**406.16**						

The APV approach suggests that the present value of equity is now $406.16m, $56.1m, and 16% higher than the $350m value given by the standard WACC approach, because it is able to take account of the relative safety (and hence increased value) of future tax shields. The increase in the enterprise value consequently reduces the debt to value ratio to 46.3%.

Modigliani-Miller (MM) WACC approach

It is, however, possible to use a different method to calculate what we term a (non-standard) WACC that takes account of interest tax shields being discounted at the cost of debt – this is known as the Modigliani-Miller (MM) WACC.

This approach holds debt at a constant monetary amount and as a result assumes that the annual tax shield is relatively safe, discounting it at the cost of debt.

The approach uses a different formula (sometimes referred to as the 'Hamada' formula) for levering the asset beta to calculate an equity beta. This formula is set out below:

$$\beta_e = \beta_a \left(1 + (1 - T) \, {}^D\!\!\big/\!_E\right)$$

The formula for the MM WACC is also different. It is rather an odd looking WACC formula and is set out below:

$$\text{MM WACC} = K_a \left[1 - T\left({}^D\!\!\big/\!_{D + E}\right)\right]$$

The MM WACC is calculated using the unlevered cost of equity, K_a, that is calculated using the asset beta rather than the equity beta used in the CAPM. The MM WACC formula does not include the cost of debt, which can be thought of as consistent with the 1958 Modigliani-Miller theory that capital structure does not have any effect on the value of a business – and therefore does not have any effect on WACC.

The Hamada levering/unlevering formula and the MM WACC formula must be used in conjunction with one another, although a long-form way of calculating the MM WACC is also to use the Hamada levering/unlevering formula in conjunction with the standard WACC formula seen earlier in Chapter 1.

In Example 8.5 we use exactly the same assumptions as in Example 8.4 to produce the same results as the APV model, using the MM WACC approach.

Example 8.5 Present value of a business – MM WACC

The debt to value ratio is now 46.3% due to the 16% increase in market value implied by the APV approach. The new equity beta is lower as the Hamada levering formula includes a downward adjustment for corporation tax. The MM WACC approach produces the following results:

Debt to value ratio	46.3%	Debt to equity ratio	86.2%
Equity beta	1.844	Cost of equity (unlevered)	10.75%
Cost of equity (levered)	14.22%		

These results allow us to calculate the MM WACC as follows:

MM WACC = 10.75% * (1 – 30% * 46.3%) = 9.26%

$m	0	1	2	3	4	5	Terminal value
Cash flows: pre-int, pre-tax	0	100	100	100	100	100	1080.23
Cash flows: pre-int, post-tax	0	70	70	70	70	70	756.16
Discount factor (MM WACC)	*1.00*	*1.09*	*1.19*	*1.30*	*1.42*	*1.56*	*1.56*
Present value	0	64.07	58.64	53.67	49.12	44.96	485.70
Enterprise value (PV)	**756.16**						
PV of debt	**350**						
PV of equity	**406.16**						

The Modigliani-Miller WACC approach produces the same figure for the present value of equity ($406.16m) as the APV approach, when the interest tax shield is discounted by the cost of debt.

It should be noted, however, that the MM WACC will only produce estimates that are consistent with APV if the level of debt remains constant in perpetuity. This is a central assumption of the Modigliani-Miller approach.

Miles-Ezzell (ME) WACC approach

The ME WACC approach makes slightly different assumptions about the value of the tax shield. The first year tax shield is treated as being as secure, as it is based on a level of interest payments that is already known – the first year tax shield is therefore discounted at the cost of debt. Subsequent tax shields are discounted at the unlevered cost of equity as they remain as uncertain as is assumed in our standard WACC approach.

The ME WACC approach uses the same levering/unlevering formula as our standard WACC approach (i.e. the Harris-Pringle formula), as set out below:

$$\beta_e = \beta_a(1 + \frac{D}{E})$$

The ME WACC formula is even more odd-looking than the MM WACC formula. The ME formula is as follows:

$$\text{ME WACC} = K_a - K_d T \left[\frac{1 + K_a}{1 + K_d}\right] \left[\frac{D}{D + E}\right]$$

If we were to apply these formulae to the assumptions made in the earlier examples, with gearing fixed at 50%, we would calculate a Miles-Ezzell WACC of 9.96% and find that the present value of the equity is $351.44m. This is only marginally above (by 0.4%) the value calculated by our standard WACC approach, as the increase in value only applies to the first year's tax shield. It is also possible to show that the APV approach produces the same result. The reader may wish to try to replicate these results as an exercise (full details can be found at *www.costofcapital.net*).

The formulae must be used consistently

The three sets of formulae presented above for calculating an appropriate WACC (standard, Modigliani-Miller, and Miles-Ezzell) under different assumptions for the uncertainty of interest tax shields are only mathematically consistent with APV results in the right circumstances. For instance, a common mistake made by cost of capital practitioners is to use the standard WACC formula with the Hamada levering/unlevering formula in circumstances where debt is free to vary and tax shields are risky. This is inappropriate because the Hamada levering/unlevering formula incorporates a tax term that is only correctly applied where the *level* of debt remains constant and tax shields are known with certainty. As shown in Example 8.6, the mistake can have a significant impact on value.

Example 8.6 Incorrect use of formulae

In this example we illustrate the potential discrepancy that can arise from using the standard WACC formula with the Hamada levering/unlevering formula in circumstances where debt is free to vary. We use exactly the same assumptions as Example 8.1, but we use the Hamada formula to calculate the equity beta from the asset beta. The adoption of the Hamada formula results in an estimate of the levered cost of equity, and hence the WACC, which is significantly lower than it should be in a world where debt is free to vary.

$m		0	1	2	3	4	5	Terminal value
Debt to value ratio	50%			Equity beta				1.955
Cost of equity (levered)	14.75%			Incorrect WACC				9.1%

$m	0	1	2	3	4	5	Terminal value
Cash flows: pre-int, pre-tax	0	100	100	100	100	100	1094.39
Cash flows: pre-int, post-tax	0	70	70	70	70	70	766.07
Discount factor (WACC)	1.00	1.09	1.19	1.30	1.42	1.55	1.55
Present value	0	64.14	58.77	53.85	49.34	45.21	494.77
Enterprise value (PV)	766.07						
PV of equity	383.04						

The estimate of the present value of equity ($383.04m) is 9.4% in excess of the estimate produced by our standard WACC approach ($350m). The $33m discrepancy is due to the assumption in the Hamada formula that interest tax shields are discounted at the cost of debt, when in actual fact the rest of the example assumes that we are in a world in which they should be discounted at the cost of equity.

Choosing the methodology

Practitioners seem to have an overwhelming preference for WACC in the same way that for calculating the cost of equity capital the CAPM is most commonly used. However, WACC may not describe the real world satisfactorily in many situations that require value to be calculated.

None of the assumptions in the three sets of formulae presented above for calculating WACC (our standard, MM, and ME) are entirely realistic and, in practice, they are seldom fulfilled. Rarely will the level of debt of a company be constant or be kept at a target gearing ratio. For instance, debt finance may be closely linked with working capital management, such that it fluctuates depending on level of business activity rather than being a relatively fixed item making up part of a company's capital structure.

Nor will interest payments and their associated tax shields be constant or even that easy to predict. For example, international groups may use a complex series of intergroup loans to manage the location of the interest deductions on their debt financing, in order to maximize the tax rate at which the interest deductions attract relief and make sure that interest obligations are located in territories where the group has sufficient profits to cover the obligations. This process can make it difficult (or impossible) to identify the tax rate at which finance costs are relieved and the timing of tax relief.

Therefore, when one looks at debt financing in practice, the picture does become very much more complicated and a simplistic assumption about timing of interest deductions, currency of debt, and effective rate, and timing of tax relief can be very far from the truth.

APV is a much more dynamic methodology and does allow specific treasury and tax strategies to be modeled. Also, as noted before, it is generally easier to calculate present value for a business in which the rate of gearing changes over the forecast period (such as a capital investment project) using APV than it is using the WACC approach. Therefore, as a valuation tool it is thought by some to be superior, particularly in the following circumstances:

- Where changes in the level of gearing are expected during the forecast period, perhaps as a project shifts from being primarily debt financed to primarily equity financed.

- Where changes in corporate taxes, interest payments, and other factors affecting the interest tax shield are expected and the valuation could be improved by modeling these effects explicitly.

- Where the appropriate discount rate for the interest tax shields is neither the unlevered cost of equity (as implicit in our standard WACC approach) nor the cost of debt (Modigliani-Miller WACC approach).

On the other hand, doing the calculation means that the financial modeler has to understand the cost of financing and model the interest tax shields that arise from debt financing. When a lack of detailed information leads the practitioner to assume that the company maintains a target gearing ratio and has a constant WACC, it is probably simpler to employ our standard WACC approach to valuation.

Valuation with personal taxes

In this chapter we have focused on the impact of corporate tax but have ignored the implications arising from personal taxes. However, investors are interested in returns after all taxes have been paid, and thus it is the equilibrium relationships after payment of both corporate and personal taxes that in theory need to be understood.

But while this may appear obvious, in practice most valuation analysis is conducted on a post-corporate but pre-personal tax basis. This is because the introduction of personal taxes makes the analysis more complex and introduces a number of uncertainties and problems that are not easy to solve:

- First, not all investors are subject to the same tax rates – but the personal tax relationships generated by academics typically assume that they are.

- Second, personal taxes may be complex. For example, investors may pay tax on dividends on overseas shares but may also be subject to withholding tax on top of this – unless a double taxation treaty exists between the country in which the investor is domiciled and the country in which the shares were purchased. From a cost of capital perspective, this sort of complexity is difficult to model.

- Third, as we saw in Chapter 6, some academics argue that it is the marginal investor who sets the cost of capital – and so what we need to know is the tax position of the marginal investor. The identity of this investor may be very difficult to determine, and not all academics and practitioners would accept that such weight should be put on the impact of one individual.

- Finally, having worked through the algebra, in some situations the impact of personal taxes may not actually be that great, or it may swing this way and that depending on the assumptions adopted. It may well, therefore, be sensible to ignore the complications and avoid the spurious precision that would come from trying to model personal taxes 'correctly', and simply focus on the post-corporate tax (but pre-personal tax) relationships and answers set out earlier in this chapter.

For these reasons we do not consider personal taxes here. However, readers who are interested in the impact of personal taxes can find some more material at our website, *www.costofcapital.net*.

Key points from the chapter

This chapter has been about using the cost of capital in DCF techniques to value businesses. The key points from this chapter are:

■ There are three fundamental DCF techniques: the WACC approach, the FTE approach, and APV.

■ The WACC approach is the most commonly adopted and involves discounting expected post-tax operating cash flows at a rate that reflects the blended returns required by all investors – the weighted average cost of capital.

■ The FTE approach discounts cash flows attributable to shareholders at the levered cost of equity.

■ The APV technique splits the value of an asset into its two constituent parts – the value associated with operations, and (any) value created by the capital structure adopted. In APV, post-tax operating cash flows are discounted assuming the asset has no leverage, with the value of the tax shield (tax relief on debt) separately identified and discounted at the appropriate rate and added to the base value to calculate the full present value of the asset.

■ In certain situations – for example, where gearing is expected to remain fairly constant – use of the WACC technique may be the most relevant approach. In other contexts, for example, valuing banks, it may be easiest to adopt FTE. In circumstances where gearing is expected to change, APV is probably the most reliable technique; the WACC approach can lead to unsound conclusions if not properly executed because, with changing gearing, discount rates must change in each year based on market gearing.

■ In addition, there are in fact three different WACC approaches – all based on different assumptions. Our standard WACC is based on an assumption of a constant gearing ratio (into perpetuity), a constant corporation tax rate, and a constant interest rate on debt (also into perpetuity). It implicitly discounts interest tax shields at an unlevered cost of equity. The beta unlevering formula that should be used in these circumstances is known as the Harris-Pringle formula – and does not include any term for tax.

■ There are other approaches. The Modigliani-Miller WACC approach effectively assumes that debt is held at a constant monetary amount and as a result assumes that the annual tax shield is relatively safe, discounting it at the cost of debt. This approach can only be used in conjunction with the Hamada unlevering formula – which includes a term for tax. Use of the Harris-Pringle formula would lead to incorrect and inconsistent results.

■ The third approach is known as the Miles-Ezzell WACC approach. This makes a slightly different assumption about the value of the tax shield. The first year tax shield is treated as being secure as it is based on a level of interest payments that is already known – the first year tax shield is therefore discounted at the cost of debt. Subsequent tax shields are discounted at the unlevered cost of equity, as they remain as uncertain as is assumed in the standard WACC approach. The Miles-Ezzell WACC approach must only be used in conjunction with the Harris-Pringle beta unlevering formula.

Notes

1   It is worth mentioning that this does not give a value on a controlling basis (see Chapter 10 for more details and a discussion on the practice of adjustments), because the share price is set by investors who have no overall control of the company.

2   This method is also known as 'adjusted cost of capital' ('ACC') by some practitioners.

3   We never said why constant gearing is an assumption in our standard WACC approach, but a comparison of the APV example with our earlier standard WACC example shows this to be the case. It is difficult to explain intuitively why our standard WACC approach includes this assumption. As we shall see in a moment, it is because all of the formulae have been mathematically derived using different operational assumptions.

4   When rates of gearing, interest rates, or tax rates change, it is only possible to calculate value using a WACC approach if separate estimates of the WACC are calculated for each year (necessary because the WACC input variables are changing creating a different WACC in each year). In these circumstances, the calculations become much more complex. For example, if gearing is expected to change and it's difficult to estimate the economic level of gearing in each year (because the present value of equity in future years is not known), it is necessary to calculate the present value of each period's cash flow by a process of backward iteration (working back from the last period and progressively discounting value in line with each period's individual WACC). This level of complexity can be avoided by adopting the APV approach instead.

5   This is why we call our standard WACC approach 'the standard approach'. If debt is free to vary and gearing can remain constant then a WACC approach adopting the Harris-Pringle formula is clearly simple to execute, and preferable to APV. On the other hand, if debt is not free to vary – because it is fixed – APV becomes the preferred methodology because it is easier to execute. The corresponding MM WACC approach using the Hamada formula is problematic, because the assumption behind the formula implies that gearing is likely to change in every year. This means that it is necessary to calculate different WACCs for different years, and in these circumstances APV is easier to use. In fact, we would not adopt an MM WACC approach in this situation, so to us this style of WACC analysis is non-standard.

9

INTERNATIONAL VALUATION AND APPRAISAL

Chapter 6 of this book provides a comprehensive guide to estimating the international weighted average cost of capital ('WACC') in global markets. This chapter builds on this foundation and examines how international WACCs can be used in the context of international valuations.

The chapter describes how to compare and assess nominal costs of capital in different countries, and provides insight into the nature and drivers of currency exposure and currency risk. It also shows that two different methods of handling currency conversion when appraising investments in foreign countries give the same result, so long as consistent assumptions are used.

Consideration is also given to the question of whether it is possible for a business to raise capital more cheaply in one market than in another.

Introduction

When contemplating investment opportunities in emerging markets, investors from developed countries typically face greater risks than for comparable investments at home. These include country (sovereign) risks such as expropriation or capital controls, more volatile business environments, withholding taxes, and additional volatility associated with currency exposure. Information asymmetry and scarcity of information may also create problems.

But it is not all doom and gloom, as there may be potential benefits. These include the greater number of opportunities available, the ability to tap into faster growing markets, and the possibility to export technology or intellectual capital.

These opportunities have not passed investors by – globalization has meant that international considerations have become increasingly important when assessing financial and economic capital. One phenomenon this has given rise to is the number of businesses that have transferred their stock exchange listing from one market to another in an attempt to raise capital more cheaply. A good example of this is provided by South African Breweries (SAB) – now SABMiller – which transferred its listing from Johannesburg to London in early 1999. Other notable examples include Daimler-Benz (Frankfurt to New York), and Billiton (Johannesburg to London).

In this chapter we look at approaches to carrying out business valuations and comparing costs of capital in the international environment.

International valuation approaches

We have discussed the general approach to using the cost of capital as the discount rate in discounted cash flow (DCF) analysis in Chapter 7, and described in more detail how this technique is used to value businesses in Chapter 8. In the international environment, when applying DCF analysis to businesses in other countries, the main complexities which arise concern, first, what model to use to calculate the WACC or cost of equity; and second, what to do about the complexities of dealing with cash flows affected by differences in relative inflation and currencies.

The approaches to the first of these complexities are described in Chapter 6; this chapter considers how to deal with cash flow complexities in the international environment.

Treatment of cash flows in international valuation and investment appraisal

There are two basic options for performing valuations. Both start with cash flows stated in the foreign currency (i.e. in the currency of the country where the business or investment opportunity is situated rather than the country of the valuer – this is consistent with the manner in which the cash flow figures are likely to be prepared). However, they differ in terms of their manipulation of these cash flows.

The two options are set out in Figure 9.1.

- **Method one** converts the foreign currency cash flows into familiar domestic currency values using forecast exchange rates. It then applies a familiar home country discount rate (including a country risk adjustment assuming that the cash flows to which the discount rate is to be applied have not already been adjusted for country risk – see Chapter 6) to calculate a home currency NPV.

- **Method two** applies a foreign currency discount rate to the foreign currency cash flows to estimate a foreign currency NPV. This can be converted into a home currency NPV at the prevailing spot exchange rate between the two currencies. Note that, unless an adjustment is made to remove the country risk element from the local discount rate, Method 2 implicitly assumes that the cash flows have not been adjusted for country risk, since the foreign currency cost of capital already includes a country risk premium component in the local currency risk-free rate component of the calculations.

FIGURE 9.1
The two main methods of international valuation

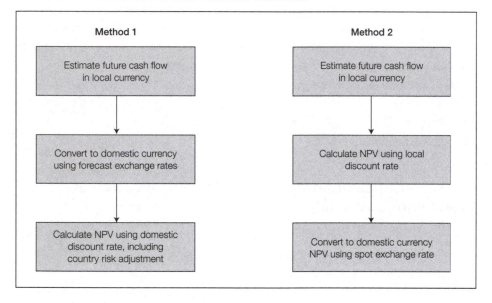

Implications of the two methods

Method one

Method one requires forecasts of the future exchange rate between the currency of the investor's home country and that of the country where the investment opportunity is located.

Currency conversion

This can be problematic. In principle it is best to use forward exchange rates quoted in the market as these can be assumed to be unbiased forecasts reflecting the consensus view. However, in practice these do not usually cover a period more than a couple of years ahead, inadequate for the typical valuation.

Currency forecasts by specialist economic forecasters are typically available to five years ahead, but even this length of time is insufficient for many valuations. It is often necessary, therefore, to produce longer-term forecasts. This is generally done by assuming that 'purchasing power parity' (PPP)[1] holds. PPP, or the law of one price, states that because of the possibility of arbitrage, the prices of products should be the same internationally. This implies that if inflation is higher in one country than in another then the value of its currency should depreciate in relative terms to offset the differential inflation. Example 9.1 shows how this assumed relationship can be used to produce an exchange rate forecast.

Example 9.1 Using a purchasing power parity ('PPP') technique to project long-run exchange rates

Let us return to the US investor considering a joint venture ('JV') investment in the Vietnamese telecommunications business that we saw earlier in Chapter 6. In this example, the inflation differential between the two countries is 5.9% – based on an inflation projection of 8% per annum for Vietnam and 2.0% per annum for the US (since 1.08/1.02 = 1.059). Let us also assume that the spot Vietnamese dong / US dollar exchange rate is currently 10,000 dong / $ and that there are no exchange rate forecasts available beyond this spot figure. This information is reproduced below.

Spot dong / $ exchange rate	=	10,000 dong / $
US inflation projection	=	2.0% per annum
Vietnamese inflation projection	=	8.0% per annum

If PPP can be assumed to hold, then one might expect the dong to depreciate in line with the inflation differential between Vietnam and the US. Put another way, because inflation is higher in Vietnam than the US, if the dong / $ exchange rate did not rise then PPP would be contravened. This is because the prices of goods are increasing by 8% per annum in dong terms, but by only 2% per annum in US dollar terms, and so goods are becoming relatively cheaper in the US than in Vietnam. The dong must fall in value against the dollar, by the exact amount of the inflation differential (per annum) for PPP to be preserved.

The corresponding calculations are shown below:

Inflation differential = (1.08) / (1.02) = 1.059 (per annum)	
Projected exchange rate depreciation = 1.059 (per annum)	
Annual exchange rate projections	= 10,000, 10,588 (10,000 * 1.059), 11,211 (10,588 * 1.059), and so on

For more information on these techniques – and to download a skeleton spreadsheet model to help with these calculations – see our website: *www.costofcapital.net*

Of course, the actual outturn exchange rate could, and almost certainly will, deviate from the forecast exchange rate used for the valuation. Thus the second issue faced in international valuation is the investor's exposure to currency risk. From a valuation perspective, it is important to consider a range of different profiles for the exchange rate and test the value assigned to the investment as the cash flows vary with this range.

Currency risk

But there is also a further issue – should a premium be added to the discount rate for currency risk? Some practitioners contend that a currency risk premium is unnecessary. They argue that if appropriate exchange rate forecasts have been used to convert the foreign currency cash flows (perhaps using a technique such as that set out in Example 9.1), then there is an equal probability that the outturn exchange rate will exceed the forecast exchange rate as there is that it will fall below it. In other words, the risk associated with subsequent exchange rate fluctuations is likely to be symmetric about an expected value.

In these circumstances, while currency exposure may make the cash flows more volatile than a comparative home investment, the currency risk should be diversifiable. By holding a portfolio of overseas investments, investors can diversify the risk of adverse exchange rate movements in one country against another.

> By holding a portfolio of overseas investments, investors can diversify the risk of adverse exchange rate movements in one country against another. This is an intuitive result, with great practical appeal.

This is an intuitive result, with great practical appeal. It is, however, important to be clear that, in the example above, the exchange rate forecasts would need to be true expected values and take account of any asymmetry associated with potential one-off currency devaluations. This is particularly prevalent in the context of those currencies tied to a fixed exchange rate or managed to a peg. It may also be important to take into account the potential covariance of devaluations – as has frequently occurred in emerging markets.

And there is a further fly in the ointment. Even if the above one-off currency devaluations are taken into account, some academics disagree with the contention that currency risk is diversifiable: they believe currency risk may actually command a premium. These academics argue that there is a slight difference between the forward rate and forecasts of the future spot rate, and believe that to ignore currency risk, currency forecasts should be expressed as *risk-adjusted* expected values rather than just expected values. If liquid forward markets exist, this risk-adjusted expected value is given by the forward rate. However, practitioners should also be aware that there is likely to be very little difference between the forward rate and forecasts of the future spot rate and, where no liquid forward market exists, the same academics offer little guidance as to the potential scale of the currency risk premium (although we are led to believe that it may be rather small).

Method two

Method two deals with the currency conversion issue by implicitly assuming that PPP holds. The foreign currency discount rate used in the DCF analysis takes into account inflation in the country where the business is situated. Assuming that inflation is higher in that country than in the country of residence of the investor (as in the case of Example 9.1) then this implies that the nominal discount rate used in Method two is higher than that in Method one due to the inflation rate differential. This has the effect of converting future cash flows back to an NPV to be converted at today's spot rate as if the exchange rate were to depreciate by the amount of the inflation rate differential – this is equivalent to the PPP methodology.

> The foreign currency discount rate used in the DCF analysis takes into account inflation in the country where the business is situated. Assuming that inflation is higher in that country than in the country of residence of the investor then this implies that the nominal discount rate used in Method two is higher than that in Method one due to the inflation rate differential.

A further point to note about differential inflation is that, based on certain assumptions,[2] the practitioner can use the nominal cost of capital in a particular country as the basis for calculating the nominal cost of capital in another country. This is because the nominal cost of capital in one country will differ from that in another by differences in the relevant country risk premia ('CRPs') and differences in inflationary expectations. So, for example, if a business is estimating the cost of capital in the context of a foreign acquisition (or project) it is possible for it to start from a familiar nominal home cost of capital and use an estimate of the CRP and forecast differential inflation to compute the appropriate cost of capital for the relevant foreign country. This is demonstrated in Example 9.2.

Example 9.2 International comparison of nominal costs of capital

Returning again to our Vietnamese telecommunications example, we are able to adjust the US dollar denominated Vietnamese country risk adjusted cost of capital into a country risk adjusted cost of capital denominated in Vietnamese dong.

The arithmetic for this is set out below.

US dollar country risk adjusted
telecoms JV WACC: **9.65%**

Vietnamese dong country risk
adjusted telecoms JV WACC: $[1.0965 * (1.08 / 1.02)] - 1 =$ **16.1%**

So, for example, if one were discounting cash flows for the Vietnam investment that had already been converted into US dollars, one would use the 9.65% discount rate. Alternatively, if the same cash flows were quoted in Vietnamese dong, the appropriate discount rate would be the 16.1% figure.

Reconciliation of the two methods

It can be shown that both methods produce the same result as long as consistent assumptions and inputs are made.

It can be shown that both methods produce the same result as long as consistent assumptions and inputs are made. The proof for this is set out in Example 9.3, using the familiar Vietnamese telecommunications example.

Example 9.3 Reconciliation of the two international valuation methodologies

The underlying assumptions that are used in the Vietnamese telecommunications example are:

US inflation	2.0%
Vietnamese inflation	8.0%

This implies an inflation differential between the US and Vietnam of 1.08/1.02 = 5.9%.

Let us also assume that the underlying WACCs are 9.65% in US dollar terms and 16.1% in Vietnamese dong terms, as in the earlier example.

Suppose the spot dong/US$ exchange rate is 10,000 dong/$. This information is summarized below:

Dong discount rate	16.1%
US $ discount rate	9.65%
Spot exchange rate (dong/US $)	10,000

In the Vietnamese telecommunications example we are interested in evaluating the value of the business to our US investor. We therefore need to assume some real cash flows to populate the comparison of the two international valuation methodologies. We assume real cash flows of 50,000m dong in each year for five years.

Cash flow periods	1	2	3	4	5
Cash flows (million)	50,000	50,000	50,000	50,000	50,000

We are now ready to compare the two techniques. Two additional variables are required to complete the calculations. These are:

- forecast dong/US$ exchange rates; and

- discount factors (derived from discount rates) denominated in Vietnamese dong and US dollars.

These figures are set out below. The forecast exchange rate is estimated by depreciating the spot dong/US$ exchange rate by 5.9% per annum (10,000 * 1.059 = 10,588 and so on), and the discount factors are calculated using the formula $(1 + r)^n$ where n is the number of years (cash flow period).

Cash flow periods	1	2	3	4	5
Forecast exchange rates	10,588	11,211	11,871	12,569	13,308

Cash flow periods	1	2	3	4	5
Dong discount factors (r = 16.1%)	1.16	1.35	1.56	1.82	2.11
US $ discount factors (r = 9.65%)	1.10	1.20	1.32	1.45	1.59

So, using Method one, we employ a US dollar set of discount factors to cash flows that have been converted into US dollars using the projected dong/US $ exchange rates. This arithmetic is set out below:

Method one   **Cash flows**

	1	2	3	4	5	
Real cash flow (million)	50,000	50,000	50,000	50,000	50,000	
Nominal dong cash flow (Using inflation of 8%)	54,000	58,320	62,986	68,024	73,466	
Nominal US $ cash flow (Using forecast e/rates)	5.10	5.20	5.31	5.41	5.52	Total NPV
US $ discount factors (r = 12.2%)	1.10	1.20	1.32	1.45	1.59	in US $
PV in US $ (millions)	4.65	4.33	4.02	3.74	3.48	20.23

Using Method two, we employ a Vietnamese dong set of discount factors to cash flows denominated in Vietnamese dong, and then convert the ensuing dong NPV into a US dollar NPV at the prevailing dong/US $ spot rate. This arithmetic is set out below:

Method two   **Cash flows**

	1	2	3	4	5	Total NPV in Vietnam dong
Real cash flow (million)	50,000	50,000	50,000	50,000	50,000	
Nominal dong cash flow (Using inflation of 8%)	54,000	58,320	62,986	68,024	73,466	202,294
Dong discount factors (r = 18.8%)	1.16	1.35	1.56	1.82	2.11	NPV in US $
PV in dong (million)	46,512	43,267	40,248	37,440	34,828	20.23

The US dollar NPV from both methods is the same, at $20.23 million. Thus, the two international valuation techniques can be reconciled, and practitioners should feel comfortable using either technique provided that appropriate assumptions are adopted.

Stock market listing changes and the cost of capital?

Having considered the key issues of international valuation, and having described some of the key principles of international finance, we can now address the related issue of whether it is possible to raise capital in one market more cheaply than in another. It is helpful to test this proposition by considering an example.

Our example is South African Breweries ('SAB') – now SABMiller – and the analysis is based early in 1999. We assume for the purposes of simplicity that we can ignore the impact of tax and that SAB can be considered to be a business with wholly South African interests (to make the country risk calculations that are necessary less complex). We also assume that the home CAPM approach (see Chapter 6) is the right methodological approach in the circumstances.

Using publicly available information, it is possible to compare equity and weighted average costs of capital in two different capital markets and see what this might mean for a company such as SAB looking at the options for its listing. In our example, we will consider London and Johannesburg listing options.

As a first stage, it is possible to calculate a cost of capital for SAB on the two exchanges; however, in order to do this using CAPM it is necessary to arrive at a beta for the operations (see Chapter 2). Since our sector is brewing, we look at quoted companies in the brewing sector. The asset betas are calculated from equity betas estimated with reference to their local listed market index. So, for example, the SAB asset beta has been calculated from SAB's equity beta as benchmarked against the Johannesburg stock exchange, while the Heineken asset beta has been calculated from Heineken's equity beta as benchmarked against the London Stock Exchange.

This analysis is summarized in Table 9.1.

TABLE 9.1
Brewing company asset betas

Exchange	Company	Asset β
Johannesburg	South African Breweries	0.78
London	Heineken	0.55
London	Carlsberg	0.73
London	Diageo Plc	0.95
London	Allied Domecq	0.81
London	Scottish & Newcastle	0.85
London	Bass	1.04

Could our South African business have an advantage in raising equity capital if it located in London? Could one of the London-listed companies gain an advantage through listing elsewhere?

On the face of it, Table 9.1 suggests that SAB's asset beta does not seem to be higher than those of the brewers listed in London – in fact it is lower, leading to suggestions of a lower cost of capital in Johannesburg. This is, however, only one part of the cost of capital and to answer the question properly it is necessary to consider the costs of capital for the SAB business if it were listed in either London or Johannesburg.

Johannesburg listing

The first issue to address is the equity cost of capital, particularly the relevant beta and the currency of the calculations was the business listed in Johannesburg:

■ Using the home CAPM approach the asset beta for the South African business is clearly best proxied by an asset beta that is linked to an equity beta calculated with reference to the Johannesburg index. Table 9.1 provides an asset beta of 0.78.

■ The relevant risk-free rate is the local South African risk-free rate denominated in Rand. This is based on a bond that has been issued by the South African government, and therefore the yield on this instrument will include a component for country risk. There is therefore no need for any additional country risk adjustment to the cost of capital. To do so would constitute double counting.

■ Moving on to the EMRP, as the Johannesburg Stock Exchange has been significantly more volatile than the London Stock Exchange, this might indicate a case for reflecting a higher EMRP for Johannesburg than for London (see Chapter 3). Since there is, however, no firm data to support this, no assumption has been made on this in the calculations summarized in Table 9.2.

■ And finally, the debt margin for the business is estimated as 1.5%.

Table 9.2 shows that these figures yield an overall South African WACC of 18.8% in nominal Rand terms. This is equivalent to a real WACC of 11.9% once the impact of South African inflation of 6.1% has been eliminated.

London listing

In terms of the same business listing in London, the calculations are largely similar but with a number of differences:

■ The risk-free rate is estimated based on a UK government bond yield. This is denominated in UK pounds sterling and does not include any premium for South African country risk (associated with the underlying business) because the UK government is not exposed to South African country risk.

■ A country risk premium of 4.5% for South Africa is therefore included separately in the calculations.

■ The asset beta is arguably different from *any* of those set out in Table 9.1. This is because the London businesses listed in Table 9.1 may have different business activities and characteristics to SAB. If this is so, an alternative – as highlighted in Chapter 6 – is to regress movements in SAB's Johannesburg share price against the London index. Although not shown in Table 9.1, the corresponding asset beta once the equity beta has been unlevered using this approach is 0.95.

■ The EMRP is 5% – as assumed previously.

■ The debt margin is 1.5%.

Table 9.2 shows that these figures yield an overall London WACC of 14.0%, denominated in UK pounds sterling. This is equivalent to a real WACC of 11.2%, once the impact of UK inflation of 2.5% has been eliminated.

If a dollar WACC is required for the London listed business, the only modification required to the London listed calculation denominated in UK pounds sterling is the substitution of a US dollar (for a UK sterling) risk-free rate, assuming that the US and UK governments are both free of country risk. For conversion into a real WACC, the final adjustment is based on US rather than UK inflation.

The figures that need to be compared are the real WACCs – the nominal WACCs are distorted by relative inflation in different countries. Not surprisingly, the final real WACCs are relatively close, but there are small discrepancies that can be exploited – for example, the analysis above suggests that SAB may have experienced a small reduction in its cost of capital on relisting (despite the higher asset beta adopted). This conclusion would have been reinforced further had we adopted a higher EMRP in South Africa (for reasons of illiquidity and non-integrated capital markets); and, in any case, from SAB's perspective, there would have been other benefits from relisting such as changing the shareholder base and the general perception of SAB as a business.

TABLE 9.2
Comparison of South African and London costs of capital

	South African perspective	London perspective	
Currency of:			
• cash flow reporting	Rand	Sterling	Dollar
• discount rate	Rand	Sterling	Dollar
Risk free rate (long-dated government bond)	14.5%	4.4%	5.0%
Estimated 1999 country risk premium (see Chapter 6)	–	4.5%	4.5%
Asset β (see Chapter 2)	0.78	0.95	0.95
Gearing (D/E)	35%	35%	35%
Equity β (see Chapter 2)	1.05	1.28	1.28
Illustrative EMRP (assuming no premium for emerging markets)	5.0%	5.0%	5.0%
Estimated cost of equity	19.8%	15.3%	15.9%
Debt margin	1.5%	1.5%	1.5%
Estimated cost of debt	16.0%	10.4%	11.0%
Nominal WACC	18.8%	14.0%	14.6%
Inflation	6.1% (RSA)	2.5% (UK)	3.0% (US)
Real WACC	11.9%	11.2%	11.3%

Key points from the chapter

This chapter has dealt with international financial relationships and valuation techniques in an international context. The key points are as follows:

■ It is possible to compare and assess nominal costs of capital in different countries, and provide insight and understanding into the nature and drivers of currency exposure and currency risk, based on certain principles underpinning international finance.

- We describe two basic international valuation techniques. Method one converts foreign currency cash flows into home currency values and applies a home cost of capital. Method two keeps the cash flows in foreign currency terms and applies a foreign currency discount rate.

- The two techniques will give the same NPV, providing that cash flows have not been adjusted for country risk, that Method one includes a proper country risk adjustment, and consistent assumptions are used for both approaches. This can be demonstrated arithmetically.

- It is unlikely that the real cost of capital will vary significantly between different markets for the same business. While small differences in the real cost of capital can exist, the biggest differences usually arise from nominal comparisons in different currencies. These can almost always be attributed to differences in relative inflation between two markets. Nevertheless, there may be practical reasons why a company may choose to change the country where its shares are listed.

Notes

1 PPP is one of five key international financial relationships upon which the methodologies and reconciliations in this chapter are based. The others are interest rate parity, the expectations theory of future exchange rates, the Fisher effect, and the international Fisher effect. Further details can be found at our website, *www.costofcapital.net*.

2 The international Fisher effect – see *www.costofcapital.net*.

3 In this example we use an additive CRP. A similar calculation could also be made using a multiplicative CRP. See Chapter 6 for further details.

10

PREMIA AND DISCOUNTS

Practitioners typically make quite large adjustments – as much as 50% or more – to valuations of businesses and investments to reflect factors such as the liquidity of the investment and whether the holding is a controlling stake. They do so because standard valuations techniques such as price-earnings multiples and net present value essentially rely on the use of comparator investments. Where the investment to be valued has different characteristics to the comparators, adjustments are needed to derive a satisfactory valuation.

The valuations literature provides guidance on the appropriate level of discounts/premia to be applied for the key comparability factors. For example, empirical studies typically suggest that a discount to the value of 20%–60% should be applied when valuing a minority stake in a closely held[1] (as opposed to publicly traded) investment, and that value should be increased by 10%–15% when a controlling stake in a company is being valued compared with a minority stake in a publicly traded investment.

Such factors generally affect valuations because they impact on expected cash flows, not because they alter the cost of capital. Thus it is in principle inappropriate to adjust the cost of capital to reflect them. In any case, the valuations literature does not offer any guidance on the appropriate size of any change in the discount rate. The effect of a given percentage increase in the cost of capital on a net present value calculation will vary depending on the timing profile of cash flows. Any valuation derived using an adjusted cost of capital may be unreliable.

Introduction

Those readers who have got this far may now well be feeling confident that there is a secure methodological basis for calculating the cost of capital, whether it be in a domestic or overseas environment. While the theory is not easy to master, it can be applied consistently and gives clear guidance in most situations. Earlier chapters have given practical examples to aid application.

When the cost of capital is calculated in a business environment, however, it is far removed from being a controlled, theoretical exercise. The figure is required to underpin some business decision – to carry out an investment appraisal, to value a potential acquisition, to set prices for a regulated industry, or to judge whether profitability is reasonable in an antitrust case.

In business life, therefore, the precise level of the cost of capital can have a real influence on such decisions, and hence on company profitability and managerial success or failure. With so much riding on the calculation it comes as no surprise to find that it is common for the cost of capital suggested by the normal application of the theory to be adjusted for application in a particular business context. Cost of capital practitioners will frequently find themselves under pressure from business decision takers to make such adjustments because of what are argued to be 'special circumstances.'

This chapter discusses both the theory and practice of the adjustments commonly applied in the commercial world. The adjustments covered in this chapter are:

- *Adjustment for the lack of marketability associated with a privately held business.* The basic rationale here is that the cost of capital should be higher for a privately owned company than for a publicly traded company because of the extra risk that shareholders face through not having a readily available liquid secondary market in which to trade their shares.

- *Adjustment for control.* Those who support this adjustment argue that having a controlling stake in a company justifies a lower cost of capital because it enables the shareholder to direct company policy.

- *Adjustment for small companies.* It has been observed that historically equity returns for small companies have been higher than the theory would suggest. Some analysts therefore argue that a premium should be added to the cost of equity when calculating the cost of capital for a small company.

- *Other miscellaneous adjustments.* These include a key-person adjustment (reflecting the additional risk which may be attributed to a business where there is considerable reliance on a particular manager or managers); an adjustment for investment appraisal optimism (increasing the cost of capital to compensate for the perception that cash flow forecasts are too optimistic); and an adjustment for companies which operate in a range of diverse areas (because of the risk that such companies will not be able to trade successfully in each of the different areas).

Valuations and adjustments

The title of this chapter refers to 'premia' and 'discounts' rather than adjustments to the cost of capital. This terminology is taken from the literature on valuation techniques, which is the source for the methodological underpinnings for most of the major adjustments that the cost of capital practitioner is likely to come across. In this literature the terms apply to valuations, not the cost of capital or discount rate. Hence, those engaged in company valuations talk about, for example, a 'premium for control' and a 'discount for nonmarketability.' These discounts and premia are generally derived from studies on share price behaviour and thus are relevant to the equity of a company.

Where adjustments to the cost of capital are considered for such factors the change is, of course, in the opposite direction – for example, if it were thought appropriate to adjust the discount rate to allow for the benefits of control, then the appropriate adjustment in the cost of capital would be downwards, thus implying a lower discount rate and a higher valuation.

Price-earnings multiples and valuations

The basic reason for valuation practitioners applying such premia and discounts is that they are often concerned with *comparability*. Many company valuations are performed on the basis of price-earnings multiples. If it is commonly found that consistently within a group of companies in a particular sector and a particular country the value of each company is the same multiple of its annual profits then this observation can be used to derive the value of another comparable company purely on the basis of its current earnings level.

Such rule of thumb valuations rely on choosing good comparator companies. Factors to consider in selecting these comparators include the activities undertaken by the companies, the degree of maturity, and market position. Typically, publicly traded companies are used as comparators because more information is readily available on such companies than is the case for privately held businesses.

Implications of using information on publicly traded comparators

Price-earnings ratios derived from analysis of publicly traded companies reflect the value attached by shareholders to such companies given the access they have to a liquid secondary market in which they can trade their shares (and hence convert their investment into cash). Typically, therefore, valuation practitioners make downward adjustments to a valuation of a minority interest in a privately held company if they have used information on publicly traded companies as the source for their price-earnings ratio analysis. The underlying principle is one of making adjustments in order to achieve a 'like for like' valuation.

Similarly, the share prices and market capitalization of publicly traded companies reflect the value attached to the companies by shareholders who generally hold only minority stakes in those companies. Valuation practitioners therefore recognize that they need to adjust their valuations upwards where they are considering a situation where an investor has (or will have) a controlling stake and the comparators used are for companies where no single investor or group of investors has control.

Consistency and comparability

Before going any further, the reader should consider the difference between enterprise value and equity value as explained in Chapter 8. A clear appreciation of the distinction is important when navigating the waters of premia and discounts.

Enterprise value is arrived at by capitalizing cash flows using a suitable multiple, or by discounting a series of cash flows by a suitable cost of capital. Enterprise value reflects the value of the enterprise before taking into account debt financing obligations, which are then deducted to arrive at the value of equity shares. On a company sale, the equity changes hands.

> Enterprise value reflects the value of the enterprise before taking into account debt financing obligations, which are then deducted to arrive at the value of equity shares.

The adjustments to value that we explore in this chapter are driven by observations on the behavior of equity prices. Therefore, generally speaking, application of the measures to enterprise value, or to the weighted average cost of capital that is used to discount enterprise cash flows, would be inconsistent with this. The cost of capital debate here is around equity value and whether the equity cost of capital should be adjusted.

The four levels of value associated with marketability/control

There are four levels of equity value defined by the degree of marketability and control enjoyed by the investor:

1. *Controlling marketable interest.* Generally a controlling marketable interest represents a majority interest in a publicly or freely traded business. The owner of such an interest has access to the public markets and the unrestricted ability to transfer or sell that interest. Furthermore, the ownership of a controlling stake gives the investor absolute control over the use of the company's cash resources. The valuations literature suggests that investors are willing to pay a premium for such control, on the basis that the cash flows or earnings of the business may be enhanced through synergies and other means.

2. *Controlling non-marketable interest.* This represents the valuation of a majority interest in a privately held business. While the business is valued as a whole, and the owner of the subject interest has the unrestricted ability to transfer or sell this interest, the investor does not have access to the public markets and therefore lacks a certain level of liquidity or marketability.

3. *Minority marketable interest.* This is a noncontrolling interest in a publicly or freely traded business. The owner of such an interest has access to the public markets, but has very limited control over both the operations and management of the business. An example of a minority marketable interest is the published share prices of freely traded common stock in a public, secondary market (e.g. the New York or London Stock Exchanges).

4. *Minority non-marketable interest.* This represents the lowest level of value. The owner of such an interest does not have access to the public markets and therefore attaches less value to the investment due to a lack of marketability. Furthermore, he or she also lacks control over the operations and management of the company.

Application to the cost of capital

Some analysts argue that the same logic should apply to cost of capital estimates derived using the capital asset pricing model (CAPM) to calculate the cost of equity. They argue that the basic information embodied in the CAPM relates to minority investments in liquid, publicly traded assets:

- The risk-free rate is derived from the market yields on *publicly traded* government securities.

- The equity market risk premium estimates the additional return that an investor requires over and above the available returns on risk-free assets in order to compensate for the extra risk associated with holding equities. This is usually estimated by examining historical returns on equities or forward looking techniques based on investor requirements. Either way, the calculation uses information based on investments in *publicly traded, minority* interests.

- Estimates of beta are derived from stock market information, again involving assets which are both *publicly traded* and (generally) held by *minority* shareholders.

Against this background, therefore, some argue that any figure for the cost of capital derived using the CAPM is applicable only to investments which are both liquid (publicly traded) and which do not give the investor a controlling stake. They argue that it is necessary to make adjustments to the cost of capital derived from the CAPM when the figure is to be applied in situations involving privately held investments or where the investor has control.

Value does not depend on the identity of the investor(s)

While this logic seems initially appealing it needs more careful consideration before it is used as the basis for adjusting cost of capital estimates based on a rigorous application of a model such as the CAPM. A particular concern is that it appears to contradict one of the important tenets of modern financial theory set out in Chapter 7 – that the value of an enterprise depends only on the cash flows it generates and the risks to which it exposes investors (in the sense of its contribution to non diversifiable risk). It does not depend on the identity of the investor(s).

In contrast, the implications of the analysis of the valuation practitioners is apparently that companies are inherently more valuable where:

- They are floated rather than privately held.
- They are controlled by one individual or connected group of shareholders rather than owned by a number of minority shareholders.

To understand how this might be the case, and yet not contradict the principles of financial theory, it is necessary to consider the underlying source of the additional value for the investor:

- *Either* the change in ownership, or increase in marketability, must affect the intrinsic value of the enterprise in some fundamental way.
- *Or* it must deal with only a part of the enterprise (i.e. be concerned with the effects of these factors on the division of enterprise value between different investors, rather than the impact on total enterprise value).

How having control increases value

Looking first at the issue of the control premium, it appears that the source of the extra value associated with control implicitly stems from both factors. The reason that individual investors are prepared to pay a premium to gain control of a company is usually given as being that this enables them to exercise full control over the company's activities. Implicitly this appears to suggest that:

- This will enable the investor with control to boost the effective overall enterprise value by improving management of the enterprise and achieving synergies with other businesses (the latter may or may not boost returns to other investors).

- To the extent that *overall* enterprise value is not affected, the individual with control is able to ensure that the enterprise's cash flows are distributed in a way which is favorable to themselves (i.e. minority shareholders may receive a disproportionately small share of the cash flows).

How marketability increases value

Turning to the possible reasons for there being extra value to the investor associated with marketability, this appears to be associated with an increase in overall enterprise value to the investor. An investment which is publicly traded can be sold easily. From the investor's point of view, therefore, the cash flows which the enterprise yields to the investor are affected by whether the company is floated or not – if it is privately held there is a possibility that the investment cannot be realized at a time required by the investor, resulting either in actual costs being incurred in finding a buyer for the investment, or in timing costs associated with the delay in finding a buyer, or both. In either case the expected cash flows associated with the investment are lower if it is privately held than if it is publicly traded.

There are also suggestions that a company whose shares are listed on a major exchange is subject to more rigorous reporting and corporate governance procedures and this therefore gives a greater measure of financial transparency to investors in reporting its cash flows/earnings. Also there may be a clearer dividend policy. It is not clear that this should increase the intrinsic value of an investment, but investors may attach some value to this feature in addition to the marketability issue dealt with above.

Implications for the cost of capital

There is therefore some rationale, consistent with modern financial theory, for making *valuation* adjustments to reflect the differences in marketability and control (further discussion of this is included in the following sections).

But does this mean that the equity cost of capital should be adjusted when calculating value using a discounted cash flow approach? In principle there are three possibilities for reflecting the differences in marketability and control, only one of which would involve adjusting the cost of capital. These are:

1. Calculate the present value of an investment or company using unadjusted cash flows and discount rates, then simply adjust the resulting value upwards or downwards by a percentage to reflect differences in control or marketability.

2. Adjust the cash flows for the estimated effects of the difference in control/marketability, and discount these adjusted cash flows using an unadjusted cost of capital.

3. Adjust the cost of capital to reflect differences in control/marketability, and use this adjusted discount rate in conjunction with unadjusted cash flows to calculate the present value.

Only the third approach would involve any change to the way in which the cost of capital is calculated.

Approach (1) – adjusting the present value once calculated

Taking the three approaches in turn, approach (1) involves adjusting the present value calculated using unadjusted cash flows in conjunction with the correct (unadjusted) cost of capital discount rate. The big advantage of doing this is that it is consistent with the approach used in the valuation literature. This means that the evidence compiled in this literature on the level of the adjustments can be directly applied. It is the practical solution usually adopted in the context of a valuation.

The drawback to this approach is that the cost of capital is often calculated and used in situations where there is no present value calculation to be adjusted. For example, the cost of capital may be compared with an IRR to determine whether a company, project, or subsidiary is earning (or is expected to earn) adequate returns.

Furthermore, where the cost of capital is being used as a discount rate in discounted cash flow analysis to appraise investment projects, the present value adjustment approach is less helpful because it precludes the possibility that, because of factors such as marketability or control, an otherwise value-enhancing investment opportunity will be value-destroying. If the project is calculated as having a positive present value before adjusting for lack of control/marketability discounts, it will still have a positive present value after such adjustments (albeit a greater or smaller present value).

Where there are constraints on capital spending, making such an adjustment would cause the project to be given a different priority, but it is clear in principle – and desirable in practice – that if considerations of control and marketability are real and material, the methodology by which they are dealt with should leave open the possibility that certain investments will be rejected outright as a result of such considerations, rather than simply be given a different priority.

Approach (2) – adjusting cash flows

Approach (2) involves adjusting the expected future cash flows associated with an investment or company for the estimated impact of the difference in control/marketability, and applying a standard cost of capital discount rate in order to calculate the appropriate present value. The advantage of this approach is that it best reflects the underlying reasons why value is affected by control and marketability factors.

For both the control premium and marketability discount the fundamental reason for the change in value is associated with the effects that the factors have on expected cash flows, not with a change in the rate of return required on investments in the enterprise. Gaining control of an enterprise or increasing the marketability of an investment affects the level and timing of the cash flows available to the total enterprise and the individual shareholder respectively. It is therefore legitimate that the value associated with the investment should change to reflect this, and adjusting the cash flows used to derive the present value is the most appropriate way of calculating this accurately in the case of the control premium. The implication of this is that if a valuation has been carried out using cash flows that have already been estimated to reflect the synergies of an acquisition, to add a full control premium would probably be double counting. For the marketability discount, data on the effect of investor perceptions is the only solution widely used by practitioners.

> Gaining control of an enterprise or increasing the marketability of an investment affects the level and timing of the cash flows available to the total enterprise and the individual shareholder respectively. It is therefore legitimate that the value associated with the investment should change to reflect this, and adjusting the cash flows used to derive the present value is the most appropriate way of calculating this accurately in the case of the control premium.

Note that, in contrast to approach (1), approach (2) allows for the possibility that an investment could be evaluated as being value enhancing (positive NPV) where the investor would have control and/or a marketable interest, but value destroying (negative NPV) where the investor would not have control and/or a non-marketable interest. This is a desirable property for the appraisal methodology.

A drawback is that the valuations literature tends to focus on the empirical evidence regarding the end result, i.e. the equity value, in terms of changes in value for control and marketability. It therefore gives much clearer guidance on how to adjust the final present value rather than how to adjust the underlying cash flows attributable to an investment.

Approach (3) – adjusting the cost of capital discount rate

So neither of the first two approaches is ideal. Approach (1) is practical to implement but is arguably flawed as an approach to investment appraisal as it cannot result in control or marketability issues changing an investor's view of whether an investment adds or subtracts value. Approach (2) is theoretically preferable, but difficult to implement practically.

Thus, while *it is inappropriate from a theoretical perspective* to alter the cost of capital to reflect factors such as control and marketability, because neither of the two alternatives are entirely satisfactory, for practical reasons there is a tendency for some businesses to contemplate changing the cost of capital to reflect control/marketability factors when valuing acquisitions or undertaking investment project appraisal.

While this is understandable, such a policy of altering the cost of capital should be undertaken with extreme caution. Because there is no theoretical underpinning to such an adjustment, it is impossible to give firm guidance on the amount by which the cost of capital should be adjusted.

Indeed, to do so, could lead to absurd results. Example 10.1 gives an example of this. It demonstrates that the implicit reduction required in the cost of equity to adjust for a premium for control could take the overall cost of equity below the risk-free rate of return, an absurd result.

Example 10.1 Dangers in adjusting the cost of equity to reflect control

Suppose a company is expected to generate cash flows for its equity investors of $10 per annum to perpetuity. The value of the equity on a marketable, noncontrolling share basis is calculated using the standard CAPM analysis:

Risk-free rate	5%
Equity market risk premium	4%

▶

Equity beta	0.5
Cost of equity	7%
Annual cash flow	$10
Value of equity	$142.86

Given these assumptions, the value of equity is $142.86.

Now consider the valuation of the same company on a controlling share basis. Suppose it is believed that there is a 50% premium for control, i.e. if all of the enterprise's equity is owned by one individual it will be worth 50% more than when it is spread among a number of minority shareholders. On this assumption, the equity of this company is worth $142.86 when spread among minority equity investors, but it rises to $214.29 when it is owned by a single investor.

From this it is possible to infer the appropriate adjustment to the cost of equity discount rate needed in order to adjust for the premium placed on control. The appropriate cost of equity is the rate which values an annual cash flow of $10 in perpetuity at $214.29:

$$10/r = 214.29$$
$$\text{i.e. } r = 4.67\%$$

It turns out that the adjustment to the cost of equity required to reflect the control premium changes it from 7% (derived from the CAPM) to 4.67%. This is clearly absurd, as the cost of equity thus derived is now below the risk-free rate of 5%.

While the figures in Example 10.1 are exaggerated (there is little evidence to support such a large control premium, for example – see below) it demonstrates the fundamental objection to altering the cost of capital. In strict terms the appropriate response to such adjustments is to alter the expected cash flows and not the cost of capital/equity.

Example 10.2 further emphasizes the difficulty of making cost of capital/equity discount rate adjustments in the absence of any theoretical or empirical basis for doing so.

Example 10.2 Difficulties in changing the discount rate to reflect marketability

Suppose a company is contemplating an equity investment in a privately held business. Using standard CAPM methodology it calculates that, given the risk characteristics of the business, the cost of equity is 10%. However, it notes that the valuations literature typically suggests a discount of around 50% to value for a privately held company compared with a publicly traded one (see below). The investment appraisers therefore decide to adjust the cost of equity upwards to reflect the disadvantages associated with the lack of marketability.

Suppose that the investment opportunity under consideration has very simple cash flows. There is an initial outlay of $1,000 in the first period, followed by nine periods of positive cash flow of $271 per period. Using an unadjusted cost of equity of 10% as the discount rate, the NPV of the project is $510 (visit our website at *www.costofcapital.net* for details of all these calculations).

If the cost of equity is now increased by 50%, to 15%, to reflect the fact that this is a closely held investment, the NPV falls to $255, half the previous level. Thus, the value of the investment to the company is indeed reduced by 50%, just as the valuations literature suggests.

Does this imply that it is always appropriate to increase the discount rate by 50%? The answer is no. Suppose that instead of generating cash at $271 per period in periods 2 to 10 the investment generated $400 per period. Increasing the discount rate from 10% to 15% would then reduce the NPV from $1,185 to $790, a reduction in value of not one half (as suggested by the empirical evidence) but one third.

Furthermore, if the cash flows in periods 2 to 10 were $200 per period then increasing the discount rate from 10% to 15% would result in a *positive* NPV of $138 becoming a *negative* NPV of $40, a reduction in value of around 130%. As a result of adjusting the discount rate the investment would no longer appear viable, which might or might not be the appropriate conclusion. This emphasizes the need to exercise caution in applying the empirical findings of valuations experts through adjustments to the cost of capital: the arithmetic implications are not clear.

Implications

Overall therefore the cost of capital practitioner needs to be alert to premia and discounts. These can have a genuine influence on the value of investments, although those who urge adjustments to be made for them may not have thought through clearly the ways in which they impact on value.

Close analysis suggests that in general the appropriate reaction to these adjustments is probably to alter the expected cash flows used in any discounted cash flow modeling exercise. Failing this, an adjustment to the final present value calculated may be a reasonable compromise, although it has drawbacks in project appraisal terms. Adjusting the cost of capital is not the most theoretically robust response, and no practical guidance exists on the scale of adjustment that should be made.

While, therefore, premia and discounts do not generally have an impact on the calculation of the cost of capital, and to this extent are not relevant to this book, they are intimately related to the use of the cost of capital in DCF applications. The remainder of this chapter discusses some of the most common premia and discounts to value which the authors have come across when applying the cost of capital in business situations. These are:

- discount for lack of marketability;
- premium for control;
- discount for small companies;
- other miscellaneous adjustments.

Discounts for lack of marketability

The first adjustment we shall consider is that for the lack of marketability, or liquidity, of an investment. While an equity investment in a publicly traded company is typically highly liquid (the stocks can be sold almost instantaneously at a quoted price) this is not the case for an investment in a closely held company. Such investments are worth less as a result, because it may take longer to sell the asset, it may need to be sold at a discount, or costs may be incurred in finding a willing buyer.

Clear evidence that investors value liquidity is all around us:

- Banks offer higher rates to savers for money committed for a longer period.
- US government bonds that are newly issued ('on-the-run') trade at a slightly higher price than comparable established bonds, due to their extra liquidity.

The liquidity of different types of investment

There are three key factors which influence the extent of marketability of an investment:

1. Whether the asset is privately (closely) held, or publicly traded.

2. Whether there are restrictions on the sale of the investment.

3. Whether the market for the investment is thin or active.

Figure 10.1 sets out a hierarchy for the liquidity of different types of investments based on these three criteria.

FIGURE 10.1
Marketability of different types of investment

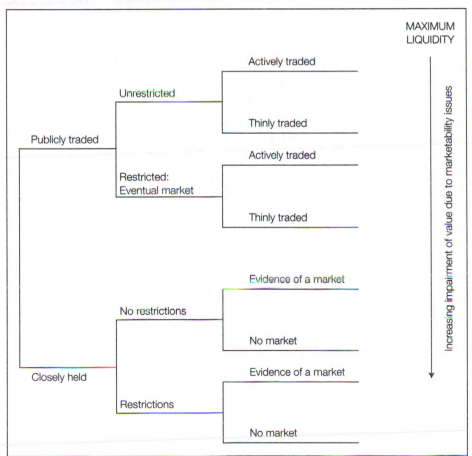

Factors influencing the illiquidity discount

Figure 10.1 shows that the most liquid type of investment is one in an unrestricted, publicly traded stock, traded on an active market. An example would be the purchase of a minority holding of the common stock of a company traded on a well-established and liquid stock market such as the New York Stock Exchange (NYSE) or London Stock Exchange (LSE).

If the value of such an investment is used to benchmark the value of an investment where liquidity is impaired (e.g. because of thin trading on the stock exchange concerned, because of restrictions on the sale of the stock, or because the stock is privately held) then it is necessary to make adjustments to value to reflect this lower level of liquidity. The size of this discount depends on a range of factors. These include the following:

- The general commercial situation facing the company is important. Illiquidity implies that an investor may be constrained as to when and how they dispose of the investment. If the company in which the stock is held is itself risky, this compounds the problems of illiquidity because it increases the risk that the investment will be disposed of at an unfavorable price.

- The dividend policy of the closely held company is important. If a company pays no or low dividends this increases the reliance on appreciation in the stock price for returns. In these circumstances the difficulty in realizing the appreciation in price is a real issue.

- The amount of control that a shareholding gives (e.g. to appoint management, acquire or liquidate assets, declare dividends, or determine business policy) has an effect on the disadvantages of illiquidity. During any period of delay in disposing of the shares it is valuable for the shareholder to have influence over company policy.

- The disadvantages of illiquidity may be affected by any provisions restricting the transferability of shares (e.g. a right of first refusal option of other owners) and by any redemption policy (e.g. an option to sell the interest back to the entity at a specified price).

- If there is a satisfactory history of transactions in the closely held shares, this reduces the disadvantages of illiquidity.

- The better the prospects for achieving an initial public offering (IPO), and the lower the cost of achieving this, the less the discount for lack of marketability.

Quantifying the discount for illiquidity

There have been numerous studies which have attempted to estimate the reduction in value as a result of an investment being illiquid. These have looked at evidence relating to the three key sources of the impairment to value identified above: first, studies examining discounts in the value of restricted stock; second, studies examining the lower value attributed to closely held as opposed to publicly traded stock; and, finally, studies relating to discounts resulting from thin trading.

> There have been numerous studies which have attempted to estimate the reduction in value as a result of an investment being illiquid.

Discounts for restricted shares

The analysis of the prices of restricted shares gives a direct valuation of illiquidity. Restricted stock issued by a public company is identical in all respects to its counterpart freely traded stock with the exception that it is restricted from trading on the open market for a certain period. Such restricted, or 'letter,' stock is generally issued when a company is making an acquisition or raising capital, because of the time and costs associated with registering the new stock with the Securities and Exchange Commission (SEC).

The reduction in value associated with restricted stock has been specifically recognized by the SEC:

> restricted securities are often purchased at a discount, frequently substantial, from the market price of outstanding unrestricted securities of the same class. This reflects the fact that securities which can not be readily sold at the public market are less valuable than securities which can be sold, and also the fact that by the direct sale of restricted securities, sellers avoid the expense, time and public exposure which registration entails.[2]

Many studies have been conducted on the difference in value between restricted trades and public market trades in the US on the same date. For trades which took place before 1990 the studies came up with remarkably similar results, suggesting an average discount in value for restricted stock of around 30%–35%. Since 1990 a loosening of the rules relating to restricted stocks in the US appears to have reduced the size of the average discount. Later studies suggest the discount has fallen to 20%–30%, and possibly even as low as 15% or less based on the latest rules (although the evidence since the latest rule change is scant).

Estimating the discount for closely held stock

It seems clear that there should be a bigger illiquidity discount associated with a closely held stock than with restricted stock. In many cases, purchasers of restricted stock secure rights to register the stock for sale in the existing public market at some future date. By contrast, a purchaser of closely held stock has no established market in which he or she can eventually trade the stock.

Studies seeking to estimate the discount in value for closely held stock have concentrated on the difference in the transaction prices between IPOs and private transactions conducted immediately before an IPO.

The size of the illiquidity discount for closely held investments depends on whether the investment represents a majority or minority interest. For a majority interest there is still some discount; courts in the US have allowed discounts for lack of marketability on controlling interests from as low as 3% to as high as 33%. For minority interests the potential size of the discount is likely to be larger – perhaps as high as 60%. However, there is a wide range for this discount, and its level depends on the particular circumstances affecting the marketability of the minority interest (for example, whether there is a near or medium term prospect of a sale, whether dividends are paid, whether there is any ownership abuse etc.). A range of 20%–60% is typically applied, although lower figures are possible where circumstances favor the minority shareholder.

Evidence on discounts for thin trading

Lucinda Spicer and Paul Ginocchio of PricewaterhouseCoopers carried out a UK study in 1997 that examined the effects on stock value of the illiquidity of the market in which a company's stocks are traded.

Specifically they looked at the three UK markets in which shares are publicly traded. They ranked the shares listed on these markets according to turnover percentage (total trading activity by value divided by current market capitalization) and concluded that of the three markets the London Stock Exchange ('LSE') was by far the most liquid, with the Alternative Investment Market ('AIM') the next most liquid, and the Ofex market being least liquid. The PwC team examined companies which switched exchanges, and looked at the effect on share price of the announcement of the switch. It found no evidence of a discount for illiquidity between the LSE and the AIM, but evidence of a 10% discount on value for companies quoted on the Ofex compared with the other two markets.

Discounting enterprise or equity value?

In principle value discounts for lack of marketability could affect the enterprise value of a business (i.e. the value of both debt and equity) since all investors will attach less value to investments which are illiquid. However, in practice all the evidence presented by valuation practitioners on these discounts apply to share values, and hence the discounts should be applied to the value of equity rather than the enterprise value.

Conclusions on discounts for lack of marketability

Overall, therefore, the best empirical evidence suggests that:

- By comparison with the benchmark of a fully liquid investment in the shares of a company quoted on a highly liquid public market such as the NYSE or LSE, the biggest reduction in value for lack of liquidity is associated with holding a minority stake in a closely held company. Empirical studies suggest a typical reduction in value of 20%–60%.

- The value is also reduced, but by a lesser amount, if the investment takes the form of a shareholding in a publicly quoted company, but where restrictions are placed on disposal of the shares. Empirical studies suggest a reduction in value of about 15%–35% in such situations in the US, depending on the date considered.

- Value is reduced even where the stock is publicly quoted and freely tradable, if there is a lack of liquidity in the market. One study of this suggests a discount in value of around 10%, although this figure is likely to depend on the market in question.

Control premium

It is generally recognized by valuation practitioners that an investment which gives an investor control of a business is worth more than a minority stake. In valuation terms, there is thus a control premium, or its inverse, a minority discount. In the US this has been formally recognized by the US Internal Revenue Service in Revenue Ruling 59–60, which states that:

> control of a corporation, either actual or in effect, representing as it does an added element of value, may justify a higher value for a specific block of stock.

Similarly, the US Tax Court, in *Ward* v *Commissioner* (87 TC 78, 105; 1986) stated that:

the minority discount is recognized because the holder of a minority interest lacks control over the corporate policy, cannot direct the payment of dividends, and cannot compel the sale or liquidation of the assets.

The sources of extra value in control

This latter quotation summarizes neatly what most valuation practitioners appear to mean when they say there is a premium for control. The additional value conferred on the individual with a controlling stake stems from two sources:

- Control over the distribution of cash generated by the enterprise. An individual with a controlling stake can have a direct influence on such matters as the timing and level of dividends, the payment of director salaries, and the liquidation of the business. Depending on precise legal rights, a minority shareholder in a private company faces difficulties in realizing a fair return on her/his investment. Often there will be restrictions on the sale of minority shares.

- There is an effect on the actual amount of cash generated by the enterprise. This appears to assume that investors place a premium on control, either because they will be able to direct policy and hence ensure that the enterprise is well-managed, or they will be able to direct the company's policy in a way which will enhance value to them (e.g. by accessing synergies with other businesses in which they have a shareholding, or through controlling what would otherwise be a competing business).

Both factors undermine the fundamental principle of separation of ownership and management. They suggest that shareholders will attach value to achieving direct control of a business:

- *Either* because they do not trust the managers to maximize value.

- *Or* because they want to run the business in such a way so as not necessarily to maximize the actual individual business value, but to maximize the total value of all the businesses in which they have an interest.

- *Or* because they want to operate the business in order to ensure a disproportionate flow of cash to themselves rather than other shareholders.

Irrationality and the valuation of the control premium

There is clearly some credence in these factors, particularly as they apply to privately held companies. However, it also seems clear that some of the additional value attached to control stems more from human nature rather than disinterested analysis of value creation. The view that gaining control adds value because it confers rights to direct a business often reflects an arrogant assumption that the investor is better able to manage the business than anyone else. This may or may not be the case.

In considering whether such assumptions of increased value from control are realistic it needs to be borne in mind that while a public company may be owned by millions of investors, each with a small minority stake, these investors appoint a single set of managers to run the company on their behalf. And as we saw in Chapter 7, using realistic assumptions about individuals' preferences and how markets work, these managers can be set a clear objective – to maximize present value. So a minority held company is controlled by a single management team which should be incentivized to maximize the value of the company. Care needs to be exercised before increasing value for control given this.

> The view that gaining control adds value because it confers rights to direct a business often reflects an arrogant assumption that the investor is better able to manage the business than anyone else. This may or may not be the case.

Furthermore, the acquisition of controlling rights often takes on the form of a hunt, particularly if there is a competitive or hostile takeover situation. In these circumstances managers and investors can let their emotions run away with them, leading to a desire to gain control at any cost. The final price paid to acquire the business can be out of all proportion to the real cash flow advantages generated; the successful bidder is the one that is prepared to pay more than anyone else to acquire the company and is doomed to receive an inadequate return on its investment (the 'winner's curse').

Evidence on the size of the control premium

Typically estimates of the size of the control premium are based on data relating to the analysis of premia paid by companies which acquire majority stakes in other companies and therefore control. One of the most frequently cited sources of information is Mergerstat/Shannon Pratt's Control Premium Study™ (see *www.BVResources.com*). Of course, a problem with such information is that it can only give an indication of the level of additional payments actually made to gain control of companies. It does not indicate the commercial logic behind making such payments.

As we saw earlier, if in carrying out a valuation you have reason to believe that securing control will boost value then it is preferable, if possible, to analyze

> if in carrying out a valuation you have reason to believe that securing control will boost value then it is preferable, if possible, to analyze the source of this increased value objectively and model it explicitly in cash flows rather than making a simple adjustment to value after the present value has been calculated.

the source of this increased value objectively and model it explicitly in cash flows rather than making a simple adjustment to value after the present value has been calculated. Such a methodology will focus attention on the reasons why it is anticipated that gaining control will enhance value.

Nevertheless, the alternative approach often used by valuation practitioners is simply to calculate a value in the standard way (either by discounted cash flow analysis or some other technique such as price-earnings multiples) and then adjust the resulting valuation. A discounted cash flow valuation carried out using a cost of capital applied to the free cash flows of a business gives the appropriate value for a publicly traded company where control is being exerted over the business, but no shareholder or group of shareholders has strategic control giving them access to synergies. The valuations literature argues that this valuation needs to be adjusted where either:

- a strategic controlling stake giving access to synergies is being valued; or
- a minority stake in a publicly traded company is being valued.

Where a strategic controlling stake is being valued the size of the control premium will depend on the specific circumstances of the situation, and in particular the value of the synergies resulting from having strategic control. Sources such as the Mergerstat/Shannon Pratt study give information on the typical premia paid in the market where investors acquire control. Such bid premia can be as much as 40% above the value of a marketable minority stake. Where a minority stake in a publicly traded company is being valued, the general guidance of the valuations literature is that a reasonable guideline minority interest discount (i.e. reduction in value) is between 10% and 15%. However, it is important to consider each case on its own merits and explicitly consider the sources of additional value and evidence available from market data.

The benefits of control depend on minority shareholder rights

To adjust the valuation for the effects of a minority stake in a privately held company it is necessary to understand what rights the shareholder enjoys. Some of the most important of these are set out in Table 10.1.

Consideration also needs to be given to the track record (if any) of the business – for example, has there been any history of the controlling interest siphoning off distributable cash flow? Recognition should also be paid to the overall balance of shareholdings. For example, a shareholding of less than 50% can still effectively confer control if no other shareholding is as large. Furthermore, even a quite small shareholding may have importance if it gives the holder potential to act as a 'swing voter' on issues of company policy. When examining privately held companies it is often important to understand the relationships between individual shareholders, e.g. some shareholders may be members of the same family, and their holdings may effectively be combined for voting purposes.

TABLE 10.1
Factors affecting discount for lack of control

Election of directors
Ability to select management
Control over dividend policy
Ability to establish compensation and benefits
Ability to set corporate strategies
Ability to acquire or liquidate the assets
Control to compel the sale of the company
Ability to liquidate, dissolve, or recapitalize the company
Establish buy/sell agreements
Revise the articles of incorporation and bylaws
Restrictions on an initial public offering
Ability to affect future earnings
Control efforts for growth potential

As always the general guidance holds – the best approach is to understand the implications of the size and structure of the shareholding arrangements for company cash flows and the allocation of those cash flows between shareholders, and to adjust the cash flows used in the discounted cash flow model as appropriate in order to reach the correct valuation.

Discounting enterprise or equity value?

It is clear that in principle if there are benefits in controlling a business that should boost the entire value of the enterprise. The evidence on the size of the control premium, however, is based primarily on studies of differences in equity values so generally it is at this level in the valuation that the control premium is applied.

Small company discount

In contrast to the previous issues in this chapter, this discount is accepted by some as being a factor that could legitimately change the cost of equity.

Much attention has been paid by financial economists to the possibility that company size is an important determinant of the cost of capital, (see, for example, the Fama-French Three Factor Model described in Chapter 4). A large number of studies of historical data have shown that the returns actually achieved by those investing in small companies have been higher than would be implied by the application of standard CAPM analysis. The fact that these returns have not been driven down through arbitrage to the levels suggested by the CAPM methodology suggests that investors require additional returns for the risks of investing in small companies.

Operational leverage

It must be emphasized that in practice the CAPM framework generally suggests that the required returns on investment in small companies are higher than for their larger counterparts. Empirical analysis of the betas of groups of companies of different sizes shows that they are higher for small companies. One likely explanation for this is that a small company will probably be exposed to a greater degree of *operational leverage*. This occurs where the proportion of costs which are fixed is high in relation to turnover, so that free cash flow fluctuates by a large proportion as revenue moves up and down with the state of the economy. Example 10.3 illustrates how this happens with a simple numerical example.

Example 10.3 How small companies are exposed to more operational leverage

Consider two firms operating in the same industry over a 12-year period. Each has the same cost structure, incurring fixed costs of $300 per annum and variable costs of $5 per unit of output. However, in a year of normal demand assume that Firm A produces 100 units of output while Firm B is smaller, producing only 80 units of output. Assume that the product they both produce sells at a price of $10 per unit. This implies that in a year of normal demand the revenue, costs, and cash flow for our two companies are as follows:

	Firm A	Firm B
Output	100	80
Price	10	10
Revenue	1,000	800
Fixed costs	300	300
Variable costs	500	400
Total costs	800	700
Cash flow	200	100

Assuming a discount rate of 10%, the 12-year value of Firm A is $1,362.74, while that for Firm B is half this amount at $681.37.

Now consider the impact on value of a fluctuation in demand of 20% in either direction. The table below gives the impact on Firm A and Firm B of an increase in demand of 20%.

	Firm A	Firm B
Output	120	96
Price	10	10
Revenue	1,200	960
Fixed costs	300	300
Variable costs	600	480
Total costs	900	780
Cash flow	300	180

When demand is 20% higher Firm A generates 50% more cash – $300 per annum rather than $200 per annum. Its NPV therefore also rises by 50% to $2,044.11. Firm B, on the other hand, now generates 80% more cash ($180 compared with $100 per annum), and its value has therefore increased by 80%, to $1,226.46. Similarly, a 20% reduction in demand would result in a 50% fall in the value of Firm A but an 80% fall in the value of Firm B.

So for the same change in basic economic conditions there is a disproportionately larger fluctuation in the value of an investment in Firm B than Firm A. This is because Firm B is smaller. Because it produces less output, and therefore has a smaller revenue base than Firm A, fixed costs represent a larger proportion of its total revenue. This means that net revenue – cash flow – is smaller and so any given absolute change in this revenue stream represents a bigger proportionate change.

There are generally fixed costs associated with any form of business, and these contribute to small businesses having more fluctuations in earnings. This is termed operational leverage. The financial effects of such fixed costs incurred for operational reasons are similar to the effects of increasing debt (financial leverage).

> There are generally fixed costs associated with any form of business, and these contribute to small businesses having more fluctuations in earnings. This is termed operational leverage.

The problem is that the increase in the cost of equity explained by higher betas due to such factors is insufficient to explain the overall high level of returns historically achieved by small companies. This has led some commentators to suggest that there are other risks associated with investing in small companies which the standard CAPM systematic risk framework does not pick up.

Some suggested reasons for higher returns

In some of the valuations literature the explanation for the existence of extra risks associated with small companies relies on arguments such as the fact that small companies are often privately held; that they are more likely to rely on individual managers for their success; or that investors find it difficult to obtain information in order to help them make judgments about the companies.

Certainly all of these factors add to risk (although it should be noted that these risks are not unique to small companies, albeit they are often more relevant in analysis of small companies). The problem with this explanation is that all of these risks are in principle diversifiable. Ex-ante, they certainly affect the investor's view of the expected cash flows, but they should not affect the required return on the investment for an individual with a well-diversified portfolio. Investments which ex-ante do offer an additional return for such factors should not exist, because they should attract an excess number of investors, driving expected returns back down to the appropriate risk-related level.

Financial distress and 'survivor bias'

This line of thought suggests one possible explanation for the observed high returns on small companies – 'survivor bias.' As it is undoubtedly the case that the cash flows associated with small companies are subject to relatively high degrees of risks (both systematic and diversifiable), and that their size makes them vulnerable to bankruptcy in the event of an adverse performance, it is clear that there will be a large number of small companies which fail. Historical measurements of small company profitability, therefore, will be biased upwards as they will include only those companies which continue to operate. A better measure of overall returns on small companies would include the negative returns of those which exit the market.

Against this background, one argument would be that the high level of observed ex-post returns on small companies does not necessarily indicate that investors require ex-ante higher returns on such companies – they simply demonstrate that such companies are subject to a great deal of diversifiable risk which means that an analysis of surviving companies will inevitably show that they make high returns (to offset the negative returns on those companies which fail).

Financial distress and 'shadow' investment

A second way of looking at these additional risks of financial distress suggests that they do imply that there is a genuine investor requirement for higher returns on small companies. In this approach, investors implicitly regard their investment as being larger than it actually appears (because they factor in implicitly the 'shadow' cost of possible expenditure on dealing with financial distress) so that observed returns on actual investments overstate the effective returns on perceived total investment. From this perspective, the investor does require an additional return on small companies.

This explanation accords with evidence found by some analysts that additional risk premia for small companies are much more important in times of economic hardship. It is at this stage of the economic cycle that the risks of financial distress for small companies are highest.

Finally, two other possible explanations also imply that investors genuinely do require higher returns on investments in small companies. It is sometimes suggested that investors need to achieve higher returns in order to compensate them for the lower liquidity and higher transaction costs associated with investing in small companies.

Reconciling the two approaches

The first approach ('survivor bias') implies that whilst observed historical returns may have been higher for small companies, this does not necessarily imply that ex ante investors required higher returns. The second approach suggests that there are additional 'shadow' costs associated with investing in small companies (associated with the greater likelihood of financial distress, with illiquidity and with transactions costs) and that as a result investors do require the prospect of a higher return ex ante.

The latter approach would suggest that the forward looking cost of equity derived from the CAPM framework should be adjusted upwards in the case of a small company. However, if this approach is taken, this is only appropriate if the expected costs of possible financial distress, illiquidity or transaction costs are not taken into account in the cash flows, and the size of the investment is not adjusted for these 'shadow' costs.

Evidence on the small company risk premium

To determine what the level of such a premium should be it is necessary to consider empirical studies of past evidence on returns on small companies. One such study was conducted in 1999 by Roger Grabowski and David King[3], who were then working for PricewaterhouseCoopers. They looked at evidence on historical returns over the period 1963 to 1998. They divided up the companies on the New York Stock Exchange into 25 equally sized portfolios based on the eight different measures of company size set out in Table 10.2.

TABLE 10.2
Company size measures in Grabowski/King study

Market value of common equity

Book value of common equity

Five-year average net income

Market value of invested capital

Total assets

Five-year average EBITDA

Sales

Number of employees

Having created the 25 portfolios for the NYSE companies Grabowski and King then added companies from the American Stock Exchange and the NASDAQ National Market System (thereby greatly increasing the number of small companies in the survey).

In an attempt to eliminate some of the 'survivor bias' discussed above, the survey imputed a 30% loss in the month of delisting for those companies which were recorded as delisting for performance reasons (e.g. due to bankruptcy or insufficient capital). This figure was based on an estimate produced by Tyler Shumway in March 1997.

Table 10.3 sets out the results based on ranking companies by market value of equity.

TABLE 10.3
Evidence on the small company premium – ranked by market capitalization

Companies ranked by market value of equity
Historical equity risk premium: average since 1963
Data for year ending December 31 1998

Portfolio rank by size	Average mkt value ($m)	Log of average mkt value	Number as of 1998	Beta annual since '63	Standard deviation of returns	Geometric average return	Arithmetic average return	Arithmetic equity risk premium	Smoothed average equity risk premium	Average debt/ MVIC
1	64,877	4.81	49	0.91	15.86%	12.99%	14.17%	6.61%	3.04%	17.66%
2	16,054	4.21	49	0.94	15.98%	11.32%	12.48%	4.92%	4.94%	23.90%
3	10,011	4.00	48	0.89	15.16%	10.58%	11.64%	4.08%	5.58%	26.63%
4	7,417	3.87	43	0.98	16.80%	12.82%	14.07%	6.51%	5.98%	27.06%
5	5,357	3.73	47	0.99	17.37%	11.18%	12.54%	4.98%	6.43%	27.99%
6	4,342	3.64	52	0.99	17.39%	12.55%	13.89%	6.33%	6.71%	28.72%
7	3,440	3.54	51	0.94	16.79%	12.99%	14.22%	6.66%	7.03%	27.40%
8	2,816	3.45	54	1.00	18.04%	13.44%	14.85%	7.29%	7.30%	27.33%
9	2,485	3.40	51	1.03	19.01%	12.99%	13.95%	6.39%	7.47%	26.09%
10	2,072	3.32	56	1.19	20.68%	13.31%	15.17%	7.61%	7.71%	25.83%
11	1,733	3.24	56	1.11	20.05%	13.78%	15.52%	7.96%	7.96%	25.45%
12	1,431	3.16	52	1.05	18.76%	14.84%	16.35%	8.79%	8.21%	27.20%
13	1,190	3.08	70	1.15	21.66%	12.89%	14.99%	7.43%	8.46%	28.02%
14	1,015	3.01	70	1.05	19.95%	14.49%	16.20%	8.64%	8.68%	28.19%
15	875	2.94	73	1.14	20.74%	14.40%	16.38%	8.82%	8.88%	28.21%
16	753	2.88	77	1.19	22.11%	14.48%	16.66%	9.10%	9.09%	26.61%
17	616	2.79	83	1.22	23.10%	13.54%	15.85%	8.29%	9.36%	27.09%
18	510	2.71	72	1.17	23.83%	14.97%	17.35%	9.79%	9.61%	27.60%
19	448	2.65	79	1.28	24.71%	14.46%	17.17%	9.61%	9.79%	28.47%
20	386	2.59	85	1.23	24.94%	13.69%	16.40%	8.84%	9.99%	28.12%
21	305	2.48	95	1.21	24.00%	15.80%	18.20%	10.64%	10.31%	28.49%
22	234	2.37	109	1.26	25.78%	14.98%	17.83%	10.27%	10.67%	30.11%
23	179	2.25	130	1.31	26.24%	16.41%	19.32%	11.76%	11.03%	28.90%
24	124	2.09	223	1.31	26.75%	16.57%	19.61%	12.05%	11.53%	30.33%
25	44	1.64	588	1.39	33.24%	18.63%	22.88%	15.32%	12.93%	31.73%
Large stocks (Ibbotson SBBI data)						12.59%	13.72%	6.16%		
Small stocks (Ibbotson SBBI data)						14.99%	17.77%	10.21%		
Long-term Treasury income (Ibbotson SBBI data)						7.53%	7.56%			

Source: Grabowski and King, 1999.

Exhibit A

Equity Risk Premium Study: Data through December 31 1998
Data smoothing with regression analysis
Dependent variable: average premium
Independent variable: log or average market value of equity

Regression output	
Constant	18.063%
Std err of Y est	1.131%
R squared	80%
No. of observations	25
Degrees of freedom	23
X coefficient(s)	–3.121%
Std err of coef.	0.323%
t-Statistic	–9.67

Smoothed premium = 18.063% – 3.121% * Log (Market value)

Smoothed premium vs. unadjusted average

(Equity premium vs. Log of average market value of equity)

Table 10.3 shows that in general the level of the equity beta is inversely related to the size of the company. For example, the portfolio containing the companies with the largest market capitalization (portfolio 1 with an average equity market value of equity of $64.9 billion in the year ending December 31 1998) had an average equity beta over the period 1963–98 of 0.91. Portfolio 25, which includes the smallest companies (with an average market value of only $44 million in 1998) had an average equity beta of 1.39.

Similarly, the achieved arithmetic average return over the period 1963–98 also appears inversely related to firm size. The portfolio of the largest firms achieved average annual returns of only 14.2% over the period, while the portfolio of the smallest firms achieved returns of 22.9%.

Grabowski and King carried out a regression, seeking to estimate whether there was a systematic relationship between the historically achieved equity premium for the different portfolios and the differences in market value of equity. This suggested a high degree of correlation; the relationship plotted is shown in Table 10.3, and demonstrates how good the fit is.

Some analysts have pointed out that there is an inherent logical difficulty with such analysis. If Grabowski and King's analysis is to be believed, there is an inverse relationship between the returns that equity investors require from a company and the market capitalization of the company. This might be interpreted as suggesting that the smaller a company is, the higher the returns investors will require. But the causality could equally be argued to work the other way: the more risky a firm, the lower will be its market capitalization (all other things being equal) because investors will apply a higher cost of capital discount rate in assessing its value and hence what price they are willing to pay for its shares.

For this reason, Grabowski and King also used seven other measures of company size, as listed in Table 10.2, to give an overall view. Table 10.4 shows the analysis using one of these – the number of employees.

All of the measures appeared to demonstrate the same result – that returns have been negatively correlated with company size.

It is also clear from the analysis that the higher returns achieved by small companies are in excess of those that would be suggested by a standard application of the CAPM. Table 10.5 demonstrates this, using as an example data for portfolio 16 of the companies ranked by market value of equity (taken from Table 10.3).

TABLE 10.4

Evidence on the small company premium – ranked by number of employees

Companies ranked by number of employees
Historical equity risk premium: average since 1963
Data for year ending December 31 1998

Portfolio rank by size	Average number of employees	Log of number of employees	Number as of 1998	Beta annual since '63	Standard deviation of returns	Geometric average return	Arithmetic average return	Arithmetic equity risk premium	Smoothed average equity risk premium	Average debt/ MVIC
1	184,237	5.27	48	1.15	20.08%	12.37%	14.19%	6.63%	6.59%	26.83%
2	67,920	4.83	47	1.03	18.26%	13.49%	14.91%	7.35%	7.30%	26.67%
3	43,921	4.64	46	0.95	16.96%	14.19%	15.42%	7.86%	7.62%	27.77%
4	33,745	4.53	48	1.05	18.30%	14.37%	15.80%	8.24%	7.80%	27.43%
5	25,670	4.41	49	1.03	18.95%	14.82%	16.37%	8.81%	8.00%	27.67%
6	19,995	4.30	52	1.04	19.51%	14.78%	16.42%	8.86%	8.18%	26.39%
7	15,322	4.19	50	1.08	20.18%	13.02%	14.77%	7.21%	8.37%	28.23%
8	12,325	4.09	63	1.07	19.64%	13.80%	15.48%	7.92%	8.52%	29.66%
9	10,527	4.02	53	1.10	20.24%	14.95%	16.73%	9.17%	8.64%	29.60%
10	8,808	3.94	57	1.15	22.51%	14.58%	16.70%	9.14%	8.76%	30.68%
11	7,406	3.87	61	1.17	22.34%	14.47%	16.65%	9.09%	8.89%	31.19%
12	6,747	3.83	60	1.16	21.65%	14.67%	16.76%	9.20%	8.95%	30.50%
13	5,759	3.76	62	1.09	20.38%	14.82%	16.66%	9.10%	9.07%	31.39%
14	5,058	3.70	72	1.15	22.21%	13.22%	15.50%	7.94%	9.16%	31.18%
15	4,167	3.62	68	1.10	21.46%	15.97%	17.96%	10.40%	9.30%	32.07%
16	3,712	3.57	68	1.17	21.97%	14.85%	17.02%	9.46%	9.38%	30.41%
17	3,124	3.49	73	1.12	21.58%	13.05%	15.25%	7.69%	9.51%	31.88%
18	2,580	3.41	93	1.20	23.24%	13.97%	16.31%	8.75%	9.64%	31.16%
19	2,148	3.33	95	1.18	22.03%	13.78%	15.91%	8.35%	9.77%	30.20%
20	1,766	3.25	97	1.18	22.83%	16.38%	18.71%	11.15%	9.91%	29.70%
21	1,454	3.16	121	1.17	23.04%	14.78%	16.98%	9.42%	10.05%	29.43%
22	1,166	3.07	133	1.17	23.01%	15.99%	18.23%	10.67%	10.21%	29.12%
23	848	2.93	158	1.21	23.08%	15.72%	18.17%	10.61%	10.44%	30.23%
24	533	2.73	224	1.19	24.95%	15.35%	17.95%	10.39%	10.77%	28.68%
25	195	2.29	415	1.37	28.79%	16.97%	20.47%	12.91%	11.49%	24.08%

Large stocks (Ibbotson SBBI data)						12.59%	13.72%	6.16%		
Small stocks (Ibbotson SBBI data)						14.99%	17.77%	10.21%		

Long-term Treasury income (Ibbotson SBBI data)						7.53%	7.56%			

Source: Grabowski and King, 1999.

Exhibit H
Equity Risk Premium Study: Data through December 31 1998
Data smoothing with regression analysis
Dependent variable: average premium
Independent variable: log of average employees

Regression output

Constant	15.257%
Std err of Y est	0.855%
R squared	65%
No. of observations	25
Degrees of freedom	23
X coefficient(s)	-1.646%
Std err of coef.	0.254%
t-Statistic	-6.49

$$\text{Smoothed premium} = 15.257\% - 1.646\% * \text{Log (Employees)}$$

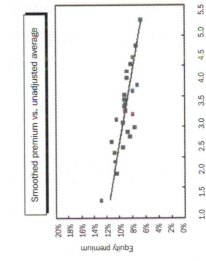

Smoothed premium vs. unadjusted average

TABLE 10.5

The cost of equity for one group of companies

From Table 10.3 it can be seen that portfolio 16 has an average equity beta of 1.2. Combining this with a large stock equity market risk premium of 6.2% and a risk-free rate for 1963–97 of 7.6% (the figures used by Grabowski and King) gives an indicative cost of equity based on CAPM:

$$7.6\% + 1.2 * 6.2\% = 15.0\%$$

In fact, as Table 10.3 shows, the actual historical arithmetic average return for portfolio 16 was 16.7%, 1.7 percentage points higher than the CAPM would suggest.

The implication of this analysis – according to Grabowski and King – is that the reader who believes there are compelling reasons why investors in small companies should require higher returns should add 1.7 percentage points to the cost of equity derived from the standard CAPM methodology when applying the analysis to a company which has a similar market capitalization to that of portfolio 16 (i.e. $750 million).

Other adjustments

Anyone who is involved in cost of capital analysis in a business environment for any length of time will come across a whole range of different reasons promoted by business managers and others setting out why the CAPM framework should be adjusted for particular circumstances. Some of these have some underlying logic associated with them, while others are simply pragmatic responses to particular aspects of the business environment in which the cost of capital is being derived. The following briefly sets out some of the most common adjustments which the authors have come across.

Key person adjustment

The logic here is that where management responsibilities are concentrated with a key individual or a few people there is exposure to the risk of severe financial consequences due to the loss of the individual(s) in the event of death, disability, departure, or adverse performance.

The effects of this would clearly be felt on cash flows, and therefore any adjustment should in principle be made to cash flows or value, not to the cost of capital or discount rate.

Information access and reliability

If investors do not receive sufficient information about strategy and performance, then they face extra risk in making investments because the financial position is less clear. They will therefore mark shares down. While investors and analysts generally get most of the financial information they need, important gaps exist in nonfinancial information, the communication of strategy, and providing peer group comparisons.

A 1999 PricewaterhouseCoopers global survey of the banking sector asked 39 banks, 51 investors, and 29 analysts to comment on how well the banks met the information needs of the markets, and how any information gaps affected the market value of the banks. Although the survey found that banks were good at providing much of the information that investors require it identified some major gaps, particularly in the area of nonfinancial information, but also in terms of value creation.

Some examples of the areas where additional information was needed by analysts and investors to assess the value of banks more effectively included data on customers and markets (e.g. customer penetration and retention, and market growth and share), on risk management (e.g. risk management practice, market risk exposure, and asset quality) and strategy.

More importantly, the participants believed that improved disclosure would have significant benefits, including increased share price. Over half of the respondents stated that improved disclosure of information would reduce the cost of capital.

Notwithstanding this finding from a survey of market participants, in principle it appears that the opacity disbenefits of poor disclosure should be reflected in more pessimistic assumptions regarding expected cash flows rather than in an increased cost of capital. Where investors have little information on which to base judgments about an investment they are likely to take a pessimistic view of cash flows.

In principle there is no reason to believe that they will assume that the cost of capital should be high. Indeed, it is possible that with partial information it might appear that the cost of capital for a firm is low (e.g. it appears that cash flows are not highly correlated with economic conditions) but that with better information it becomes clear that in fact the cost of capital is high.

Nevertheless what appears certain is that improved communication with the market is an important area where management can take action to enhance value.

Portfolio adjustment (or 'conglomerate discount')

Some valuation practitioners reduce the value of a company if they perceive that it is too widely spread among a range of heterogeneous activities. The underlying assumption is that the company, particularly if it is small, may not have the necessary management capabilities to be successful in a range of different markets and will therefore underperform.

Once again, theoretically this adjustment should be reflected in lower cash flows, not a higher cost of capital.

Investment appraisal optimism adjustment

The authors are aware of some businesses which appraise investment projects centrally using a discount rate higher than their estimated cost of capital. The reason they do this is that they anticipate that the cash flows advised to them by managers 'in the field' will be inherently too optimistic. Managers will be overly enthusiastic about their area, and will want to obtain approval for investment to increase their sphere of influence and because they have invested their own personal time and effort in developing the investment proposal.

The UK government adopted such an approach in the 1970s when it included a two percentage point premium for appraisal optimism for evaluating schemes suggested by individual spending departments.

In strict theoretical terms, adding such a premium is inappropriate as it would be far better to adjust cash flow estimates to eliminate the overoptimistic assumptions. Furthermore, it can be counter-productive, as those who are proposing projects will be aware of the premium and will be tempted simply to increase the cash flows further. Nevertheless, it is understandable why a central investment function, with limited resources to analyze cash flows for individual projects, might take such an approach for pragmatic reasons.

Headquarters premium

Some companies add a premium to the discount rate in order to cover the costs of the corporate headquarters function. The logic behind this is that cumulatively the cash flows associated with projects 'in the field' must provide sufficient cash flow to recover the costs of the central, noncash generating function.

Again, this is a highly pragmatic response by large companies to the issues they face. The difficulty with it is that it may cause value-enhancing projects to be rejected despite the fact that they have no incremental implications for central or overhead costs.

Key points from the chapter

- Valuation practitioners adjust the value of a business (e.g. from a discounted cash flow model) to take account of the particular circumstances affecting the business being valued. The most important adjustments are a downward adjustment in value where a company is privately owned or is small, and an upward adjustment where a strategic controlling interest in a company is being valued.

- Analysis of these discounts and premia suggests that the underlying reason for attaching a different value is that the expected cash flows are affected by the circumstances. Where a discounted cash flow valuation is being performed, therefore, in principle the best approach is to adapt cash flow forecasts to reflect these factors.

- As an alternative, the actual valuation resulting from the discounted cash flow analysis can be adjusted. While this is theoretically inferior, it has the practical advantage that much of the valuations literature and research data concentrates on discounts and premia to value and is hence readily applicable in this manner.

- Adjusting the cost of capital is not theoretically sound and raises practical concerns because the impact of any change will vary depending on the profile of the cash flows.

- The degree of liquidity or marketability of an investment affects value. An equity investment in a publicly traded company is highly liquid but this is not the case for a minority interest in a closely held company. Such investments are worth less as a result, because there may be a delay or costs in finding a buyer, or they may need to be sold at a discount. The literature typically suggests reductions in value of 20%–60%.

- Studies suggest investors pay a premium for control of a company. This is probably because investors attach value to being able to affect the cash generation and distribution policy of a company. The general guidance of the valuations literature is that the value of a publicly traded company is reduced by 10%–15% where a minority stake is being valued, but could be increased by as much as 40% above the value of a minority stake where a shareholder or group of shareholders have strategic control, although much will depend on the particular circumstances.

- Small companies appear to earn returns in excess of the cost of capital, and some practitioners therefore suggest that it is appropriate to make a downward revision to value when estimating the value of a small company. This can be done through an adjustment to the equity cost of capital, where studies from the US market support the level of adjustment.

- Other premia/discounts that are talked about by practitioners include the key person discount (management responsibilities being concentrated, increasing exposure to risk), information access (a discount to value where financial information is poor) and a portfolio adjustment (a discount is applied where a company is perceived as having activities which are too widely spread). These again reflect factors that should affect cash flows, but where it is not possible in practice to estimate the effect of any adjustment that may be made.

Note

1   In this chapter the terms 'closely held' and 'privately held' are used interchangeably to denote investments that are not publicly traded.
2   SEC, *Accounting Series Release No. 113: Statement Regarding Restricted Securities.*
3   Updates are published annually in the Standard & Poor's *Corporate Value Consulting Risk Premium Report* by Roger J. Grabowski and David W. King at *www.Ibbotson.com.*

EPILOGUE

What we have learned about the cost of capital in the real world

Remember the analogy in the Prologue? It suggested that trying to use cost of capital theory to help navigate the world of international investment today can seem like standing at the edge of a river and trusting to application of the laws of physics to help wade across safely. Cost of capital theory can seem arcane and inapplicable to the real world of investment and finance.

We hope that this book has gone some way to making the important lessons of the theory more practical and accessible for everyday use. If we have succeeded in the task we set ourselves in writing this book, you should now be able to come up with answers to the seven questions posed in the Prologue. These were designed to illustrate some of the practical issues in the world of international investment, risk and return, and valuation, which we typically find are of concern to investors and businesses.

1. Should a company use its own cost of capital to appraise new investments and acquisitions? For example, what cost of capital should a US regulated utility use when considering an acquisition in the construction or transport sectors? What if it can fund this acquisition by borrowing at a cheap rate?

   The cost of capital appropriate to appraisal of any investment should be that which reflects the risks of the investment itself. Thus, a company should only use its own cost of capital if the investment opportunity it is appraising has the same risk characteristics as its business as a whole. This is highly unlikely to be the case for a US regulated utility contemplating an acquisition in the construction or transport sectors. These are higher risk sectors, and any acquisition would increase the overall riskiness of the utility's business. The cost of capital used in the appraisal should therefore be higher than that for the business as a whole. Similarly, while the utility might be able to borrow the required cash at cheap marginal rates, as its risk profile would increase as a result, the overall cost of capital for the whole business would increase. The cost of capital in the appraisal needs to reflect this (see Chapter 7).

2. What cost of capital should a US company use when appraising an investment in, say, the Philippines? What kind of risks should you be reflecting in the discount rate in international valuation and which are in cash flows – which emerging markets deserve a higher discount rate and why?

According to the theory, it is not necessarily appropriate to increase the cost of capital for investments in emerging markets. As long as the cash flows used in the appraisal are true, 'expected' cash flows (i.e. they reflect the full range of possible outcomes, weighted by the probability of each outcome) a cost of capital the same as that which the company would use for equivalent investments in the US is appropriate. However, in practice the authors have found that cash flow forecasts are adjusted only for risks which the appraiser can readily identify as being relevant to the particular investment. Appraisers find it difficult to adjust for generic risks associated with emerging markets, such as the risks of civil disorder, macroeconomic collapse, etc. These are low probability, high-impact risks, affected by social, political, and economic factors which are unfathomable to the average business manager. We therefore often add a country risk premium when appraising investments in emerging markets such as the Philippines, deriving our estimates of the premium from observed spreads on internationally traded sovereign bonds. When this approach is adopted it is important that the expected cash flows should be appropriately probability-adjusted for all risks associated with the investment, except those which are generic to any investment in the country, since the country risk premium added to the cost of capital adjusts value for these factors (see Chapter 7 on probability-weighted cash flows, and Chapter 6 on the international cost of capital and country risk).

3. For a typical investment, which type of risk is more important – specific risk or systematic risk? How should these risks be reflected in, say, a venture capital situation?

For a typical investment specific risks (i.e. risks which are specific to the investment concerned) are quantitatively more important – in other words, variations in cash flows away from the mean are more likely to be associated with specific rather than systematic risks (i.e. risks which are generic, and affect most or all investments). This means that specific risks are more important when considering the calculation of probability-weighted cash flows and the promised cost of debt. However, because equity investors can 'diversify away' specific risk by investing in a portfolio of investments, only systematic risk affects the cost of equity, increasing its importance. Venture capital projects generally exhibit a high level of specific risk but low systematic risk. This implies that venture capital funds making equity investments should require a low return on their investment. However, often the full downside impact of specific risks is not reflected in the cash flow forecasts, and instead investors target a high required return (sometimes referred to as a hurdle discount rate) to compensate for this (see Chapter 1 on systematic and specific risk, and Chapter 7 on probability-weighted cash flows and venture capital).

4. Debt is cheaper than equity – so why don't companies raise more debt than they do? Why isn't the world full of companies financed using high gearing levels, or is there an optimal capital structure that can be achieved?

It is true that debt finance is cheaper than equity finance, not least because of the tax advantages of debt. However, as more debt is introduced into a company or investment, so the underlying cost of both debt and equity start to increase. This is because debt providers become more nervous about the ability of future cash flows to repay the debt (and hence they require a higher interest rate to reflect the increased risk) and the risk borne by equity investors also increases because debt takes precedence over equity in the allocation of cash flows and there is more debt to service. It is possible to calculate an optimum cost of capital which occurs at the point where the benefits of any further increase in gearing in terms of substituting cheap debt for expensive equity is just offset by the disbenefits of increases in both the cost of debt and the cost of equity. There is an optimum point for most companies because as the proportion of debt finance increases, so lenders set a significantly higher 'debt premium' to reflect the increasing danger of the company going into financial distress and defaulting on interest payments and principal repayment (see Chapter 5).

5. Most practitioners use the weighted average cost of capital ('WACC') in valuation and appraisal – but do they understand when it should not be the preferred approach and how to use other approaches?

There are three techniques that can be used to estimate Present Values ('PVs'): the WACC technique, the Flows To Equity ('FTE') technique, and the Adjusted Present Value ('APV') technique. The WACC approach is the most commonly adopted and involves discounting expected post-tax operating cash flows at a rate that reflects the blended returns required by all investors – the weighted average cost of capital. The FTE approach discounts cash flows attributable to shareholders at the levered cost of equity. The APV technique splits the value of an asset into its two constituent parts – the value associated with operations, and (any) value created by the capital structure adopted. In APV, post-tax operating cash flows are discounted assuming the asset has no leverage, with the value of the tax shield (tax relief on debt) separately identified and discounted at the appropriate rate and added to the base value to calculate the full present value of the asset. In certain situations – for example, where gearing is expected to remain fairly constant – use of the WACC technique may be the most relevant approach. In other contexts, for example, valuing banks, it may be easiest to adopt FTE. In circumstances where gearing is expected to change or there are tax losses, APV may be the most reliable technique; the WACC approach can lead to valuation errors and unsound conclusions if not properly executed. This is because, with changing gearing, discount rates must change in each year based on market gearing (see Chapter 8).

6. Risk can be reflected in valuation through the use of real option modelling – how does this so-called innovative thinking sit with a net present value approach and discount rates?

There are two principal approaches to valuing real options. One of these, decision analysis, involves an extension of the conventional net present value approach through the introduction of a decision tree. For any investment this allows future options (e.g. growth, deferral or exit options) to be identified and net present value to be calculated on the basis of assumptions that the investment will be managed proactively to take advantage of any upside opportunities and to avoid downside risks. Such options can add greatly to value because the effects are asymmetric – upsides add to expected future value but downsides do not need to be considered. Real option modeling can therefore be regarded as being closely related to net present value modeling, but the results can be quite different. The other approach to real options modeling is to apply financial options modeling techniques, such as the Black-Scholes formula. These techniques differ radically from the traditional approach. However, they require deep technical and mathematical skills, and are only applicable in certain specific circumstances (see Chapter 7).

7. Are global capital markets integrated? Does the Equity Market Risk Premium ('EMRP') differ across markets and how should it be calculated?

Global capital markets are not perfectly integrated, meaning that it is perfectly feasible for investors to require different EMRPs in different territories. Of course, it is quite difficult to validate this contention because in practice the more emerging the market, the harder it becomes to source concrete data on the EMRP. So we have something of a Catch 22. The more emerging the market the less likely it is to be integrated with main world markets, but the harder it is to substantiate what this may mean in empirical terms. While it is clear that if world markets were fully integrated there would be one global market for capital and thus one aggregate world EMRP, in the absence of full integration the suspicion may be that emerging markets are likely to have higher EMRPs than their more developed counterparts – perhaps owing to the greater illiquidity of these markets and perhaps also due to the relatively small size of the traded companies and the lack of traded history and overall transparency (Chapter 3).

INDEX